EMBRACING RACE

Why We Need Race-Conscious Education Policy

EMBRACING RACE

Why We Need
Race-Conscious Education Policy

MICHELE S. MOSES

FOREWORD BY GARY ORFIELD

Teachers College, Columbia Universitiy
New York and London

Published by Teachers College Press, 1234 Amsterdam Avenue, New York, NY 10027

Library of Congress Cataloging-in-Publication Data

Moses, Michele S.
　　Embracing race : why we need race-conscious education policy / Michele S. Moses.
　　　　p. cm.
　　Includes bibliographical references and index.
　　ISBN 0-8077-4237-6 (pbk.) — ISBN 0-8077-4238-4 (cloth)
　　　1. Discrimination in education—United States.　2. United States—Race relations.
　　I. Title.
　　LC212.2 .M67 2002
　　306.43—dc21　　　　　　　　　　　　　　　　　　　　　　　　2001060380

ISBN 0-8077-4237-6 (paper)
ISBN 0-8077-4238-4 (cloth)

Printed on acid-free paper

Manufactured in the United States of America

09　08　07　06　05　04　03　02　　8　7　6　5　4　3　2　1

To my parents, Maria Teresa and John J. Moses,
who taught me the most important lessons in life

Contents

Foreword

The United States is a society with a deeply rooted and dominant political philosophy of individualism, a tradition of defining liberty as freedom from government, and a set of profoundly institutionalized social divisions that are based on race and ethnicity. Equal opportunity is a central American tenet, particularly for education and work. These are the keys to mobility and self-improvement, to attaining the American dream: Learn, work hard, show your talent and your determination and you will be rewarded. Both historical experience and social science analysis, however, strongly suggest that in a highly stratified society with intergenerational inequality and many institutions and beliefs that perpetuate unequal treatment, there is no individualistic set of policies that will produce anything like genuinely equal opportunities. Inequalities are transmitted through generations and reinforced both by active prejudice and discrimination and by institutions and connections whose neutral operation tends to perpetuate inequalities. Most of the time this contradiction between the promise of equal opportunity and the perpetuation of unequal chances is simply ignored, since the inequality is either invisible to most white Americans, ignored or rationalized in American law, or attributed to the failure of nonwhite groups to take advantage of the opportunities they have been offered.

The civil rights movement of the 1960s, along with the federal government's brief but serious effort to change outcomes and remake the institutions of apartheid in the South, brought this contradiction out into the center of public debate for the first time. The major institutions of government in the most liberal period in American history reached the conclusion that race-conscious, group-oriented policies were essential to reverse deeply rooted inequalities produced by a history of racial subordination. Prosecuting one case of voter discrimination at a time in areas where there had never been a significant black vote, transferring one black student at a time into white schools in a district where everything was defined by race and where whites never transferred into black institutions, or trying to deal with job discrimination by suing over each individual case of hiring or promotion discrimination changed almost nothing. The resulting policies included the Voting Rights Act, which simply suspended local control of elections where minorities had always been excluded; affirmative action plans, to create real integration of work forces; school reassignment and desegregation plans that actually integrated all the schools in a district; and affirmative admissions plans for colleges that made selective universities significantly interracial for the first time in their history. These policies were, however, bitterly challenged by a rising conservative movement that polarized white voters, changed the federal courts into the most conservative branch of government, and attacked the policies in the name of an individualistic policy of nondiscrimination, a policy that dismantled remedies that had produced significant changes during the civil rights era.

This movement dominated the era from the late 1960s to the present, an era in which six presidential elections have been won by anti-civil rights Republicans receiving very few minority votes, interrupted only by three terms of moderate Southern Democratic governors who made only tepid defenses of the need for broad race-conscious policies and appointed only two Supreme Court justices in a third of a century.

The 2000 census marks a watershed in American history, showing that we are clearly on a path to becoming a predominantly non-European country in which historically excluded groups will be a much larger presence and often a majority of the population of states, regions, and communities. In this era, the questions of civil rights remedies arise with special urgency and in a multiracial rather than a black–white context. In fact, the census shows that the largest "minority" group is now Latinos, a group that is not a distinct racial group since many of its members are from multiracial backgrounds, not a nationality, only partly defined by language, and extremely diverse. Latinos are the most segregated group in American schools and extremely disadvantaged in terms of high school completion and college access. The 2000 data also shows a very rapidly growing presence of Asians, who are on average exceptionally successful in American society, but whose numbers include some refugee populations with problems much like those of the Latinos. The huge Latino migration brings issues of language into focus as never before. Neither Latinos nor Asians experience the extreme caste-like separation from whites in terms of marriage and residence that blacks have historically experienced. It is no simple matter to decide how to apply civil rights policy in these more complex settings. To add to the complexity, this is a time when whites are the most isolated population and have the most isolated schools but need to become successfully "integrated," not only so that a healthy democracy can function, but also so that they can succeed in increasingly multiracial communities and institutions. The experience of other deeply multiracial democracies is a sobering one and the dangers of balkanization, polarization, or domination by a declining white minority are all serious issues.

Obviously, neither simple individualistic assumptions nor the remedial assumptions and practices rooted largely in the black–white experience of a society defined by two intensely separated and sharply bounded communities will be adequate. We are entering a period in which we need to rethink our understanding of our changing society and the essential principles of justice needed in the new context. This is a very difficult challenge requiring both analytic originality and a well-grounded knowledge of the complex realities that the principles must come to terms with. This is the task that Michele Moses has taken on in this study—wildly ambitious, risky, impossible for one person to fully master, but essential in moving the discussion forward.

This is a bold, provocative, and important study. No one will agree with all of the judgments and conclusions she reaches in this complicated and many-sided argument ranging from the broadest philosophical claims to policy analysis about the effects of various remedies, but I believe that all readers will benefit from her work. Moses strongly rejects the theory that racial and ethnic divisions have been solved and that whites are being harmed by unneeded and arbitrary civil rights policies that discriminate against them. Rather than try to reinforce the traditional arguments for affirmative policies, however, she tries to reconstruct the entire debate with a different set of basic terms and constructs. She argues that the individualism that critics of race-conscious policies say they are defending is fundamentally opposed to real and informed self-determination for all students. The white students in institutions that convey nothing but white experience do not have enough knowledge of others to overcome their intellectual isolation and limited perspectives; the minority students cannot have real self-determination without a fair chance to overcome their unequal origins and preparation and learn in a setting that sufficiently respects and reflects them and their culture. If anyone doubts the importance of the work of young "minority" scholars for America's future, this book should make that reader think again. Here is a young scholar who takes ideas very seriously but starts from issues and perspectives that rarely arise in mainstream American political thought—the central importance, not only of individual autonomy but that of groups, particularly the groups who have been historically subordinated, devalued, and excluded by discrimination. Moses' perspective produces a different and important set of ideas about rights and equality and allows her to recast the philosophical and social arguments over policies ranging from bilingualism to affirmative admissions in selective universities. She makes the reader come to terms with the implications of an important, different set of fundamental assumptions and first principles. This is a solid contribution to the vital work of rethinking American democracy for a transforming society.

Gary Orfield
Harvard University

Preface

The ideas examined in this book have been swirling around in my head
for many years. My life experiences have shaped the way that I view
education and what I believe to be essential within education policy if
our policies are going to contribute to meaningful opportunities for students of color and poor students. Of course, as a child growing up in
Queens, New York, I did not yet place such expectations on education.
I just knew that I loved school, and I liked it when my teachers and
peers liked me. Although that was a good thing, I cared a bit too much
what they all thought of me. And there were some things about my
family (at least from my perspective) that made me more different than
I wanted to be. My mother worked outside the home. This is not such
a novelty now, but back then it was a big deal. To me, it meant that
she did not walk me to elementary school or pick me up to take me
home for cookies and milk. Instead, my *abuelita* was there each day.
That was another different thing about my family. My grandmother lived
with us and took care of me while my parents worked. She had recently
come to the United States from her native Bolivia and did not speak
more than five words of English (*hello, no home, thank you*), so I had
to speak to her in Spanish. What did I know about bilingualism being
an asset? I just felt weird, and embarrassed by her seemingly odd ways.
I even hesitated to invite friends to our apartment after school. Imagine
an 8-year-old's mortification when her grandmother would answer the
door with curled green leaves stuck on her head to cure her headache
and, instead of pop-tarts, would offer us snacks of *humintas* and *chuño*!
An outside observer likely would have been surprised by my fears of
feeling different at school, because many of my classmates came from
immigrant families and were "different" in their own ways too. In hind-
sight, the subtle message in my public school classes was that we should
all be the same. The curriculum reinforced that message. What I did not
then realize was that it did not have to be that way.

Still, as I said, I loved school. I also knew that school was very important; my family made that abundantly clear. Although I did not com-

pletely understand what it meant at first, I had learned that education was the ticket to a different world, one rife with choice and possibility. I was good at school and looked forward to the move to junior high school. But there were stories of guns showing up at my neighborhood junior high, so with luck and guts my family managed to move to the suburbs, and my schooling continued on Long Island, where as a multi-ethnic bilingual kid, I really *was* different. By the time I got through high school, though, I was adept at ignoring my diverse roots. I was admitted early to the University of Virginia, which I chose because it was not too far away, had an excellent academic reputation, and was relatively affordable given its status as a so-called public ivy. Affirmative action policy likely helped my admissions case, since I had checked the "Hispanic" box on the application. I never thought that I did not deserve my admittance, however. I felt confident in my academic and personal record. In college, my choice of courses that had a multicultural focus opened my eyes to a multicultural world. As a student, I was affected by the race-conscious policies discussed in this book, especially multi-cultural education (its absence from my public schooling and its presence in my college courses) and affirmative action.

It is this story, my early story, which has so influenced my perspective on the place of education in our society. Throughout the book, I will present a variety of people's stories as illustrative examples that make the sometimes abstract philosophical analysis more real and meaningful. Policy theory is important, but it is the persons affected by the policies that are most important. In many ways, I have written this book to remind educators, policymakers, and scholars that our emphasis should be on students, who deserve an education that serves to foster a sense of possibility for their education and their lives. My hope is to help improve the educational system for students of color by providing a new philosophical foundation for race-conscious education policy, as well as by raising educators' and policymakers' awareness about these policies' ties to fundamental educational aims.

Martha Nussbaum (1991) has written about the importance of "caring about the characters" in the novels we read and "being moved by their fate" (p. 894). The race-conscious education policies that I address in this book—bilingual education, multicultural curricula, affirmative action in higher education admissions, and remedial education—require educators to care about and respect the real characters in the stories that make up our social lives. This necessitates not merely letting them into these stories, but inclusion on terms consistent with who they are and from where they come. As John Dewey (1938) wrote, "[w]hat avail is it to win prescribed amounts of information about geography and history, to win ability to read and write, if in the process the individual loses his own soul . . . ?" (p. 49). Hopefully, my analysis of race-conscious education policy can contribute to the realization of an educational ideal in which individual students receive a good education but do not have to lose their souls in the bargain, an ideal that will allow them to write the stories of their own lives.

ACKNOWLEDGMENTS

Before beginning, I must express my heartfelt thanks to the many people who have helped me along the way. I first owe a very special debt of gratitude to Ken Howe, the best colleague and advisor anyone could hope for, and even more important, a wonderful friend. His guidance is always insightful and wise, and his heart always generous. He is truly an inspiration.

My sincere thanks go to Rubén Donato, María Fránquiz, Ernie House, Catherine Lacey, Patricia Marin, Linda McNeil, Robert Nash, and Ramona Thomas for their thoughtful comments on various portions of this work, and especially to Claudia Mills, who gave generously of her time to help me clarify my arguments in Chapter 2. Marina Gair helped me immeasurably with research updates and manuscript revisions as the book neared completion.

Special thanks also go to the Spencer Foundation, for generously providing the funding and intellectual support necessary for me to complete this work. Predissertation and dissertation Fellowships supported my initial research and analysis in Chapters 1 to 5, and a small research grant facilitated my work on what became Chapter 6.

This book contains more detailed versions of some pieces that I published along the way. Parts of Chapter 2 borrow from "The Relationship Between Self-Determination, the Social Context of Choice, and Authenticity," in *Philosophy of Education 2000* (pp. 294-302), edited by Lynda Stone, 2001, Urbana, IL: Philosophy of Education Society. A portion of Chapter 3 comes from "Why Bilingual Education Policy Is Needed: A Philosophical Response to the Critics," 2000, *Bilingual Research Journal*, 24(4), pp. 333-354. And part of Chapter 5 is adapted from "Affirmative Action and the Creation of More Favorable Contexts of Choice," 2001, *American Educational Research Journal*, 38(1), pp. 3-36. All articles have been rewritten for this volume.

During the time it took to complete this project, I leaned on many friends and relatives, who provided valuable support and encouragement all along the way. I am grateful for Beth Krensky, Patricia Marin, and Deb Holloway, friends and colleagues whose wit, imagination, and deep commitment to social change never cease to inspire me. Very special thanks also go to Maria Moses and Lois Bell, whose generous help and support made it truly possible for me to think and write with a clear head and heart in the early stages of this work. I am deeply appreciative of my grandmother, Helen Moses, for her unwavering encouragement every day and for sharing her amazing life experiences with me. I am indebted also to my *abuelita*, Maria Antonieta Boyán, who, without realizing it, taught me profound lessons about culture, immigration, and home, all of which are reflected in my ideas. My mother, Maria Teresa Moses, taught me what courage means, how important educational opportunities can be, and the endless possibility life holds. My father, John Moses, my first and most important advisor, helped me always to keep perspective and believed in my capabilities even when I did not. Finally, a most important thank you goes to Gabriela and Natalie Bell, who blessed me with their patience and spirit and deepened my commitment to possibility and justice.

And to Chris Bell, who, it seems, labored with me over every idea and somehow knew just what to say to make me smile at each step of the process, thank you for reminding me of all things important, especially dreams and laughter and love.

Introduction

Hope. Possibility. Justice. Education holds the promise evoked by these three words. The problem is that for far too many students—students of color, poor and working-class students, and female students of all kinds—the educational system in the United States is failing grossly to fulfill its promise. As Kenneth Howe (1997) points out, the effort toward equality of educational opportunity has largely failed. Rather than nurturing hope, education causes despair. Instead of creating a sense of possibility, it constrains students' choices. In lieu of fostering social justice, it perpetuates oppression. History has shown us that important social changes are not often achieved in the United States without the force of law to compel them. In order for our educational system to fulfill its promise, we need to have education policies that are explicitly concerned with social justice.

A law professor at the University of Texas at Austin has said that students of color are unable to compete with white students at selective universities because within their cultures educational success is not held in high regard and academic "failure is not looked upon with disgrace" (Lino Graglia quoted in Mangan, 1997, p. 1). Perhaps it comes as no surprise that during this time of rightist resurgence, people in the United States might hold such opinions. But that such a comment can be made by a professor, at a press conference no less, shows that something is profoundly amiss within our educational institutions. W. E. B. DuBois anticipated that the main problem of the twentieth century would be the problem of the color line. Similarly, Manning Marable (1995) prophesizes that the main problem of the twenty-first century will be the problem of a

> "multicultural democracy:" whether or not American political institutions and society can and will be radically restructured to recognize the genius and energy, the labor and aspirations of millions of people of color—Latinos, Asian Americans, American Indians, Arab Americans, African Americans, and others. (p. 117)

Indeed, issues of race and ethnicity comprise today, and will continue to comprise, some of the most controversial, thorny, value-laden, and passion-filled ethical and political debates in the United States. What is more, they are central to our country's history and identity (House, 1999). Their relationship to education in general and education policy in particular has resulted in no small amount of scholarship from within the educational research community as well as from a variety of other disciplines (e.g., Altbach & Lomotey, 1991; Appiah & Gutmann, 1996; Fullinwider, 1996). According to Amy Gutmann and Dennis Thompson (1996), "racial injustice may be the most morally and intellectually vexing problem in the public life of this country" (p. 107). Through this book, I hope to make a unique contribution to the important debate surrounding that problem.

Research and experience remind us that students of color and poor students are losing out within our public educational system (Anyon, 1997; Della Piana, 1999; hooks, 1994; House, 1999; K. Howe, 1997; Kozol, 1991; Weis & Fine, 1993). At all levels, they are forced to assimilate, left out of the curriculum, steered away from pursuing higher education. Since the celebrated *Brown v. Board of Education of the City of Topeka* (1954) decision, the federal government and some state and local governments have voiced a commitment to equality of educational opportunity. Mere rhetoric would never erase inequalities, so measures designed to promote greater access and equitable outcomes were put into place by educators and policymakers during the civil rights movement of the 1960s and 1970s. The most substantive and far-reaching initiatives have included *bilingual education, multicultural curricula, affirmative action in higher education admissions*, and *remedial education*.[1]

This book provides a philosophical defense of these four race-conscious education policies. What must the educational system do to promote social justice for students of color and poor students? What is required to help these students develop self-determination? Where and how do race-conscious education policies fit into this? These are the general questions addressed herein. I should note that I am using the term *race-conscious* not because I see race as a signifier for some kind of immutable biological or genetic difference between humans, but because of the socially constructed place that "race" has in our society. Marable (1995) makes a relevant point:

> Race only becomes "real" as a social force when individuals or groups behave toward each other in ways which either reflect or perpetuate the hegemonic ideology of subordination and the patterns of inequality in daily life. These are, in turn, justified and explained by assumed differences in

physical and biological characteristics, or in theories of cultural deprivation or intellectual inferiority. (p. 186)

I chose these four policies because I believe that it is important to consider them together, where each in its own way serves to foster the development of self-determination and, subsequently, social justice. They have most often been examined separately, a practice that neglects the importance of the role each one plays within education for social change. John White (1991) posits that a "*justifiable* government policy is one which seeks to promote the autonomy of all its citizens and does not favor some at the expense of others" (p. 22). This is a crucial point, for it can be argued that race-conscious policies sometimes do favor some people at the expense of others. Critics of race-conscious policies point out that members of the dominant culture end up losing out when, for example, available monies are spent on things that do not benefit them directly, such as bilingual programs or the recruitment of students of color. The question, then, is whether or not those policies are still somehow justifiable. I contend that race-conscious education policies are defensible because they play a central role in the development of self-determination of students who otherwise are left with a deficient education.

To support my contention, I briefly trace the histories of each policy, identify underlying principles and assumptions, and examine relevant empirical research. I then measure these against a contemporary liberal framework. Here, the use of the term *liberal* draws on the tradition of liberal theory within political philosophy; this should be distinguished from common uses of *liberal* in reference to specific politicians or ideas. The main argument in *Embracing Race* hinges on the premise that self-determination (i.e., personal autonomy[2]) is required for justice. Race-conscious education policies are thus critical because they systematically foster the ideal of self-determination through the support of authenticity and favorable "contexts of choice" (Kymlicka, 1991, p. 166). It is important to point out that I see this ideal of self-determination as a moral one. I mean this in the sense that Charles Taylor (1991) outlines, that a moral ideal serves as a "picture of what a better or higher mode of life would be, where 'better' or 'higher' are defined not in terms of what we happen to desire or need, but offer a standard of what we ought to desire" (p. 16). I embarked upon this task because my early research on multicultural education indicated that race-conscious policies often lack solid footing (Moses, 1997). In this time of political backlash against most race-conscious education policies, it is critical to be able to provide educators and policymakers with a principled and nuanced foundation, a foundation that is clearly and thoughtfully articulated, not taken for granted. Often the real aims of these policies get lost within the turbulent political debates. While I am aware that these analyses involve complex sets of issues and that very difficult moral choices must be made, my aim is to show that these policies, though by no means perfect and perhaps outdated in some forms, in general promote greater self-determination for students of color and, consequently, social justice. The argument from self-determination provides a new perspective that goes beyond previous arguments for race-conscious policies. Although these policies have been defended on righteous and political grounds, the defenses have been vulnerable to charges of political correctness and identity politics. I want to appeal instead to the central importance of self-development for students of color, because all persons deserve a meaningful opportunity to become self-determining.

K. Howe (1992) observes that in discussing complex issues, the goal should be to "devise philosophically defensible interpretations that have some chance of winning broad acceptance" (p. 458). My hope is that this investigation of bilingual education, multicultural curricula, affirmative action, and remedial education as importantly related to the development of self-determination will win that type of acceptance.

OVERVIEW OF ARGUMENTS AND CHAPTERS

The debates over bilingual education, multicultural curricula, affirmative action, and remedial education policy are passionate and complicated. People take these issues very personally and end up having deeply entrenched opinions regarding them. However, missing from these discussions is an analysis of the policies that takes into account students' vastly different social contexts of choice. Oppressive societal structures may constrain individuals' contexts of choice and thus limit individuals' *real* choices in such a way that their *nominal* choices do not reflect their potential talents, abilities, and aspirations. For example, Jonathan Kozol (1991) describes the experiences of students of color who attend woefully underfunded and inadequate public schools. For many of these students, schooling does not lead to any opportunities, much less to ones that have meaning. It is no wonder that dropping out of school sometimes seems like the best available option. As Kozol (1991) has shown, schools in neighborhoods of different race and class makeup provide their students with quite disparate educations.

Simone de Beauvoir (1952) makes a relevant distinction between a life of immanence and one of transcendence. A life of immanence is characterized by a passive acceptance of the roles into which we are socialized. By contrast, a life of transcendence is characterized by the active and free pursuit of one's possibilities in order to redefine one's future. Supporters of race-conscious education policy emphasize that the persistence of institutionalized racism in the U.S. educational system and the country as a whole halts the ability of marginalized students to lead lives of transcendence. They argue that measures taking racial and ethnic factors into account in the distribution of opportunities are sometimes warranted and justifiable in the interests of social justice (Gutmann, 1987). Hence abolishing race-consciousness in education policy will likely result in a return to a more unequal, pre-*Brown* state of affairs; students of color would be able to achieve only the inauthentic life of immanence that de Beauvoir describes.

Now, self-determination, like the concept of autonomy, can be seen as being at odds with a concern for persons' social and cultural backgrounds. Nevertheless, the ideal of self-determination as I conceptualize it is actually centrally concerned with social and cultural contexts and authenticity. I rely heavily on the work of philosopher Charles Taylor (1991, 1994) in making this important connection. We must first understand that human life is fundamentally dialogical, relational in character. It is through our acquisition of what Taylor (1991) calls "rich languages of expression" that we become fully human actors, capable of understanding ourselves and defining our identities. The only way to learn these languages is in relation and exchange with others, especially those who are most significant in our lives, who matter to us. The idea here is that one's identity and sense of oneself are not formed just through self-reflection, as strict individualism might have us believe; they are formed through relationships with important forces in one's life: family, community, peers, teachers, and the like.

So, authentic identities are defined in dialogue with (whether in harmony or struggle) the identities our family and community want to recognize in us. Even as we grow and develop, these defining relationships last a lifetime. Thus one's schooling can serve to enhance or it can serve to harm one's developing sense of oneself and consequently one's ability to imagine options and possibilities for one's life. When it serves to enhance one's development of self-determination, the end result is threefold: Self-determining persons can make unforced and meaningful choices about their lives without having to sacrifice their secure sense of personal and cultural identity; they can make these choices from among good options; and they can act with the knowledge that who they are is worthy of public respect and recognition.

To go along with all of this, readers have to accept the following controversial points. First, education *ought to* play a central role in diminishing oppression. To do this, one must reject the notion that education is not (at least partially) responsible for combating social problems. In doing nothing, it actually serves to perpetuate the injustices; hence, it should certainly strive to combat them. Second, self-determination is a valid aim of education. One must therefore reject the criticism that self-determination is too individualistic a notion to do any good for marginalized students. And third, these arguments can actually matter. To accept this, one must believe in the power of thought to provoke action.

Both those who support race-conscious policies and those who oppose them tend to agree on the value of the ideals of equality, freedom, and justice. Because of this, a defense of race-conscious policy based on self-determination as a fundamental aim of a good education hopefully will resonate with those on both sides of the debate. This type of principled defense can add to the conversation by speaking to both liberals and conservatives. Those left of center still may protest that the principle of self-determination is too individualistic, while those on the right may take issue with how I apply it. My challenge, then, is to show that personal autonomy as self-determination is indeed a key aim of an education that supports justice and democracy, and that race-conscious policies are the best way to help oppressed students to become self-determining in a meaningful way. These are the main aims of this book. In the next chapter, I concentrate on the first aim. Subsequent chapters focus on the second aim.

The book is made up of seven chapters. Following this introduction, Chapter 2 focuses on self-determination as a crucial underpinning of an education for justice and democracy. The ideal of an education that fosters social justice is largely rooted in hope—hope that the social and structural situation into which a student is born will not predetermine her or his aspirations and possibilities in life. A good education should help students to develop in ways not necessarily imagined by dominant society. With this in mind, Chapter 2 examines the concept of personal autonomy within political philosophy. I begin by establishing that in liberal political theory there is a strand of liberalism that recognizes the critical importance of not only the individual, but of the individual within her or his community context. It is important to distinguish this contemporary liberalism from the more traditional strands of liberalism in order for it to adequately support race-consciousness in policy efforts. This type of liberalism has its roots in the philosophy of John Dewey (1927, 1930), and is now supported by scholars like Taylor (1991) and Joseph Raz (1986). It embraces a perfectionist stance on the good, rather than a neutral one. This is significant because a perfectionist liberal tradition allows for a focus on an ideal such as self-determination as a specific constituent of the good life.

There are two main conditions associated with self-determination. The first condition of self-determination is that persons have a favorable social context within which to make the significant choices about their lives. This affects the character of people's choices; even if a choice is not directly coerced, it cannot properly be thought of as a meaningful choice if it is made within an impoverished context. The second condition is that persons maintain or develop an authentic cultural identity. The identity that individuals subscribe to is one that they want to have, not one that they internalize due to oppression or one that is forced upon them. This enables people to avoid having to sacrifice their authentic personal and cultural identity in order to attain success as defined by mainstream culture. Thus, they can be true to themselves and become self-determining. Education policies must play a part in this process.

The next four chapters focus on the application of the contemporary liberal framework developed in Chapter 2 to race-conscious education policies. I investigate how each one is related in different and complex ways to the framework. For each policy has its own connection to the development of self-determination, and some connections are more direct than others. Each of the policies and practices I examine leads directly to the creation of a favorable context of choice, whereas they have both direct and indirect relationships with the development of authentic cultural identities. In addition, these policies affect both K–12 and higher education. Rather than maintaining a strict separation between K–12 and higher education, the analyses underscore the important linkages between them in the struggle for social justice.

Chapter 3 examines bilingual education policy in light of Arizona's Proposition 203 and California's Proposition 227, its farthest reaching challenges to date. I defend bilingual education policy as an important way of ensuring that English language learners (who are primarily Latino and Asian American) receive an education that improves their contexts of choice and supports the worth of their cultural identities. When English language learners are able to learn English while at the same time progress academically in all other subjects, they have the best chance to achieve academically and to have meaningful educational opportunities. Bilingual education thus helps English language learners to become self-determining by publicly recognizing their particular cultures and by expanding their range of options for choice.

In Chapter 4, I explore the controversy surrounding multicultural curricula at both the public school and college levels. I view multicultural education as an educational approach that teaches students what they need to know in order to grow and succeed within a multicultural democracy. Students are taught that there exists a mainstream culture, but that it is not superior to other cultures, and that different cultures are

worthy of public recognition and respect. The main points of argument
I use to defend a broad policy of multicultural education are that it contributes to an equal respect for different cultures and to a substantial reduction of oppression. Students of color and white students alike learn
about multiple perspectives and thus can begin to question dominant societal structures. The nature of the school curriculum has a deep impact
on the quality of students' social contexts of choice. It also affects how
students feel about their own cultures and those of others. This is why it
is so important for students to receive an education that is multicultural.
A monocultural curriculum serves to stunt the students' sense of self and
their ideas of what is possible in life. If, to take an obvious example, a
history class shares only the stories of white leaders and heroes, or a
literature class highlights only white male authors, students collaterally
learn that Latinos and African Americans, among others, contributed little
to our nation's history or to the canon of literature. Multicultural curricula
provide one avenue for the educational system to ensure that it does not
perpetuate an exclusive and oppressive status quo.

In Chapter 5, I look at perhaps the most controversial race-conscious education policy of all, affirmative action. The discussion is limited to affirmative action in higher education admissions. There have
been many challenges to affirmative action policy, including California's
Proposition 209, which abolished affirmative action in that state, and
court cases against the University of Texas Law School, the University
of Washington Law School, and the University of Michigan. These challenges have not adequately taken into account the crucial role that affirmative action policy plays in fostering the self-determination of students
of color. In this chapter, I undertake a thorough review of the most
common arguments against affirmative action: it amounts to reverse discrimination; it causes unqualified students to be admitted to college; it
harms more than helps students of color in the long run; it overlooks
those students who need it most; and it perpetuates a society that is far
too race-conscious already. After responding to each argument, I then
fashion my own positive argument for affirmative action, relying in part
on Gutmann's (1987) claim that affirmative action is just inasmuch as
race, ethnicity, and sex constitute relevant qualifications for admission
to colleges and universities. I bolster the qualifications argument with
the contention that affirmative action is required because it contributes
greatly to the development of self-determination of students of color,
primarily by vastly improving their social contexts of choice.

Chapter 6 focuses on the debate over remedial education policy. I
am concerned with remedial education at the college level, most specifically the types of courses that are offered at 4-year institutions in order

to help students rise to college level in basic subjects. There has been little philosophical attention to the remedial education controversy.[3] Of course, that fact in itself is not a justification for the need for such research. The remedial education debate is important both for its own sake, in terms of how the availability of remedial courses affects college opportunities, and how it fits into the larger debates over race-conscious education policies discussed in this book. The debate about remedial courses centers on the question of whether or not remediation belongs at prestigious four-year institutions, and concomitantly, whether or not students who may need such courses merit admission. Remedial education opponents argue that remediation should take place at lower level and lower status institutions. In examining the controversy, I aim to defend the place of remediation at 4-year colleges. I argue that remedial education, like the other race-conscious policies I discuss, plays a meaningful role in creating more favorable contexts of choice for oppressed students. It supports students after they have gained admission to college so that they may succeed.

Ultimately, if we do nothing and we say nothing to protest the move away from race-conscious education policies, then we will be left with nothing but the empty and meaningless rhetoric of democracy and opportunity. This work is my attempt to say something worthwhile in defense of bilingual education, multicultural curricula, affirmative action, and remedial education. These initiatives are linked in important ways in their ability to foster self-determination among students of color and thus contribute to educational and social justice.

Let us now begin unraveling just how this is so.

NOTES

1. Not all of the four policies and practices I will examine are federally mandated; while bilingual education and affirmative action are federal policies, multicultural curriculum policy and remedial education policy are local ones that are generally established by individual schools and colleges.

2. Herein I will be using *self-determination* and *autonomy* interchangeably. The type of personal autonomy for which I argue will be fleshed out in Chapter 2 as self-determination. Briefly, it is characterized by the positive freedom to rule one's own life, which is a more robust notion than merely the absence of coercion (negative freedom).

3. I have seen only one piece within political philosophy and none within the philosophy of education (see Fullinwider, 1999).

2

Toward Self-Determination: Taking Context and Identity into Account

The 1959 film *Imitation of Life* tells the story of Sarah Jane, a young light-skinned African American woman, and her struggle to find her place in a society that would likely oppress her if her racial heritage were common knowledge. This same society would celebrate her talents if she kept her race a secret, allowing others to believe she was a white person. Unfortunately, her choice to pass for white causes her much internal pain and suffering because in order to pass, she must reject her African American mother and, in so doing, deny a crucial part of her self.

I recount a portion of this story because it exemplifies the heart of the problem this book addresses. Sarah Jane's case provides a dramatic instance of how the racial oppression a person faces can lead her to make choices within an impoverished "social context of choice" so that she can receive certain social advantages (Kymlicka, 1991, p. 166). In other words, Sarah Jane feels forced to make the choice to deny publicly her personal and cultural identity as an African American in order to improve her context of choice and, consequently, her life chances. Because she cannot then be her authentic self within a family she loves, she cannot determine meaningfully the way her life will go. In order to be truly self-determining, she would need instead a good range of options within which she could pursue a good life without having to sacrifice a significant portion of her personal and cultural identity, without foregoing public recognition of the worth of her race and culture, of who she truly is.

In a liberal democratic society,[1] which embraces autonomy and equality as virtues, how can we avoid situations like Sarah Jane's? Can we support a notion of the "good life" entailing that individuals will be respected for who they authentically are within the context of their particular histories and identities?

In this chapter, I argue that we *can* (and indeed ought to) support such a notion of the good life, specifically one that places personal autonomy and authenticity at its center. In order to do so, I sketch a contemporary liberal framework within which I conceptualize a notion of personal autonomy as self-determination. This notion of personal autonomy is one where a person's life choices are not merely uncoerced choices, but choices that are in keeping with the person's authentic sense of self. Self-determination is importantly connected to one's social context of choice and feelings of authenticity. Accordingly, these bear directly on one's personal and cultural identities and their place in a just society. "Cultural membership," Will Kymlicka (1991) notes, "affects our very sense of personal identity and capacity" (p. 175). I focus on cultural identity as an essential part of self-determination because of the special significance that race and ethnicity have in our society in particular. Thus, for the purposes of the argument put forth in this book, I characterize cultural identity as having three main facets: (1) racial and ethnic heritage, including bicultural or multicultural heritages; (2) connection to one's cultural community; and (3) a sense that one's race and culture have worth and deserve respect. I view self-identification and identity development as continuous processes, and, as such, identities as fluid, not static; open, not monolithic; and multiple and contingent, rather than unalterable essences (Ginsberg, 1996). Therefore, I want to stress that, as Martha Nussbaum (1997) points out, cultures are diverse within themselves, according to things such as religion, class, thought, or values. When I refer to cultural identities herein, I mean to invoke this complicated characterization.

The past and present oppression of nondominant groups in the United States renders an authentic and publicly recognized cultural identity important in order for persons to be able to determine the course of their own lives within a more favorable social context of choice. That being the case, I lay the foundation of an argument for self-determination as a primary aim for people within a just and democratic society, one that is constituent of the good life. I specifically maintain that the social institution of education and its concomitant policies play an important role in students' development of this concept of self-determination. This will frame the analyses of bilingual education, multicultural curricula, affirmative action, and remedial education that I undertake in subsequent chapters.

PERSONAL AUTONOMY WITHIN CONTEMPORARY LIBERAL POLITICAL PHILOSOPHY

For a long time the political theory of liberalism has been charged with being too atomistic, too oriented toward the individual, too blind to social and cultural embeddedness, and too noncommittal (neutral) about the good. Taylor (1991) points out that individualism has a prominent dark side that encourages people to be so self-centered that they lose concern for others. This, in turn, eventually causes their lives to become narrower and ultimately devoid of meaning. Perhaps certain strands of liberalism are guilty as charged. However, the contemporary strand of liberalism I embrace strives for equal consideration of both the individual and her or his community.

The perspective I adopt, then, is grounded in what has been called the "dominant political philosophy of our times," the liberal philosophical tradition, but is radically different from the received wisdom on traditional liberalism (Arthur & Shaw, 1991, p. 242). As do the traditional strands of liberalism, contemporary liberalism supports important goods such as individual liberty, human equality, and religious tolerance, to name a few (MacLean & Mills, 1983). However, the contemporary perspective, championed first by Dewey (1927, 1930) and currently by scholars such as K. Howe (1997) and Kymlicka (1991), can be distinguished from the traditional libertarian and utilitarian strands of liberalism in that it joins liberal individualism with people's societal and communal contexts, resulting in what Dewey calls a radical form of liberalism. This type of liberalism promotes an ideal in which flourishing both as individuals and as social beings are inextricably bound up. Contemporary liberal theory transcends traditional liberal theory precisely because of its central concern with placing the responsibility for oppression and disadvantage within dominant societal structures, rather than with individuals. It acknowledges as essential people's cultural and social contexts, within which a context of choice is framed by a society's history and structures in interaction with a person's cultural background (Kymlicka, 1991). It is thus important to distinguish contemporary liberalism from the traditional strands of liberalism that view social problems as the responsibility of the individual, in such a way that social policy must somehow compensate for individuals' cultural deficiencies. Instead, contemporary liberalism attempts to move liberal political theory beyond the idea that education policy needs to remedy individual cultural deficits, toward the idea that oppressive social structures and systems need to be changed so that oppressed persons in general, and students of color in particular, may flourish.

Dewey (1930) reacted against the reigning rugged individualism that was primarily associated with self-interest by conceptualizing the notion of a great community. This community is formed when all individuals participate actively in shaping the values of the group. In it, he wanted people to feel a profound sense of responsibility for others as well as for themselves and to act in reflection of those feelings. Dewey called for this when he urged changing society to foster a new type of individual. This new individualism is based on respecting autonomous individuals while taking centrally into account their community context as an essential component of self. Rather than being at odds, the individual and the collective make up the two main parts of Dewey's great community.

Still, liberalism often is seen as dismissive of social and cultural contexts. The main critics of liberalism, even in its contemporary form, come out of feminist and postmodern philosophy, and most prominently out of communitarian philosophy. Feminist critics charge that liberals support only compensatory notions of justice, focusing on mere tolerance rather than on emancipation, which serves to condone a culture that denies women (and people of color) opportunities and treats them as inferiors (MacKinnon, 1989; Young, 1990a). Similarly, postmodernists claim that some basic themes espoused by liberalism, such as individual liberty, tolerance, and autonomy, support the unequal status quo. Communitarians claim that liberalism separates people by playing individualistic politics and denying the importance of public morality (Sandel, 1991).

Daniel Bell (1993), for one, a self-identified communitarian, maintains that liberalism is too focused on individual self-choosers who are independent from the social world and its shared ends. Similarly, Michael Sandel (1991) criticizes the liberal conception of self as empty because it is not properly embedded in the communal contexts within which choices are made. Contemporary liberalism is able to answer these criticisms. It is true that the individual is at the center of liberal theory. However, contemporary liberal theory also stipulates that individuals can be understood only within their social and communal context. But what makes liberalism different from (and better than) communitarianism is that liberalism explicitly does not cherish the notion of community-defined shared ends because more often than not they are exclusionary and oppressive. Too many people are forced into taking on those ends even though they had and have no part in formulating them (Kymlicka, 1991). As Bruce Ackerman (1980) points out, liberalism is essentially concerned with constructing a power structure within which all community members feel they have an equal voice in the dialogue.

I move now to a more in-depth look at the communitarian critique of liberalism. By most accounts, Sandel has been the leading communitarian critic of liberalism. While he does not specifically call himself a communitarian, theorists on both sides place him in that camp (e.g., Bell, 1993; Kymlicka, 1991, 1992). Sandel's responses to what he calls "deontological liberalism" in the Kantian tradition of placing individual rights and justice as central have led the communitarian critique of liberalism (Sandel, 1982, p. 176). The main criticisms have focused on the liberal notion that the right is prior to the good and on the liberal conception of the self.

For my purposes here, I would like to concentrate on the critique of the liberal notion of the self.[2] Sandel (1982) posits that the self, when held separate from meaningful attachments, ends up disempowered rather than liberated. He interprets the liberal notion of the self as devoid of attachments and unencumbered by historical or community contexts. John Rawls's (1971) original position is the best-known and most criticized example of the ideal of the autonomous individual who is detached from historical and social context. Communitarians place society as prior to the individual and thus view the self as deeply embedded in society and community. Bell (1993) tries to outline a communitarian moral vision stemming from the critiques of communitarians such as Sandel and Alasdair MacIntyre (1981). He states, "We are first, and mostly, social beings, embodied agents 'in the world' engaged in realizing a certain form of life" (Bell, 1993, p. 31).

There is a fundamental problem with this communitarian interpretation of the liberal notion of the self and its place within community and society. It exemplifies a deep misunderstanding of the actual liberal notion of self, especially within contemporary liberalism. Communitarians assume an extremely individualistic liberalism that sees the individual as completely detached from society and culture. As mentioned above, since the time of Dewey at least, liberals have purposively maintained the crucial importance of understanding individuals within their specific culture and society in general. Contemporary liberalism is much more concerned with social and cultural identity than its critics allow. This is, in fact, similar to the importance that communitarians place on the social and cultural embeddedness of the person.

What is different is that, for liberals, the individual is prior to society, for they believe that the society and community should not dictate a common good made up of what Bell (1993) calls "shared meanings" (p. 63). All too often those shared meanings are shared only by those who have had enough power and status to formulate them in the first place. Indeed, as Kymlicka (1992) points out,

> communitarians often write as if the historical exclusion of various groups was just arbitrary, so that we can now include them and proceed forward. But the exclusion of women, for example, wasn't arbitrary. It was done for

a reason—namely, that the ends being pursued were sexist, defined by men to serve the interests of men. (p. 86)

As a result, members of marginalized groups are called upon to adapt themselves and make sacrifices in order to understand the shared meanings and fit into the shared ends of the majority. This places an oppressive burden on nondominant groups. Thus contemporary liberals believe that in the name of justice we should focus on people's autonomy and free choice, but always within the context of their history and culture, not detached from them. In significant ways, this is not so very opposed to the communitarian project. Consider Sandel's (1991) point: "open-ended though it may be, the story of my life is always embedded in the story of those communities from which I derive my identity— whether family or city, tribe or nation, party or cause" (p. 248). Yes!— contemporary liberals would likely agree with Sandel here.

The key distinction between contemporary liberalism and communitarianism, then, and the one that makes contemporary liberalism more defensible than communitarianism, is the liberal emphasis on the individual as prior to society, in a moral sense. This is tied to the vital need for individuals to be included in the formulation of societal meanings and social institutions. Contemporary liberalism builds upon a solid liberty-enhancing tradition with a significant emphasis on social context and cultural membership. In so doing, it enjoys not only a completeness, but a focus on social justice that communitarianism sorely lacks.

LIBERAL NEUTRALITY VS. LIBERAL PERFECTIONISM

Within contemporary liberalism itself there is some debate about the essential nature of the good life and the state's role in defining it. In the tradition of Rawls (1971) and Ronald Dworkin (1978), there are competing notions of the good life, and the liberal state is, for the most part, neutral about what the good life is to entail.[3] This neutrality is an attempt to respect people's personal conceptions of the good, at least what is the good for them. Thus one can criticize another's conception of the good only on grounds of inconsistency with her or his overall life plan, not because it is somehow wrong or misguided. Other contemporary liberals such as Taylor (1991) and Raz (1986) take issue with such a neutral or stripped-down conception of the good. Although still pluralists, they embrace instead a more perfectionist liberal stance on the good. Christopher Wolfe and John Hittinger (1994) put it well: "The future of liberalism lies, not in a working out of the anti-perfectionist impulse, but in a dialogue with more . . . 'perfectionist' philosophical positions" (p. xvii). My argument here comes out of a perfectionist liberal tradition in an attempt to advocate for the ideal of self-determination as part of the content of the good life.

Still, there is a potential problem with perfectionist liberalism that liberal neutrality does not encounter. This is the risk of being labeled "illiberal." Illiberal states often see it as their primary state function to oversee the morality of society, whereas liberal states claim to avoid such strict oversight. The antiperfectionist fear is that even well-intended and well-researched policies can still backfire in the hands of government bureaucracies (Raz, 1986). By supporting personal autonomy as a moral good, do we risk illiberalism? This is a fair question. It would be easy for me to assuage critics' fears by telling them not to worry, that my version of the good really is good, and not at all oppressive or exclusionary, if that is their worry. However, such an answer, while it may be true, does no real work. It is better to point out that placing a value on personal autonomy as a good is entirely in keeping with liberal tenets of justice. In fact, autonomous agents can best decide how to live their lives and what particular conception of the good to pursue. In this way, autonomy is a special kind of good that, when promoted, actually enhances a tradition of liberty rather than compromising it in an illiberal manner. In addition, while the American state claims neutrality about the good, its actions actually reveal the promotion of a specific conception of the good life. Consider these examples: Schooling is compulsory until the age of 16, except in limited circumstances; there are laws restricting the labor of children; and steps must be taken by public school districts to ensure that English language learners have adequate opportunities to learn, as per the *Lau v. Nichols* (1974) decision. These policies are not neutral; in fact, they promote a specific version of the good life that places value on education and educational opportunities for all.

Liberal perfectionism contains a clear theory of the good that a just society ought to promote. It offers grounds from which to criticize others' conceptions of the good as wrong or incomplete. Raz (1986) is a perfectionist in that he argues for an objective theory of the good that revolves around the ideal of autonomy. For him, autonomy is intrinsically as well as instrumentally valuable because it is always a component of that which is intrinsically valuable. Justice involves promoting people's personal autonomy. Taylor's (1991) theory of the good revolves similarly around the concept of authenticity. He sees authenticity as a concept of essential importance rising out of liberal individualism. Because of this belief, Taylor considers himself a contemporary liberal,[4] albeit more toward the perfectionist side. I rely on both Raz and Taylor in fashioning my argument that self-determination is a main good that society, through its social institutions and policies, ought to promote. I turn now to an examination of autonomy before specifically moving on to self-determination.

Personal Autonomy

In *The Morality of Freedom* (1986), Raz aims to promote an ideal of individual freedom that can be (and should be) supported by the state. In so doing, he builds his theory around the concept of autonomy. Following John Stuart Mill, he assigns a strong, clear value to personal autonomy as a central good. Quite generally, the concept of autonomy is defined as self-government (Christman, 1989). Beyond that, however, accounts diverge; neo-Kantian and socialization accounts of autonomy tell different stories (Christman, 1989; Meyers, 1989). My conception of personal autonomy as self-determination is rooted more in the socialization accounts, such as Diane Meyers's (1989) view that autonomy is a competency that people acquire through socialization. I rely most on Raz's narrative conception of autonomy, where autonomy is seen more as a capacity (Chockley, 1997). For Raz (1986), then, "an autonomous agent or person is one who has the capacity to be or to become significantly autonomous at least to a minimal degree. . . . (Significantly) autonomous persons are those who can shape their life and determine its course" (p. 154).

Autonomous people have the freedom and self-respect necessary to make their own choices from among a range of good options. This is especially important because within U.S. society, if one is not autonomous, one is unequipped to make good decisions about which projects and commitments to undertake (Raz, 1986). In other words, without the autonomy to do so, one could not make one's life one's own in important ways. Of course, merely stating that autonomy is necessary for success in our society is not enough of a justification of its importance. We could similarly say that a belief in white supremacy was required in order to prosper in apartheid South Africa. That something is required for success in a given society itself does not make it a valuable concept. Still, the concept of autonomy is distinctive in that its value is tied to the fact that it enhances people's liberty and their capacity to pursue a good life.

In addition, Raz's conception of personal autonomy builds upon the idea that autonomy is intrinsically valuable. Eamonn Callan, too, views personal autonomy in this way. He points out that "autonomy is essential to the exercise of moral virtue and the achievement of justifiable self-respect; and because these things are plausibly regarded as very weighty intrinsic values, autonomy can be seen, with equal plausibility, as a very weighty constitutive good" (1988, p. 45). In addition to its intrinsic value as an important good, I see two main reasons why autonomy is valuable. First, it parallels the concept of empowerment. According to Mischler, "to be empowered is not only to speak in one's own voice and to tell one's own story, but to apply the understanding arrived at to action in accord with one's own interests" (quoted in G. Anderson, 1989). This conception of empowerment mirrors a liberal conception of personal autonomy in that it leads people to be the authors of their lives ("to speak in one's own voice and to tell one's own story") and to pursue their own conceptions of the good life ("to apply the understanding arrived at to action in accord with one's own interests").

Second, autonomy is valuable because its conditions require that individuals have the sufficient mental capacities and range of options in order for them to be able to make meaningful choices. The important point here is that these choices are *meaningful* ones, not merely forced choices among limited options. If one has sufficient mental capacities, one is self-aware and can understand and envision the lasting effects of one's choices. A range of options is adequate if it consists of a variety of acceptable alternatives from which to choose, including ones that give people long-term projects, commitments, and relationships. Such a range of options would allow for meaningful choices.

It is important to note that placing such a value on autonomy does not entail, as communitarians would believe, that an autonomous individual can make any choices she or he wants, regardless of life circumstances or communal contexts. While persons in unfavorable circumstances can make certain choices, often they are limited by the social context within which they are choosing. What this means is that, although these persons do make uncoerced choices from a limited range of options, these choices are less autonomous than ones within a more favorable context of choice containing an adequate range of a variety of options. I contend that individuals are able to be self-determining in meaningful ways when their social contexts are favorable, thus allowing them to choose from among good options. And a good range of options is one of the central conditions required for an autonomous life.

These conditions include independence, integrity, appropriate mental abilities, and the aforementioned adequate range of options. Independence is characterized by an ability to make choices without being coerced or manipulated to do so. In order to have integrity, people must identify with their choices and be loyal to the projects and relationships they choose (i.e., have a sense of authenticity). If people have appropriate mental abilities, they are capable of deliberating, planning, and making choices upon which they can then act. They also understand how their choices and actions may have long-term consequences for their lives. Finally, autonomous people must have an adequate range of options. An option is a personally conceivable, socially recognized, and materially possible alternative. For the range of options to be considered adequate, individuals need choices between goods, not only between good and evil. These choices have to include not only trivial ones, but significant ones as well (Raz, 1986).

Although Raz's conception of autonomy is an appealing one, it is not entirely unproblematic. For instance, T. M. Scanlon (1979) points out that the notion of individual autonomy is "notoriously vague and slippery" (p. 533). It is quite difficult to determine whether or not people have made truly autonomous decisions. In the same vein, Claudia Mills (1995) is skeptical about what might constrain autonomy. She contends that even though harm can come from things like manipulation, the fact that we have been manipulated does not necessarily "take away our fundamental autonomy" (p. 107). This is certainly true. However, to continue with her example, the harm of manipulation does not come from its completely taking away our autonomy. It comes from the fact that being manipulated tends to distort our decisions and our goals, diminishing severely our autonomy (Raz, 1986).

Accordingly, it is important to consider just how we are to judge who is self-determining. The issue of false consciousness comes into play here. How do we judge whether, for instance, peoples' articulated desires and choices are indeed their own, or due instead to their subordinated societal position and internalization of the messages of inferiority attendant to it? This is problematic because we may run the risk of intimating that people are self-determining only when they make what we deem to be good and worthwhile choices. However, we can say at least this much: Autonomous people ought to be able to know and understand what they really want, what their wide options are, what is important to them—now and for their future—and to judge whether or not their desires and choices resonate with their personal and cultural identities. In partial response to these complex issues, my conception of self-determination holds that mere freedom from coercion should not be considered the same as self-determination within favorable contexts of choice by people secure in their cultural identities.

In order to develop personal autonomy, then, people need to satisfy its requisite features and conditions. In subsequent sections, I will argue that social institutions such as formal public education serve as critical components in the formation (or lack thereof) of the requirements for self-determination, most notably in how they affect the creation of favorable social contexts of choice and persons' development of authentic cultural identities.

If one enjoys personal autonomy, it does not mean that one's choices are completely independent of or detached from one's historical, cultural, and social context. According to Kymlicka (1991), in order to lead a good life, it is most important to be true to ourselves and our beliefs about what is of value and to be able to freely question and reexamine those beliefs according to the cultural and societal information we receive. This type of self-determination enables people to lead good lives.

PERSONAL AUTONOMY AS SELF-DETERMINATION

This section centers on conceptualizing personal autonomy as self-determination. Etymologically, *autonomy* comes from the Greek for *self* and *law* and means the making of one's own law (J. Feinberg, 1989). This is translated into self-government or self-determination. Self-determination is a capacity that can be constrained or expanded by one's place within a dominant structural context and resulting life circumstances. In conceptualizing personal autonomy as self-determination, I begin with the fundamental premise that a just and democratic society requires that its citizens be autonomous, or self-determining, or, as Kymlicka puts it, able to live life "from the inside" (1991, p. 18; see also G. Dworkin, 1989). Accordingly, the development of self-determination among young people becomes most important. The education system plays a significant role in whether or not students will be able to become self-determining in a meaningful way, that is, become the primary authors of their life stories.

The notion of authoring one's own life story is essential for self-determination. According to Raz (1986),

> the ruling idea behind the ideal of personal autonomy is that people should make their own lives. The autonomous person is a (part) author of his own life. The ideal of personal autonomy is the vision of people controlling, to some degree, their own destiny, fashioning it through successive decisions throughout their lives. (p. 369)

David Richards (1989) similarly describes a strong notion of personal autonomy as the reflective freedom to plan one's own life. A person with this reflective freedom is one whose life is characterized by self-determination, one who is freely able to choose one's own goals and relationships.[5] Self-determination thus characterizes a personal autonomy that is more robust than the barest notion of autonomy defined only by the absence of coercion. Callan (1988) explains it this way:

> It is not the case that only minimal autonomy is necessary to evince moral excellence or achieve a robust and well-grounded sense of self-respect; it is rather the case that the degree to which these intrinsic values are realized necessarily depends on the degree autonomy is realized. (p. 45)

In other words, this is the difference between autonomy in name only and self-determination (i.e., autonomy that is "worth wanting" [Howe, 1997, p. 18]). Self-determining people can achieve that robust sense of self-respect. In addition, they make not only trivial judgments about, for instance, whether to wear sunglasses or a straw hat, but significant judgments about more substantial and worthwhile activities. Most importantly, they know the difference between the two. A just and democratic society ought to cultivate self-determination among its people. This way, their choices, made in relation to their historical, cultural, and social contexts, represent who they are and who they want to become, rather than who they cannot be due to unjust societal limits.

Bell (1993) characterizes this liberal position well: "The best life is still the one where the individual *chooses* what is worth doing, achieving, or being, though it may be that this choice has to be made from within a certain framework which is itself unchosen" (p. 40). The key, as I will address in the next section, is that although the framework may be unchosen, it should not be unjustly limited by constrained social contexts of choice. Personal autonomy as self-determination is characterized, then, by a significant capacity for autonomy within which one's life is not wholly determined by social factors outside of one's control. In addition, self-determination depends on private and public affirmation of a person's authentic sense of self.

As I have begun to lay out, my conception of personal autonomy as self-determination is associated with two central requirements: a favorable social context of choice (expanding rather than constraining choices) and authenticity (being true to oneself and one's social and cultural identity). In addition, in order for persons to become self-determining, it is important to promote education policies that systematically foster the development of autonomy through the creation of more favorable contexts of choice and the support of authentic cultural identities. Although it is certainly possible to be autonomous in some form without necessarily enjoying a favorable context of choice or a sense of authenticity, it is not possible to achieve true self-determination without the fulfillment of these requirements.

THE SOCIAL CONTEXT OF CHOICE

This section will highlight Kymlicka's (1991, 1995) notion of a social context of choice, where a favorable context of choice is a central requirement for the development of self-determination.[6] This is closely connected to the set of conditions that are required for an autonomous life. Consider Marcy Ford, a bright, 18-year-old African American senior in an urban high school, who did not believe that she would ever make it to college. No one in her family had been to college and her school counselors did not encourage her to apply. Despite good grades, she was afraid that she did not have the ability to do the work, so she avoided taking the college preparatory curriculum and the college entrance examinations (Wheeler, 1997). Ford resembles many other students of color in urban U.S. high schools. She also provides a good example of someone who is operating within a constrained social context of choice that serves to limit her sense of possibility. Structural constraints often limit the ability of people in similar situations as Ford to meet the conditions necessary to make self-determined choices about their life plans. As mentioned above, these conditions include independence, integrity, appropriate mental abilities, and an adequate range of options (Raz, 1986).

A contemporary liberal vision of the good as promoting an ideal of self-determination underscores the need to create more favorable social contexts of choice for people. A favorable context of choice is characterized by a social environment in which persons can conceive of their possibilities, choose freely among good options, and visualize the consequences of their actions. It is crucial for the attainment of self-determination. As R. S. Peters (1967) points out, "anyone who seriously asks the question 'What ought I to do?' is on the path to autonomy. But it is a further question whether or not he is free. This will depend on whether or not there are any constraints preventing him from doing what he has decided to do" (p. 115). Although some constraints are inevitable, constraints due to an unfavorable or limiting social context of choice are often unjust. These types of constraints, due to systemic injustices such as racism and classism, limit a student's ability not only to do what she or he has decided to do, but to see the possibilities for choice as well.

Take, for example, the African American children whose psychological interviews were cited by the plaintiffs in *Brown v. Board of Education* (1954). When they were given two dolls, a black one and a white one, and asked which doll they thought was the best, they most often chose the white doll. This finding exemplified for the court that the choices that these children were making were severely constrained. Official social policy was serving to truncate their sense of self-worth. Their supposedly separate but equal educations were contributing to internalized oppression and their cultural identities were being harmed. Now, according to Kymlicka (1991), "it's only through having a rich and secure cultural structure that people can become aware, in a vivid way, of the options available to them, and intelligently examine their value" (p. 165). Secure cultural structures are seriously undermined by societal oppression. As M. E. Hawkesworth (1990) explains, using the oppression of women as the example, oppression

> is most visible in systems that define women's existence solely in terms of the role of wife, mother, domestic laborer, and consumer; but it is no less pernicious when it surfaces in societies that encourage men and women to be active, independent agents of their own destinies, while subtly affording women fewer opportunities for self-realization than men. (p. 74)

What happens, then, not only with gender oppression, but with racial oppression as well, is that oppressed peoples no longer enjoy a wide, open sense of possibility. And when these limits in possibility are internalized, the oppressed become, in essence, complicit in their own oppression. When choices are made under conditions of inequality and oppression, we may doubt their authenticity. So, while these types of choices may not be directly coerced choices, they are made from within a severely limited range of options. It is the character of the choice that makes a difference. Individuals are certainly responsible for their choices, but an unjust situation arises when there are grave inequalities within the societal context from which people are making their life choices.

When a person makes choices in life, these choices are influenced (limited or expanded) by the social and cultural circumstances under which she or he learns about life's possibilities (Kymlicka, 1991; Rawls, 1971). Therefore, it is important to note, as Kymlicka (1991) does, that when we say that people are responsible for their choices, we must acknowledge that "it is only plausible to assign beliefs and attitudes about the good life to the person, rather than to her circumstances, if she has the good fortune to have received a sufficiently broad education to be able to conceive the various options open to her" (p. 201). Thus

a person's social context of choice acknowledges the intersection between individual choices and community context.

In addition, taking into account the social context of choice in as-
sessing persons' capacity for self-determination shows that it is important to acknowledge that persons begin life from very different starting
places. Kymlicka (1991) contends that

> the distinction between choices and circumstances is in fact absolutely cen-
> tral to the liberal project. Differences between people in terms of their
> resources may legitimately arise as a result of their choices. . . . Differences
> that are due to people's choices are their own responsibility (assuming
> that they are freely chosen, with adequate information about the costs and
> consequences of those choices etc.). But differences which arise from peo-
> ple's circumstances—their social environment or natural endowments—
> are clearly not their own responsibility. (p. 186)

Societal institutions privilege some starting places over others, even
though they are not justifiable by appeal to inherent worth or desert.
We do not choose our socioeconomic status or our color, yet sometimes
we are placed in a position of disadvantage or lowered expectations
because of these facts.

If one saw things from, say, a libertarian point of view, one might
counter that, while it is certainly true that people cannot choose their
birth circumstances, it does not necessarily follow that anything should
be done about that. After all, there is the basic issue of luck and the
differences can be caused by people's luck through no doing of their
own. Why should the state feel a responsibility to try to equalize such
differences in luck?

While it is clear that state policy cannot control people's luck, it is
equally clear that a discussion of luck begs the question about differences in people's initial life circumstances. There is a qualitative difference between whether or not I find a 100-dollar bill on the street and
whether or not I have a decent public school experience at my neighborhood school. I suppose I am unlucky if I happen to look up at a bird
rather than down at the money on the sidewalk, but I am not only
unlucky, but oppressed, if my neighborhood public school is in a sham-
bles and I cannot learn well enough to continue on to higher education.[7]
The fact is that initial life circumstances are not only arbitrary like basic
issues of luck, but they are arbitrary in a morally significant way. The
reason that some societal starting places (e.g., being Latino or being
female) are less privileged than others is because of the legacy of racism
and power relations. It was propertied white men who were able to
confer value onto certain ways of being in our society. Thus in certain

circumstances one's race, culture, class, or sex, although arbitrary, have a profound and pervasive effect on life expectations, beliefs about value, and views about the good life.

For that reason, individuals need a social context of choice that is "conducive to acquiring an awareness of different views about the good life, and to acquiring an ability to intelligently examine and reexamine these views" (Kymlicka, 1995, p. 13). This context of choice is best described as a set of conditions within which one's personal and cultural identity is either affirmed or thwarted. It does not shape one's identity; authentic identity is developed through the interaction between individuals and societal circumstances. The social context of choice, then, is the context within which one's identity can be exercised. Thus, in order to be self-determining, persons need to feel a sense of authenticity in making choices that allows them to be true to themselves, to both their personal and cultural identities. This way they can enjoy worthwhile free choices, rather than bare or empty ones that they cannot even recognize or imagine, or costly ones that require them to deny or distort their identities (Dennett, 1984; K. Howe, 1997). Such denial or distortions of one's identity often leave one with a much diminished capacity for self-determination. The development and maintenance of an authentic personal and cultural identity is thus a central feature of personal autonomy as self-determination (Taylor, 1994). Similarly, the requisite conditions for autonomy are fostered through an expanded context of choice and the development of inner capacities such as self-awareness and deliberative abilities (Raz, 1986). In order for persons to be self-determining in decisions about how to lead their lives, they need to make choices that allow them to be true to themselves from a good range of options available within their social and cultural context. For these lives to be good, the range of options must include meaningful options; the context of choice must be expansive rather than constraining.

Thus, as Raz (1986) observes, "the autonomous agent is one who is not always struggling to maintain the minimum conditions of a worthwhile life. The more one's choices are dictated by personal needs, the less autonomous one becomes" (p. 155). Entrenched societal norms and policies often leave people of color, women, and the poor less capable of becoming self-determining and self-respecting. Social policies designed to improve people's social contexts of choice are therefore necessary before we can meaningfully call people self-determining. Part of enhancing people's social contexts of choice comes when people have a sense of authenticity, especially with regard to their cultural identities, as I will now discuss.

AUTHENTICITY AND CULTURAL IDENTITY

A sense of authenticity is characterized by the ability to be true to one-self. This can occur in two ways. First, one's feeling of authenticity stems from the inside, from inner reflection upon one's personal identity. Second, it stems from one's relations with others. The second way that authenticity is shaped is fundamentally dialogical in nature, and the public recognition of one's worth is a key component (Taylor, 1991). Authenticity, then, is defined here as a state of being, within which one has the ability to act in keeping with one's true self, that is, to make uncoerced choices and to feel public affirmation of one's personal identity, of which one's cultural identity is a central part. This authenticity is not prescriptive in the sense that there are established identities into which one must fit, but is defined both privately (by the individual) and publicly (by the community and society).

Thus the notion of authenticity is woven into that of self-determination. They are similar in that both involve the idea of freedom and being part author of one's own life. Authenticity is an important facet of autonomy because it keeps autonomy grounded in the authentic personal, social, and cultural identities that shape people's lives. As Taylor (1991) contends, "modern freedom and autonomy centres us on ourselves, and the ideal of authenticity requires that we discover and articulate our own identity" (p. 81). This is crucial in order to attain confidence in one's self-worth and ability to reach one's life goals—self-respect, which Rawls (1971) called "perhaps the most important primary good" (p. 440). We must define ourselves not just within the sometimes damaging categories society might have assigned to us, but within a secure personal and cultural structure. Without such a structure, people's cultural identities are undermined or even denied, and young people especially often lose the opportunity to have solid role models and life goals.

The controversy over the U.S. census racial and ethnic categories provides a vivid example of the importance of authentic cultural identity to many people in this country, especially to people of color. The rigid traditional census racial and ethnic categories often have not taken into account people of mixed heritage, leaving some uncomfortable with their categorization (Schmidt, 1997). The issue of proper classification, proper recognition of people's identities, was important enough to warrant changes in the categories for the 2000 census. As people strive for authenticity in their identity, even filling out census forms takes on a deeper significance.

This section focuses on the concept of authenticity and its relationship with our personal and cultural identities, which makes it a primary feature of personal autonomy as self-determination. In order to flesh this out, I rely on the current work on authenticity by Taylor (1991, 1994, 1995). In his book *The Ethics of Authenticity* (1991) he follows Rousseau's project of addressing the problem of an authentic self. Taylor contends that "a society in which people end up as the kind of [inauthentic] individuals who are 'enclosed in their own hearts' is one where few will want to participate actively in self-government" (p. 9). As a result, democracy is seriously undermined. If people cannot honor their own culture and history, both privately *and* publicly, they are essentially giving in to the oppressive pressure of forced assimilation into the dominant culture. This type of assimilationist way of living is most certainly inauthentic; people cannot then be true to themselves and their cultures. Of course, all assimilation is not an evil that inevitably leads to a complete loss of authentic cultural identity. Some identity adjustment is certainly necessary for immigrants to a new society, as well as for others encountering a world they did not create. What does lead to inauthentic identity is a social context within which only the dominant culture is affirmed as worthwhile. In order to define one's authentic identity, one always must take into account one's history and background—what one has come to believe is significant, especially in one's distinctness from others. Thus the contemporary liberal idea of authenticity is both an inner concept and an outer one; while we must be true to ourselves, the only way to really do so is in relation to others, in taking into account our historical, cultural, and social contexts.

By doing this, we move away from the more radically individualistic existentialist notions of authenticity that place no constraints on what it means to be true to oneself. Søren Kierkegaard's individualistic philosophy influenced Martin Heidegger, in whose philosophy the concept of authenticity is a central theme (Solomon, 1974). For Heidegger (1927), authenticity means being one's own person in such a way that one breaks away from others to find one's true self. While Heidegger acknowledges that people encounter "thrownness" when they arbitrarily find themselves as social beings in a certain world, his notion of authenticity is of a state of being that surfaces only in separation from that world. In essence, existentialist conceptions of authenticity attempt to transcend the individual life circumstances and social contexts that contemporary liberals, such as Taylor and me, believe to be essential for the development of genuine self-determination.

The development and maintenance of a sense of authenticity in one's identity is one of the most prominent features of a sense of autonomy that is worth wanting. The concept of authenticity revolves around a person's desires and choices. It is often mentioned as at least linked with the concept of autonomy, if not as part and parcel of it (Berman, 1970; G. Dworkin, 1989; Fletcher, 2000; Taylor, 1991). Like autonomy, the concept of authenticity is criticized as too individualistic, too concerned with the inner life of the self (Taylor, 1991). And as with liberal autonomy, these critics ignore the relational and contextual character of authenticity. One can really be authentically oneself only in relation to the background, history, and culture that has shaped one.

By contrast, some scholars have seen an irreparable split between the notions of autonomy and authenticity, with autonomy falling more on the side of reason and authenticity falling more on the side of emotion (as if there could be such a stringent separation of the two). Both Robert Leahy (1994) and Alessandro Ferrara (1994) outline a fundamental distinction between autonomy and authenticity. While they admit that autonomy and authenticity are related in some way, they see the concept of authenticity as a more viable ideal for which to strive in society, because it places emotions and caring as more central to human life than reason. In addition, the ideal of authenticity does not revolve around rigid adherence to universalizable principles as the ideal of autonomy does. As such, unlike the concept of autonomy, that of authenticity does not entail that one control one's emotions with reason. Instead, authenticity hinges on one's personal identity, so that one's actions need not be strictly rational in order to be good. They conclude that authenticity has more to offer us than autonomy does.

The problem with their argument is that without some sort of stronger combination of autonomy and authenticity (akin to my notion of self-determination), the concept of authenticity is incomplete. Regarding the connection between autonomy and authenticity, Taylor (1991) makes a relevant point: "The affinity is obvious. Authenticity is itself an idea of freedom; it involves my finding the design of my life myself, against the demands of external conformity" (p. 67). Take, for example, the people who have a sense of authenticity in their identity as slaves, in that it is the only life they have ever known or conceived of. Still they cannot make autonomous choices and are not considered full, equal human beings. While I think they share important ideas about the incompleteness of autonomy as a moral ideal, by eschewing liberal autonomy altogether, proponents of authenticity such as Leahy and Ferrara are just replacing one incomplete conception of a moral ideal with another. Replacing the concept of autonomy with the concept of authenticity does not do the work necessary for theorizing about social justice.

Similarly, promoting autonomy as an important ideal exclusive of authenticity is incomplete as well. Rob Reich (2002) argues for a conception of minimal autonomy in which persons have the ability to examine and evaluate the things in life that they want and believe, and to which they are committed, as well why they feel as they do. Within this conception of autonomy, authenticity is unnecessary as a condition because all choices would be seen as at least potentially authentic. What Reich does not consider is that while choices are potentially authentic, many cannot be categorized as meaningfully authentic. For example, a choice generally is not authentic, or consequently, self-determining, in a meaningful way if it perpetuates a person's overall oppression. It would instead serve to undermine the person's self-determination. Therefore, what we need to strive for instead is more than a minimal version of either autonomy or authenticity. When viewed against the backdrop of a favorable social context of choice, a linkage, or merger, of the two concepts would move us much farther along the path to social justice.

Consider the experience of Adrian Piper (1996), a scholar who identifies as black, but looks white. People of all races often mistake her for white. She recounts one significant incident, where, when her racial identity is challenged by a powerful white professor, she feels shame and illegitimacy. She explains,

> their ridicule and accusations then function to both disown and degrade you from their status, to mark you not as having done wrong but as being wrong. This turns you into something bogus relative to their criterion of worth, and false relative to their criterion of authenticity. (p. 235)

Due to delegitimizing incidents such as these, Piper's sense of authentic cultural identity is challenged and public recognition of her true identity is denied. She therefore must find a way to feel authentic in her identity by somehow balancing her inner sense of herself with how she is perceived by others. This is an example of how personal and cultural identity are shaped publicly in relationship as well as privately through self-reflection. What is pivotal in Piper's case is that she not be forced to claim only the identity that others give her, for her self-determination would then be sorely compromised. The concept of authenticity is thus inextricably bound up in the notion of self-determination, that is, personal autonomy worth wanting. Each is incomplete without the other.

With regard to authentic identity and authentic choices in Piper's case, not only is one's identity relationally created but it is also the identity that one *wants* to have. This contrasts with an identity that is somehow forced upon one and then internalized as one's own, as we saw with the distorted identities of the African American children in the pre-*Brown* era of segregation. For Taylor (1991), authenticity is "something that we have to attain to be true and full human beings" (p. 26). It would be wrong somehow for Piper just to accept that, regardless of her heritage and upbringing, if she looks white, she must identify as white, just as it would be wrong for the African American children to accept that their cultural identity was inferior to a dominant culture identity.

PARTICULAR IDENTITIES AND THE ISSUE OF COMMONALITY

While Taylor holds that we should be very concerned about authenticity within the multicultural democratic societies of the West for reasons stemming from experiences like those of Piper, the notion of authenticity often is associated with the extreme individualism that Taylor criticizes. Critics of authenticity such as Allan Bloom (1987) maintain that a focus on self- fulfillment and identity is detrimental to the common good of American society.

A problem with Bloom's view is that he does not take into account who has been and continues to be excluded from that notion of the common good. Invariably, those commonalities were devised by an elite group of white men. Consequently, the commonalities often intended to serve the self-interest of that group of men. It is thus important to note that the result of that history is that the dominant culture remains largely "gender-coded, race-coded, and class-coded, even when women, blacks, and workers are legally allowed to participate" in its institutions (Kymlicka, 1991, p. 86). Feminist scholars such as Marilyn Friedman (1991) point out that authentic identities can be forged within what she calls chosen communities, rather than only in found communities, especially when those found communities turn out to oppress and exclude marginalized groups of people.

There is a good case for supporting multicultural efforts toward authentic cultural identities, for marginalized and dominant groups alike. For members of nonoppressed groups in the United States, public recognition of the worth of their cultures is consistent and strong. Privately, however, the cultural identity of dominant group members often is not considered important. A focus on educational efforts to foster authentic cultural identities would aid white students in seeing their color and their culture. While society clearly recognizes the worth of the dominant culture, too often social policy and societal expectations have placed marginalized people in particular on a path to inauthenticity due to the alienation from, and the devaluation, rejection, or misrecognition of, their constitutive communities. If the dominant perspective is the only essential element in society, people of color inevitably will be forced into one of two paths: to deny their own identities in order to fit into the existing structure, or to resist assimilation and risk social failure, both of which limit their self-determination. Consider Jody Cohen's (1993) story of a student who sacrifices her identity for traditional educational success; by allowing her identity as a black American to fade into the background, she can take advantage of educational opportunity. But at what price?

There is, however, a third alternative. People can try to manage some combination of the above—some sort of balance that will not result in either full denial or full assimilation—where one can feel one is still being true to oneself. This third option is in keeping with our earlier conceptualization of authenticity. Finding a balance between the inner and outer influences on one's personal and cultural identities seems to me to be the most viable way to keep a sense of authenticity and, as a result, be able to be a self-determining person.

Within the societal realm, the notion of authenticity as a primary feature of self-determination is directly related to multiculturalism and cultural identity. As Taylor (1991) notes, "however we explain it, it is clear that a rhetoric of 'difference,' of 'diversity' (even 'multiculturalism'), is central to the contemporary culture of authenticity" (p. 37). According to proponents of the multiculturalism movement, it fosters the development and sustenance of authentic cultural identities. This occurs partly through the recognition of the importance of people's cultural identities and the central part they play in the pursuit of a good life. This recognition is grounded in Taylor's (1994) concept of the politics of recognition, which is characterized by a public recognition of the worth of people's cultures in a way that transcends mere toleration, reaches toward understanding, and mitigates the effects of misrecognition and internalized oppression. If, as I have maintained, human identity is partly created relationally, which I see as parallel to being created within a certain context of choice, then recognition is critical if a person is to have an authentic sense of identity.

Critics of multiculturalism fear that the recognition of particular identities causes a damaging societal disunity (e.g., Bloom, 1987; D'Souza, 1991; Hirsch, 1996). These critics maintain that a movement that serves to bolster people's respect for their own cultural identity (as well as that of others) ends up being too particularistic. They believe that an emphasis on the worth of many cultures tends to create separation and disunity, rather than a common culture based on melting pot ideals. Dinesh D'Souza (1991) has even gone so far as to blame multicultural activists for a resurgence of racism and intolerance on college campuses. Similarly, Arthur Schlesinger (1992) believes that so-called militants of ethnicity foster an unhealthy separatism that amplifies people's differences, nourishes prejudice and animosity, and trivializes commonalities.

At first glance, their criticisms seem to make sense. No one wants a disunited society that enhances separations among people and places them at odds with one another. Nevertheless, I argue that these criticisms do not hold up under closer scrutiny because they tend to idealize a type of societal structure that neither exists now, nor has ever existed. For example, Schlesinger (1992) believes that the U.S. public education system, one of the farthest reaching social institutions, should contribute to forming "a nation composed of individuals making their own unhampered choices" rather than abandoning "historic purposes, replacing assimilation by fragmentation, integration by separatism" (p. 16). What he neglects to take into consideration is who was excluded from defining those "historic purposes," and who it is who actually can make those "unhampered choices" within a traditional educational and social system that focuses on a monocultural curriculum and forces assimilation. One of the reasons that we need to recognize multiculturalism is that the U.S. public education system was conceived by an exclusive group of Anglo men (Banks, 1994).

As a result, while the current educational system may lead certain students to develop self-determination, other students are systematically left out. Too often, students of color end up with a distorted notion of their cultural identities and feelings of inauthenticity and inferiority that damage their sense of themselves. In addition, the diminished opportunity of some to develop self-determination has profound effects not only on those individuals, but also on the proper functioning of a participatory democracy built upon equality.

The idea that I am advancing is that important social institutions, such as the public education system, ought to promote actively the development of self-determination among people. Here, I focus on the concept of authenticity and its relationship with personal and cultural identity as integral components of that development. Despite its most ardent critics, multiculturalism, with its emphasis on recognizing particular cultural identities as worthy of respect, urges our liberal democratic society to take the issue of identity seriously. Identity develops properly within the context of things that matter to individual people (Taylor, 1991). So, to exclude a person's history, heritage, community, and cultural particularity, as antiparticularists would have it, essentially would be to ignore all those things that matter.

A person's identity, cultural and otherwise, is defined as that person's understanding of her or his own self, who she or he is, the central characteristics of her or his human personhood (Taylor, 1994). This identity is defined both privately, within one's historical, cultural, and social context, and publicly, within society as a whole. Recall that one's cultural identity is characterized by one's race and ethnicity, connection to one's cultural community, and a sense of the worth and dignity of one's race and culture. Often what is most important in defining ourselves is emphasizing how we are different from others (Connolly, 1991). In a recent study, psychologists asked students to complete the following sentence: "I am _____." Invariably, white students would give an answer referring to personality traits such as "I am friendly" or "I am shy." Students of color, on the other hand, most often filled in the blank with their ethnicity, saying "I am Puerto Rican" or "I am black" (Farley, 1997, p. 89). This is just one example of the pivotal importance of race and culture in our society, especially for marginalized populations. Of course, it also suggests that if societal oppression were to diminish somehow, the students of color might be less likely to identify themselves foremost by their race. We could celebrate such a finding, as long as the students felt equal to one another and cultural differences contributed to a positive sense of the United States as a diverse nation. In the best-case scenario, we then could avoid the feelings of cultural inauthenticity that make up a large part of what Taylor (1991) calls the "malaise" of modernity (p. 1). Still, throughout the history of the United States, cultural issues have had and continue to have a deep influence on people's rights, status, and level of self-determination (Omi & Winant, 1994). Both because of the legacy of oppression and present oppression in the United States, public recognition of cultural identity is indeed vital.

WHY AUTHENTIC CULTURAL IDENTITIES ARE IMPORTANT

If cultural recognition and the development of authentic cultural identities are so vital, why is it that many people seem to lead good enough, self-determining enough lives without much attention to their race and culture? To be sure, this was more often the case during the pre–civil rights era of segregation in the United States, when most people did not really talk about identity or recognition. This is not because they did not have a sense of identity or a desire for recognition, but because cultural assimilation went relatively unchallenged.

For many people, the issue of culture just never plays an important role in their self-development, even though it is against their particular cultural backdrop that they develop a sense of what is most meaningful and significant in their lives. Usually, though, these people fit more easily into the dominant culture. According to Taylor (1989), "I define who I am by defining where I speak from, in the family tree, in social space, in the geography of social statuses and functions, in my intimate relations to the ones I love" (p. 35). As exemplified by contrasting the white students who defined themselves by their personality traits first and foremost with the students of color who right away defined themselves by their race and ethnicity, culture plays a different role in different people's lives. For some it is both privately and publicly defining. For others it can be an afterthought, even though it is no less defining. This leads to a crucial point. While specific cultural identities do give us a sense of the need for public recognition of those identities, they do not give a prescription of what those identities should mean to individual people. While I identify as part of the wider group of Latinos and Latinas in the United States, I still live out my identity in my own way. It is I who choose the way that I understand and relate to my cultural membership.

William Connolly (1991) writes about the political nature of identity and its relationship to the politics of difference. Like Taylor (1989, 1991) who views identity as dialogical in nature, he views identity as both relational and constructed. In this way, he is suggesting that one's identity is embedded in one's social context of choice, as I argued in the last section. I believe Connolly hits upon a clear conceptualization of identity as relational and importantly linked with public recognition. This conceptualization highlights how crucial it is for people to have a sense of authenticity in their identity. However, while public recognition is important, one might question what happens when a person (as in Piper's case) is repeatedly misrecognized. It becomes even more difficult for that person to feel secure with her or his inner conception of self in light of the public's (mis)conceptions. This is a thorny problem.

In order to have a sense of authenticity in their personal and cultural identities, Piper and others in similar situations have to develop that balance I wrote about earlier in this section. Thus, in order to foster one's own self-determination, one needs to find a way to present oneself as one would like to be recognized. For Piper (1996), this means "to do everything I could, either verbally or through trusted friends or through my work, to confront this matter head-on and issue advance warning to new white acquaintances, both actual and potential, that I identify myself as black" (p. 266). This, of course, places a burden on her to have to explain her own identity regularly. It is a compromise she is willing to make, for, as she observes, "no matter what I do or do not do about my racial identity, someone is bound to feel uncomfortable. But I have resolved that it is no longer going to be me" (p. 269). Perhaps it is a compromise others must be willing to make as well.

Also important in this discussion of authenticity and cultural identity is the issue of leaving one's cultural identity behind. If, as Connolly contends, identity is only partially chosen by individuals, then can people realistically choose to discard it? It seems to me that we are all born into a certain historical reality that somehow shapes how we grow up and learn to identify ourselves as similar to or different from others. This is precisely how identity is in fact relational. There are certain parts of our identities that truly cannot be chosen, or, for that matter, discarded. Kymlicka (1991) puts it well: "People *are* bound, in an important way, to their own cultural community. . . . Someone's upbringing isn't something that can just be erased; it is, and will remain, a constitutive part of who that person is" (p.175). This is especially true for many people of color, both because of the significance of their cultural community and because of the fact of their race or ethnicity. Regardless of how culturally "white" Asian Americans might feel, the very fact of their Asian physical characteristics does not allow them to fully discard that Asian American identity. They likely still would be publicly recognized as Asian Americans. For other people of color for whom "passing" is an actual possibility, or for people who choose to discard a less visible aspect of identity, the choice to do so is perhaps more viable.

Still, how can we discern if such a choice is authentic or inauthentic? Connolly (1991) would likely say that such a choice is not only inauthentic, but impossible. He maintains that only the more trivial elements of identity, ones that are not fundamental to one's self, are actually dispensable, such as changing from being a Macintosh computer user to being a PC user. Other, more constitutive elements of one's identity, such as one's race or sex rarely can be dropped at all.

I disagree slightly with Connolly on this point. I see this issue as being related to a person's context of choice. There seem to be two main situations within which someone indeed would choose to reject a particular cultural identity: (1) She or he is acting within an unfavorable context of choice, or (2) her or his choice is a free one. Whereas I see no problem with the latter situation, the former situation is one that a good education coupled with just social policies ought to combat. For people acting within an unfavorable context of choice, the decision to reject a cultural identity is, in Taylor's (1991) words, "self-defeating" because they are essentially destroying "the conditions for realizing authenticity itself" (p. 35). Truly self-determining individuals would not choose to reject completely their cultural identities under those circumstances.

Again, however, there is a third alternative. Individuals could choose to modify their cultural identity so that it resonated more completely with their private and public senses of authenticity. Take, for example, the situation of Angel in the 1988 film *Stand and Deliver*. Angel is a Chicano high school student in East Los Angeles with a gift for mathematics. He has grown up poor, raised alone by his *abuelita*, and an important part of his identity is as a tough homeboy with other young Chicanos on the streets of the city. When Angel finally has a mathematics teacher who inspires him academically, he struggles with how to maintain his identity as a tough kid on the street with his emerging interest in academics. What ends up working for Angel (albeit rather more easily in this film than probably would happen in real life) is to take a stand with his homeboys that just because he has become more interested in high school, does not mean he is any less cool in his neighborhood.

What is instructive in this story for my purposes here is that Angel learns how to compromise (in a positive way) aspects of his identity to accommodate his interest in mathematics, which, without such a modification, would not have fit into his authentic identity as it stood. Therefore, we can say that while self-determining persons would not choose to *reject* their cultural identities when operating within an unfavorable context of choice, they may choose to *modify* their identities in an effort to create a more favorable context of choice. Angel manages to do just that; he makes use of that third alternative. In so doing, he is able to make choices that have a positive impact on his life options without having to deny his identity. The key point here involves one's self-determination; these important choices need to be made within a society that fosters self-determination as a moral ideal of the good.

CONCLUSION: IMPLICATIONS FOR EDUCATION POLICY

How can the preceding discussion of self-determination and authenticity serve to help people like the character of Sarah Jane in *Imitation of Life*? I have endeavored to show that people ought to be able to live their lives according to a healthy notion of who they are, not in imitation of a life they believe is somehow more socially worthy. In so doing, I have outlined a contemporary liberal framework in which the concept of personal autonomy as self-determination is characterized by a favorable social context of choice and a sense of authenticity in one's personal and cultural identity. I have described contemporary liberalism as a political philosophy that can support a particular notion of the good. In this case, that conception of the good revolves around state promotion of the development of self-determination as I have conceptualized it in the preceding sections. This leads me to conclude that people's development of self-determination should be a primary aim of education policy in a just liberal society.[8]

Interestingly, the principle of autonomy (as negative freedom) is cited by social conservatives as a main reason why support of a specific notion of the good is not defensible. They maintain that such a version of liberal perfectionism is associated with too much state control and accordingly would *constrain* individual autonomy and freedom. In this chapter, I have begun to make a case for just the opposite interpretation: that a social policy specifically promoting self-determination as constituent of the good life actually *extends* personal autonomy.

An ideal liberal democratic society needs to provide its people with the best possible chance of becoming autonomous. The prominent social institution of public education is partially responsible for creating self-determining individuals who can participate fully within such a society. This was hinted at by Rawls (1971) when he said that it was the role of the educational system to "provide for each individual a secure sense of his own worth" (p. 101). A leading proponent of education for democracy, Gutmann (1987) also points to public education as the place in which people learn not only how to participate in our democracy, but also how to make choices that lead to the good life and support an authentic sense of cultural identity. K. Howe (1997) puts it this way: "Unless . . . inequalities are the result of morally relevant differences . . . it is education's responsibility—as a public institution that importantly affects the lives of citizens—to intervene and level them" (p. 66). As it currently stands, public education and its concomitant policies already contribute to the reproduction of a status quo that exacerbates inequality and oppression. Thus education too often contributes to a severely constrained context of choice for many students.

Shouldn't the educational system strive for something better in the name of democracy and social justice? John Stuart Mill (1859/1974) said that if someone "causes evil to others not only by his actions but by his inaction, . . . in either case he is justly accountable to them for the injury" (p. 70). Applying his sentiment to education, we can say that the educational system is therefore responsible and accountable for the injury it causes students by *not* providing them with an education for self-determination. As Colin Brock and Witold Tulasiewicz argue, "educational policies—can be used to further, transform, or destroy a social, cultural or national identity and [do] affect groups or individuals" (1985, p. 1). Thus, in order for formal education to effect positive rather than negative consequences, it should play a central role in preparing persons to shape their own life stories and live self-determined lives. But in order to do so, it must give careful attention to the fact that social, political, and historical forces in the United States have come together to deny full autonomy to a host of marginalized groups, including, of course, people of color (Appiah, 1994; Bell, 1992; Salomone, 1986). Advocates for a race-neutral approach to social and education policy systematically fail to consider the complex social history of the United States (Omi & Winant, 1994). In actuality, race-conscious policies are especially critical for the promotion of self-determination as an ideal, through education and beyond.

At their best, race-conscious education policies contribute to students' development of self-determination through the creation of more favorable contexts of choice and through the public recognition of the importance of authentic cultural identities. Without such policies, the chances for students, most specifically students of color, to become self-determining are slim. Consequently, a more just and democratic society will remain merely a dream for far too many people in the United States.

In the next four chapters, I apply the ideas developed in this chapter to four specific race-conscious education policies and practices: bilingual education, multicultural curricula, affirmative action, and remedial education.

NOTES

1. Here I am thinking of the United States specifically, although my argument likely will have implications for other liberal societies as well.

2. See Kymlicka (1991) for a contemporary liberal response to the priority of the right over the good.

3. Even so, both Rawls and Dworkin support the state's involvement on behalf of society's least advantaged.

4. Taylor (1995) himself refers to (what I call) contemporary liberalism as "holistic individualism," which he describes as "a trend of thought that is fully aware of the (ontological) social embedding of human agents but, at the same time, prizes liberty and individual differences very highly" (p. 185).

5. Here we must keep in mind that some relationships are given; we are thrown into them (Young, 1990b).

6. I realize that the particular cultures with which Kymlicka (1991) deals (indigenous Canadians and the Québecois) are quite different from U.S. cultural groups. Nonetheless, I think that he offers concepts that are very useful for analysis on education policy in the United States.

7. Consider the East St. Louis, Illinois, schools depicted by Kozol (1991) and the Newark, New Jersey, schools described by Jean Anyon (1997).

8. I am assuming Iris Marion Young's (1990a) definition of social justice as "the elimination of institutionalized domination and oppression" (p. 15). Social justice is determined substantially by the policies and social institutions of a society (Arthur & Shaw, 1991).

3

Bilingual Education

Even though various research studies have underscored the effectiveness of bilingual education (see e.g., Cummins, 1981; Hakuta, 1986; Krashen, 1996; Miramontes, Nadeau, & Commins, 1997; Ramírez, 1992; Wong Fillmore, 1991), like the other race-conscious[1] policies I will examine, it is still often the object of criticism and disdain. This is due in part to its focus on language, which is, as James Crawford (1991) observes, "a subject that is dear to all of us, bound up with individual and group identity, status, intellect, culture, nationalism, and freedom" (p. 15). Indeed, language in general, and bilingual education in particular, get to the heart of issues of culture, assimilation, and quality of life. In light of a negative political climate for bilingual education policy in the United States, this chapter focuses on a defense of the policy that centers on the relationship bilingual education has with students' sense of identity and their freedom to pursue the good life. Most specifically, I propose that if we view the development of self-determination as a central aim of a good and just education, then bilingual education is required because it plays a crucial part in both fostering English language learners' (ELL)[2] authentic cultural identities and expanding their social contexts of choice. I posited earlier that one's cultural identity is characterized by one's race and ethnicity, relationship to one's cultural community, and a sense of the value and respect deserved by one's race and culture. With a secure sense of identity and a favorable context from which to make life decisions, English language learners avoid high opportunity costs (K. Howe, 1997) and have the best chance of achieving self-determination.

Despite a history of polylingualism in the United States, bilingual education was not endorsed as national policy until 1968. Since then, however, bilingual education and its various implications have been hotly debated. The criticism of bilingual education has led to repeated attempts to decrease or abolish it, most notably the 2000 passage of Proposition 203 in Arizona and the 1998 passage of Proposition 227 in

California, both of which virtually banned bilingual education in those states. Debates center on the role that schooling ought to have in helping English language learners learn English and subsequently gain broader access to the educational opportunity structure. Few contest the idea that schools should play a role in helping English language learners learn English, especially following the 1974 Supreme Court decision in *Lau v. Nichols*, which endorsed the idea that schools must teach students in a language that they can understand. (I will discuss this case in more detail later in the chapter.) Bilingual education, in its various incarnations, is seen primarily as a vehicle for the acquisition of English. It has significant implications for students' cultural identities as well.

The controversy, then, concerns three main factors: (1) how learning (of English and other subjects) should occur; (2) what place a student's native (primary) language should have in the process; and (3) whether or not efforts should be made to preserve aspects of native culture. Proponents of bilingual education generally maintain that public schools have a responsibility to aid English language learners in learning English while at the same time—and this is a key point—helping students advance their learning in the academic subject areas and sustain their cultural identities as well. By using English language learners' native languages for instructional purposes, students receive the best start in their overall learning and academic achievement. It is most important, the argument goes, first to support students' learning in the content areas and second to teach them English (Andersson & Boyer, 1976; Cummins, 1981; Krashen, 1996; Miramontes et al., 1997). On the other side of the debate, critics of bilingual education contend that learning English should be students' central activity in such a way that the native language is barely used as a language of instruction or not at all. In addition, critics reject the importance of preserving students' cultural identities (Chavez, 1991; Ravitch, 1983; Rodriguez, 1982).

In an effort to shed some philosophical light on this sometimes hostile debate, I will address two main questions in this chapter. First, what role does bilingual education policy have in the educational opportunity structure for English language learners? And second, in what ways might bilingual education enhance students' self-determination? I shall argue that the various criticisms of bilingual education policy are myopic and focused on nostalgic notions of Americanization and assimilation, which often cost English language learners a secure sense of cultural identity, an expansive social context of choice, and consequently, their self-determination. I begin with an account of the historical origins of bilingual education and the federal policy associated with it. Next I outline the different types of bilingual education and arguments put forth against them, paying special attention to the English-only movement, which has voiced opposition to bilingual education almost from the policy's inception. With this foundation in mind, I delve into my defense of bilingual education policy. I end the chapter with an examination of the political challenges to the policy.

A HISTORICAL PERSPECTIVE ON BILINGUAL EDUCATION

It was a long and winding road to the election success of Propositions 203 in Arizona and 227 in California. In the more than 30 years of federal bilingual education policy, most of which included a Supreme Court mandate for instruction that limited English proficient students could comprehend, no campaigns to abolish bilingual education were as successful. During the legislative fervor of the civil rights movement, attention turned toward the needs of English language learners, then called limited English speakers, in 1967. Of course, students whose primary language was not English had been living in America even before the Europeans arrived, as Native Americans spoke over 500 languages. When common schooling began, non-Anglo immigrants were faced with monolingual and monocultural schools.

EARLY BILINGUAL SCHOOLING

German immigrants were the largest non-Anglo group in the colonies, and they attempted to set up bilingual educational opportunities for their children. Often they encountered xenophobia. In 1753, Benjamin Franklin expressed the fear that German language schools would encroach upon the primacy of the English language (Castellanos, 1985). With the common school movement of the mid-1800s came the opportunity to use public schooling for the purposes of assimilating non-Anglo immigrant children to the ways of the Anglo, mostly Protestant mainstream. The generally accepted idea was that language diversity was detrimental to the unity of the fledgling nation. The upcoming discussion of the contemporary English Only movement shows that this attitude continues despite the fact that the United States is no longer so new.

Even though the constitution said nothing about language, it was taken for granted that English was the language of the United States. Since German was the most common non-English language in the East and Midwest during the mid-to-late 1800s, there were some German-English bilingual schools in cities like Cincinnati and Baltimore. French was prominent in Louisiana, and Spanish in New Mexico, and there were pockets of ethnic European students whose primary languages were, for example, Italian or Polish. Still, languages other than English were rarely used as the language of instruction in schools. As a result, by the early 1900s, there were a number of private and parochial schools that used languages such as French, Chinese, or Japanese for instruction (Andersson & Boyer, 1976).

After the Mexican-American war ended in 1848, northern Mexico became part of the United States as the New Mexico territory. Approximately 90,000 Mexican people found themselves in the circumstance of now living in the United States and being part of a language minority group. For a while they were powerful enough to pass a school law in 1884 that stated schools could operate in English, Spanish, or a combination of the two. Later, though, citizens of Mexican descent declined in number as Anglos from the East moved to the Southwest in greater numbers. By 1891, a New Mexico state law was passed specifying that all schools must teach in English (Castellanos, 1985). Ethnocentrism and xenophobia had first reared their heads against the Native Americans and then against white ethnic groups such as the German, Irish, Italian, Polish, and Jewish Americans. Mexican Americans and Asian Americans had to face racism as well. According to Ronald Takaki (1993), when "Mexicans migrated to El Norte and began attending American schools, they were increasingly viewed as threatening to Anglo racial and cultural homogeneity" (p. 329). As the nineteenth century moved into the twentieth, the melting pot ideology was becoming the ruling national philosophy with an emphasis on the melting away of non-English languages. One particularly brazen instance comes from the annexation of Hawaii. Within 2 years of the annexation in 1898, all legislative proceedings had to be conducted in English even though there were few English speakers there (Castellanos, 1985).

As the United States steadily grew due to waves of immigration in the early 1900s, public schools were increasingly seen as the avenue for immigrant assimilation into the mainstream of America (Tyack, 1967). In his book, *Changing Conceptions of Education* (1909), educational historian Elwood Cubberly wrote that the aim of education should be to

> break up these (immigrant) groups or settlements, to assimilate and amal-
> gamate these people as part of our American race, and to implant in their
> children, so far as can be done, the Anglo-Saxon conception of righteous-
> ness, law and order, and popular government, and to awaken in them a
> reverence for our democratic institutions. (quoted in Castellanos, 1985,
> p. 31)

For the most part, the few bilingual programs that existed took place in segregated schools for Mexican American children where the overriding aim was, as Cubberly said, to "assimilate and amalgamate these people." Another aim often was to keep Mexican American people as a ready supply of labor for farmers. Too much (good) education was thus seen as counterproductive. "If every [Mexican] child has a high school education," asked a white sugar beet farmer, "who will labor?" (quoted in Takaki, 1993, p. 327). Said a Texas school trustee, "We don't need skilled or white-collared Mexicans. . . . The farmers are not interested in educating Mexicans. They know that then they can get better wages and conditions" (quoted in Takaki, 1993, p. 327). In fact, school officials often did not enforce compulsory school attendance laws.

To be sure, even before federal intervention there were instances of bilingual programs that included native language instruction, whether or not they actually were conducted with a purity of heart. In 1923, schools in Tucson, Arizona, used native language instruction when there was a majority of Spanish speakers in class. Mexican American students in San Antonio, Texas, followed a curriculum that involved their native language and culture. In 1931, the Burbank, California, schools started a bilingual-bicultural program for Mexican American students who could not speak English. Already the lion's share of bilingual schooling needs were for Spanish-speaking students. For example, there were 44,000 students in Los Angeles, California, schools whose primary language was Spanish (Gonzalez, 1990).

Yet, the first major Supreme Court ruling on language education issues came in *Meyer v. Nebraska* (1923). The high court ruled that it was unconstitutional for a state to prohibit the teaching of a foreign language (in this case, German) in the early grades (Salomone, 1986). This case is especially significant in providing a precedent for Supreme Court support of the use of languages other than English in schools. The *Meyer* case came about because during the early-to-mid 1900s, schools generally only used English for instructional purposes. David Tyack (1967) points out that "public schools became a wedge splitting immigrant children from their parents" (p. 230). That legacy continues today. Education can often present a catch-22 situation for English language learners and their families; while public schools stress cultural assimilation, they also provide a significant route to educational and job opportunities. In the 1930s and beyond, notes historian Gilbert Gonzalez (1990),

> through the program of Americanization, the Mexican child was taught that his family, community, and culture were obstacles to schooling success.

> The assumption that Mexican culture was meager and deficient implied that the child came into the classroom with meager and deficient tools with which to learn. (p. 45)

During the first part of the twentieth century, bilingual programs surfaced on a need basis, but the antiforeigner sentiments that came with the two world wars made the notion of bilingual education (especially for German and Japanese students) unpopular (Castellanos, 1985). As Gonzalez (1990) pointed out above, there were anti–Mexican American sentiments as well; and these were not due to the world wars, but to racism. After World War I, it was illegal in seven states to teach in any language other than English in the public schools, except in foreign language courses. By the 1950s, there were such laws in 28 states (Salomone, 1986). Language was seen as the key to the rapid Americanization of Mexican American and other language minority students, and English was seen as the language of intelligence and democracy (Baron, 1990).

By 1957, the cold war and the launching of Sputnik by the USSR prompted a reevaluation of education in the United States. A renewed focus was placed on mathematics, science, and foreign languages in order for American students to be globally competitive. In addition, the arrival of Cuban exiles to Florida in the late 1950s and 1960s brought with it the need for schooling that the Cuban children could understand. It was a unique situation in Dade County that among the Cuban exiles were trained, Spanish-speaking teachers, which made it easier to establish bilingual programs (Salomone, 1986). The first one began in 1963 at the Coral Way School, where half of the instruction was in Spanish and half in English. By all accounts, it was a huge success. Soon thereafter bilingual programs cropped up in Texas (Andersson & Boyer, 1976). Within 3 years, the National Education Association held a conference on the education of Spanish-speaking children.[3] The road to federal bilingual education policy was beginning to be paved.

FEDERAL BILINGUAL EDUCATION POLICY

On January 2, 1968, the Bilingual Education Act[4] (BEA) also known as Title VII, an amendment to the Elementary and Secondary Education Act (ESEA), was signed into law by President Lyndon B. Johnson. The bilingual education that it endorsed was meant to benefit limited English speaking students through the age of 18 who came from poor families. The BEA was groundbreaking within a country where many states prohibited teaching in languages other than English. Upon signing the ESEA, Johnson pointed out that it contained a special provision establishing bilingual education programs for children whose first language is not English. Thousands of children of Latin descent, young Indians, and others will get a better start—a better chance—in school. . . . What this law means, is that we are now giving every child in America a better chance to touch his outermost limits—to reach the farthest edge of his talents and dreams. (quoted in Andersson & Boyer, 1976, p. 1)

At that time Latino students, ages 14 and over, completed an average of 8 years of school as compared with 12 years for Anglo students of the same ages (Andersson & Boyer, 1976). In the years immediately following the passage of the Bilingual Education Act of 1968, there was an atmosphere of hope and promise surrounding efforts to educate English language learners. Proponents of bilingual education in particular were heartened by support for the maintenance approach to instruction. A mere 16 years later, Johnson's words were forgotten by a presidential administration more concerned with the speed by which English language learners learned English than by the quality of their educational opportunities.

Court Cases and Calls for Native Language Maintenance

There are two general philosophical and methodological approaches to the education of English language learners: maintenance and transitional. In general, each of the different types of bilingual programs falls loosely under one of these two approaches. And as with any complicated system, there are many overlaps. Briefly, the maintenance approach is based on an enrichment model in which programs aim to help students in second language acquisition while also capitalizing on and preserving their native language and culture. The transitional approach is based on a compensatory model in which programs provide some native language instruction, but emphasize the quick acquisition of English in order to prepare English language learners to enter into mainstream English classrooms as soon as possible, often within 3 years (Crawford, 1991). There are two main types of transitional bilingual programs, early-exit and late-exit. Early-exit programs include a small amount of instruction in the native language, usually less than one hour per day. The rest of the instruction is primarily in English, with the native language only used occasionally when clarification is needed. The expectation within the early-exit model is that students will move out of bilingual programs altogether within 2 years (Ramírez, 1992). In late-exit programs, at least 40 percent of instruction must be in the students' native language. English language learners are expected to stay in the bilingual program until sixth grade, to be sure that their English proficiency is adequate for all content areas (Ramírez, 1992). Two other programs do not easily fall into either category, as they do not include any native language instruction, and hence cannot properly be called *bilingual* programs. These are immersion programs and English as a Second Language (ESL) programs. Immersion programs aim to teach English language learners English through all-English instruction in all subjects with some attention to students' ability levels and understanding. These are different from submersion, or sink-or-swim programs, which were outlawed by the *Lau v. Nichols* decision. ESL programs are generally pull-out classes where English language learners go for special English instruction. They are plentiful and are sometimes a part of more comprehensive bilingual programs (Crawford, 1991). The maintenance approach to bilingual education generally has been endorsed by researchers and educators because it emphasizes native language instruction, native language competence, and the use of two languages within the curriculum and schooling. The maintenance philosophy had been used successfully at Coral Way not only to aid students in learning English, but to help students advance their native language literacy and culture as well. Many early critics of this approach lobbied for the transitional approach, which still used native language instruction, but only as a means to the end of English language mastery so as to move to an all-English curriculum (Salomone, 1986).

Once the BEA kicked in, there was a higher level of awareness among civil rights groups and families of English language learners regarding the importance of the approach to bilingual education that schools used. In 1972, the Mexican American Legal Defense and Education Fund filed a lawsuit in New Mexico — *Serna v. Portales Municipal Schools* — which claimed that Mexican American students faced discrimination because of inadequate teaching. The plaintiffs won the case, and the school district appealed. In the meantime, the *Lau v. Nichols* case had been decided by the Supreme Court (as I will soon discuss), so the 10th Circuit Court of Appeals affirmed the lower court's ruling in favor of the plaintiffs. What makes this case especially interesting is that the Circuit Court also deemed it within their purview to include its recommendation for a specific bilingual education plan for the Portales schools. The *Serna* court stated that "under certain circumstances, it is not an unwarranted intrusion for the federal district court, using its equitable powers, to choose among educational programs" (quoted in Castellanos, 1985, p. 118). This case, then, established a precedent that specific judicial recommendations regarding educational programs could be appropriate.

Soon after the *Serna* decision, amendments to the BEA of 1968 provided guidelines as to what bilingual education should actually look like (Salomone, 1986). The original act did not endorse any specific instructional program. According to the 1974 amendments, English language learners should be instructed in their native language in addition to English, and there should be a bicultural component as well. The amendments also lifted the requirement that students in bilingual programs be poor; and added the provision that students whose primary language was English could enroll in bilingual programs. The idea was that any student could benefit from bilingualism. In addition, there was more money reserved for staff development, curriculum development, and research. The amendments helped to clarify Title VII's instructional goals, but there was still debate over the educational approach that was endorsed—the maintenance approach.

The same year, the Supreme Court made a ruling on the *Lau v. Nichols* case stating that the *same* English-only instruction as provided to native English speakers for limited English proficient students was not necessarily *equal*. The decision was the culmination of a class action lawsuit brought by Chinese American students and their families in San Francisco in 1969. The plaintiffs argued that the students were not given equal educational opportunity because they were placed in English-only school situations even though they could not understand English. When the plaintiffs won the case, the defendants appealed the decision to the U.S. District Court of Appeals. In 1973, the District Court overturned the lower court's ruling, opining that the students' rights to equal educational opportunity had not been violated because they were receiving the same education as other students. According to the judges, the school was not unconstitutionally discriminating against the students because their inability to speak English was not caused by past discrimination (Castellanos, 1985). The plaintiff's appeal to the Supreme Court resulted in a landmark decision in the only Supreme Court case that deals directly with the educational opportunities of English language learners (Salomone, 1986). In the Supreme Court trial, the plaintiffs appealed to the Court's ruling in *Brown v. Board of Education*, arguing that an English-only education for students with limited abilities in English was not one *on equal terms* (as *Brown* stipulated) with that of Anglo students. As a result, the Chinese American students did not have access to an education that was meaningful or worthwhile. In a now well-known statement, Justice William O. Douglas noted that "there is no equality of treatment merely by providing students with the same facilities, textbooks, teachers and curriculum; for students who do not understand English are effectively foreclosed from any meaningful education" (quoted in Castellanos, 1985, p. 117). His statement seems so commonsensical it is difficult to believe that anyone would claim that instruction in a language students cannot understand nonetheless provides them with meaningful educational opportunities. One important point about the *Lau* decision is that the Court did not stipulate exactly *how* districts ought to go about bilingual education (Donato, 1997).

That same year, there was another case that did result in a specific mandate as to what a good bilingual program would look like. *Aspira of New York, Inc. v. Board of Education of the City of New York* involved Puerto Rican students in the New York City schools. Along with the students and their parents, Aspira sued the New York City Board of Education, charging unequal treatment and denial of equal educational opportunity. The case resulted in a consent decree, which cited *Lau* and required the school district to help the students learn substantive content in Spanish and maintain their Spanish skills, as well as learn English (Castellanos, 1985).

The Aspira Consent Decree had underscored school districts' need and desire for guidelines that outlined the components of a good and effective bilingual program. In response to this, the Health, Education, and Welfare (HEW) Office of Education under Terrel Bell put forth the Task Force Findings Specifying Remedies Available for Eliminating Past Educational Practices Ruled Unlawful Under *Lau v. Nichols*, which came to be known as the Lau Remedies (Andersson & Boyer, 1976; Castellanos, 1985). These addressed such things as the identification of students' primary or home language, diagnostic approaches, the implementation of a specific type of bilingual program, and training requirements for teachers. The remedies held that English as a Second Language (ESL) programs were not enough; school districts needed to give bilingual instruction at the elementary level at least (Salomone, 1986). While the Lau Remedies were not enforceable by law, they did provide schools with some guidelines for their bilingual instructional programs. Still at issue was whether it was really the federal government's role to provide such guidelines.

Amendment 1703f of the Equal Educational Opportunity Act of 1974 stipulated that an English language learner deserves equal educational opportunity, and therefore educational institutions must take "appropriate action to overcome language barriers that impede equal participation by its students in its instructional program" (Salomone, 1986, p. 100). The catch was that just what was to constitute "appropriate action" was not outlined. The *Rios v. Read* (1977) case took a step in the direction of defining what appropriate action would be. Plaintiffs from Long Island, New York, brought a lawsuit claiming that the bilingual programs of the Patchogue/Medford school district were not effective enough in terms of English learning and academic progress, and were thus meaningless for the students (Applewhite, 1979). The court in *Rios v. Read* held that merely establishing a bilingual program did not fully comply with the *Lau* ruling; more than just ESL classes were necessary in upholding a student's right to a meaningful education (Crawford, 1991). An appropriate bilingual program must include native language instruction by knowledgeable faculty (Salomone, 1986). In the majority opinion, the court pointed out that "an inadequate program is as harmful to a child who does not speak English as no program at all" (quoted in Applewhite, 1979, p. 12). Thus, some 10 years after federal bilingual education policy began, the court reaffirmed the need for native language instruction as part of a bilingual program, but it had to be a program that would last a finite period of time (Salomone, 1986). The stage was set for a turn away from the maintenance approach and toward the transitional approach to bilingual education.

Toward the Transitional Approach

When it came time to begin the process of reauthorization of Title VII in 1977, the American Institutes for Research (AIR) published their evaluation of 38 Spanish bilingual programs and found that students in programs funded by Title VII did better on achievement tests in mathematics, but worse in English vocabulary and reading, than comparison groups of students who were not in bilingual education programs. Supporters of Title VII programs believed that the timing of the release of the study's findings was politically motivated to interfere with the reauthorization process. They also believed that the research was flawed; among other things, it did not take into account that students in the study had differences in prior education experience, time living in the United States, and time in the bilingual program. Of course, those on the other side maintained that there was still little research that supported the maintenance approach to bilingual education (Salomone, 1986). This was significant in that it marked a shift in the debate from an emphasis on the need for bilingual education due to harmful ethnocentrism in public schools to worries about the actual value of bilingual instruction. Indeed, researchers Theodore Andersson and Mildred Boyer (1976) reported that in California, the word bilingual had come to have the negative connotation of *uneducated*. The BEA amendments of 1978

accordingly endorsed a more transitional approach to bilingual education. There would still be native language instruction, but only what was
needed to help students learn enough English to enter into mainstream
classrooms as soon as possible. It was no longer deemed important to
also help students maintain their primary language (Salomone, 1986).

In 1979, an attempt was made to change the Lau Remedies into
actual enforceable regulations. A huge controversy was born. The main
points of contention were over local school control, the costs of implementation, and the usefulness of bilingual education. It seemed to some
people that the Department of Education was mandating bilingual
instruction without enough research supporting that method. After
Ronald Reagan took office, he named Terrel Bell as Secretary of Education and Bell proceeded to withdraw the proposed Lau regulations,
which were a symbol of big, interfering government. Within one year,
the Department of Education dropped the Lau Remedies altogether,
maintaining that because the *Lau* decision had not endorsed one particular instructional approach, schools could use any approach that worked
for teaching English to English language learners and still be in keeping
with the law (Castellanos, 1985). Within this political mood, transitional
approaches to bilingual education were more acceptable than maintenance approaches. Indeed, in 1981 the judges of the Fifth Circuit Court
of Appeals ruled in another case concerning bilingual education, *Castaneda v. Pickard*, that schools could shape their own specific programs for limited English proficient students, as long as the programs
could be expected to help the students transition into full participation
in "regular" classes within a "reasonable" time period after beginning
school (Salomone, 1986, p. 103). The move was toward having students
learn English as quickly as possible without much attention to their advancement in other academic areas or their primary language.

William Bennett took over as Secretary of the Department of Education under Reagan. Under his leadership, the department challenged the
need for and effectiveness of any type of bilingual education except for
what he called "alternative programs," like ESL, which is really not a
bilingual program at all (Crawford, 1991).

During Reagan's 3rd year in office, the BEA came up for renewal.
His administration put forth amendments as the Bilingual Education Improvements Act of 1983, in response to a 1981 Department of Education
report that voiced uncertainty about the wisdom of continuing to federally fund and promote "bilingual education without adequate evidence
of its effectiveness" (Salomone, 1986, p. 92). Advocates of bilingual education criticized that report, especially its emphasis on the Canadian
experience of successful immersion programs as a model. There were

significant differences, they argued, between English-speaking (language majority) students learning French in Canada and language minority students learning English in the United States. Regardless, the Reagan administration chose to promote immersion-style programs and weaken federal involvement in state bilingual education programs. Proponents of bilingual education responded that the research evidence showed that bilingual instruction contributed to better school attendance, better retention and high school graduation, and better achievement. Native language instruction allowed students to master English while still keeping up with content learning in all their other courses (Salomone, 1986).

When the BEA was finally reauthorized in October of 1984, 60 percent of the funds were reserved for bilingual education programs themselves, and most of these had to be transitional in nature. As Rosemary Salomone (1986) points out, the BEA is evidence of a fairly weak national commitment to bilingual instruction because it only provides funds to school systems that are willing to apply for them. Although some school systems may not need the funds, and thus need not apply, this practice allows some school districts to withhold bilingual education from those students who may need it, just because they do not voluntarily apply for the funds. Thus bilingual education is not really seen as a right. Nevertheless, in 1987 the General Accounting Office sponsored a report that gave a strong endorsement of bilingual education and, as a result, questioned Bennett's views. The report came from a panel of 10 nongovernmental experts (6 of whom were recommended by the Department of Education) and concluded that Title VII's support of native language instruction was wise and advisable (Crawford, 1991). The Assistant Secretary for Educational Research, Chester Finn, called the report "inept" and unworthy of serious attention (Crawford, 1991, p. 79).

Despite the findings in the General Accounting Office's report, when President Reagan signed the reauthorization of Title VII, it received no funding increase, it gave the Department of Education discretion over whether or not to fund alternatives to bilingual education, and it established a 3-year rule stipulating that 3 years of bilingual education would be enough (with a few possible exceptions) to transition English language learners into mainstream English classrooms. The idea behind this was that more than 3 years of bilingual education could end up harming students, regardless of what the majority of second-language acquisition research findings said to the contrary (Crawford, 1991). Under Bennett and Finn, the Department of Education significantly scaled back federal support of any maintenance bilingual programs; and they supported only the weakest transitional programs. As John Halcón and María Reyes (1991) point out, Bennett's initiatives for educational reform "promoted the primacy of western culture and civilization at the expense of minority perspectives" (p. 318). During the 1980s and 1990s, federal bilingual education policy changed in its philosophy. While there were still funds available for bilingual programs, those programs increasingly had to forego an emphasis on students' primary languages and instead focus on a fast transition from the primary language to English. This trend continues under the leadership of President George W. Bush, whose plan for bilingual education calls for instruction in English, increased standardized assessment of English language learners, and a distanced and limited role for the federal government (U.S. Department of Education, 2001).

THE DEBATE OVER BILINGUAL EDUCATION

In this section, I explore the most common points of debate in the argument over the different types of educational programs for English language learners, paying special attention to the dispute over official English.

There seem to be three main arguments against bilingual education that surface again and again. First, bilingual education programs are not effective. According to proponents of this view, they do not accomplish the goal of mainstreaming English language learners. Many English language learners thus languish in bilingual programs and never achieve academically. In addition, these critics maintain that it is too difficult and expensive for schools to accommodate students' many different primary languages. Second, the federal government should not mandate education policy; local school officials should have control over such policy. And third, our national unity is dependent on English as the common language; bilingual education is too big of a threat.

BILINGUAL EDUCATION IS INEFFECTIVE

Detractors of bilingual education argue that it is counterintuitive to speak in Spanish, for example, in order to teach and learn English (Chavez, 2000; Unz, 2001). Students can do quite well without it, they maintain. For example, Glenn Garvin (1998) observes that "the idea that a kid will learn English by being taught in Spanish does not usually strike people outside the education field as very plausible" (p. 21). It is true that some students have succeeded without official bilingual programs, such as some immigrants in the early twentieth century. There are a variety of possible and complex reasons for this, including home environment, race and ethnicity, and school climate. Furthermore, some of the students who succeed despite having no bilingual education have been provided with the appropriate background conditions to support their success. Stephen Krashen (1996) points out that these conditions function like de facto bilingual education programs. They include literacy in the primary language, academic success and achievement in the primary language, out-of-school tutoring, access to books and materials in primary language and second language, and a high socioeconomic status.

Critics of bilingual education do not seem to be swayed by the idea that literacy and academic content knowledge in a student's primary language provides crucial skills that are transferable to the second language. They maintain instead that when English language learners receive native language instruction they have no incentive to learn English. Research evidence shows this contention to be false. According to Krashen (1996),

> when we give children subject matter knowledge through the first language, we help them adjust more easily to their new situation, and it makes the instruction they get in English more comprehensible. Because we acquire language by understanding it, this speeds their acquisition of English. (p. 6)

Good bilingual instruction, then, significantly facilitates English language learners' English acquisition.

A problem is that sometimes the quality of bilingual instruction is not high enough. There are not enough good methods of primary language instruction in use, effective methods of assessment, applications of bilingual educational theory to practice, or well-trained bilingual teachers; as a result, the quality of bilingual programs may suffer (Krashen, 1996; Miramontes et al., 1997). Of course, the quality of the education within bilingual programs does vary, but this is true of all other educational programs as well. Nonetheless, opponents of bilingual education cite the most outrageous of dysfunctional programs. Garvin (1998), for example, points out that in San Francisco over 750 African American students (whose first language was English) had been placed into Spanish or Chinese bilingual classrooms. There are similar stories of Latino students placed into bilingual classes just because they have a Spanish last name. These are examples of mistakes made by educators. At best we can blame ineptitude, at worst racism. In any case, bilingual education itself is not at fault. In addition, it is interesting to note that opponents often use examples of English language learners' families criticizing their children's bilingual programs as evidence of the indefensibility of bilingual education policy. What they and those who cite examples like the ones mentioned above seem to fail to understand is that just because the quality of a certain bilingual program may be subpar (which incidentally can be attributed to the lack of clear policy about what constitutes an adequate program of bilingual instruction) does not mean that bilingual education policy itself is useless or that the concept of bilingual education is flawed.

The Significant Bilingual Instructional Features (SBIF) study found five characteristics of effective bilingual classrooms: (1) Teachers are clear about expectations and instructions; (2) teacher expectations are high; (3) both native languages and English are used in the classroom; (4) there is integration of instructional approaches; and (5) students' home cultures are taken into account in class (Salomone, 1986). Monolingual programs like ESL do not meet these criteria. ESL can be helpful, but when it is the only program offered, students mostly learn conversational skills rather than the complex language skills that are necessary for competence in academic subjects (Krashen, 1996). For ESL to be useful, it must be provided as only part of a comprehensive bilingual program.

Instructing students in their primary language while they are learning English in school has two very positive outcomes. First, their native language literacy can be transferred to the second language; "once you can read, you can read" (Krashen, 1996, p. 4). Second, English language learners continue to learn—generally and in academic subjects—so that it is easier for them to understand more and more English. Ofelia Miramontes, Adel Nadeau, and Nancy Commins (1997) make a relevant point: "The more comprehensive the use of the primary language, the greater the potential for linguistically diverse students to be academically successful" (p. 37). Thus, as James Cummins (1981) suggests, it is important for educators to give English language learners enough time in bilingual programs so as to develop bilingual literacy. How long this could take will vary according to context—often depending on how much exposure students have to English outside of school. Consequently, Krashen (1996) puts forth three attributes of good bilingual programs: (1) primary language instruction in content areas, including reading and writing; (2) instruction in English that English language learners can understand; and (3) continued development of the first language.

Another reason cited for the ineffectiveness of bilingual education is that it is too difficult for schools to serve so many different language groups. The argument here goes something like this: it is unrealistic to think that schools, many of which have too few resources as it is, can accommodate

English language learners from myriad language backgrounds. In addition, providing bilingual education to so many different groups quite simply would be too costly. Consider the fact that in New York State alone, school-children speak 121 different languages (Garvin, 1998).

This is a difficult problem. Proponents of bilingual education recognize the burden placed on school districts when students bring so many different first languages to school. Indeed, it would be unrealistic to provide full bilingual education for each language group, especially when there may be just a handful of students representing some languages. Despite the fact that the Lau Remedies are no longer officially sponsored by the Department of Education, they are still seen as sound guidelines for bilingual education. The remedies specifically acknowledge the difficulty that school districts might have in providing bilingual instruction in less prominent languages. As such, they stipulate that a school should provide bilingual education when there is a critical mass of 20 students from a given language group (Castellanos, 1985). This way it is more likely that there will be teachers who are bilingual in English and the other language. And, with family and community support, such a bilingual program has a much better chance of thriving. If there are fewer than 20 students of the same language background, some type of action needs to be taken by schools as well, but it can be less comprehensive (Castellanos, 1985). It is admittedly a challenging proposition for schools to accommodate all students who come to school with a primary language that is not English. Nevertheless, the alternative is far more costly and will result in English language learners who lose the opportunity to keep up with learning in all academic subjects. It may be difficult for school districts to deal with all the different languages students bring to school, but they are obligated to do so in order to provide English language learners with a decent and just education. However, because the Lau Remedies are not official or enforceable, most districts actually fail to provide adequate bilingual programs for English language learners, and rely instead on English as a Second Language programs alone.

In addition, it seems that there is a telling paradox here. It is a valued activity when native English speakers learn a foreign language, yet when there is the chance to maintain the native language competence of students whose native language is not English, it is seen as a waste of time and money. Nevertheless, within this incongruity, Kenji Hakuta (1986) finds a potential for hope. "Perhaps," he says, "the rosiest future for bilingual education in the U.S. can be attained by dissolving the paradoxical attitude of admiration and pride for school-attained bilingualism on the one hand and scorn and shame for home-brewed bilingualism on the other" (p. 229). Perhaps. But it is clear that there are reasons people oppose bilingual education other than a concern for its financial cost.

With the acknowledgment that the maintenance approach is often best for English language learners, a good compromise bilingual education program takes aspects of the maintenance approach and combines them with aspects of the transitional approach (that tends to be less politically contentious). One key to making such a compromise work is for educators to make sure that students know that they are moving toward English instruction because of its prominence in U.S. society and *not* because it is somehow superior to other languages. Another is that students be given sufficient time for transition between program levels. A late-exit program would help ensure this. In addition, English monolingualism must not be endorsed. Krashen (1996) describes one model that aims to use native language instruction in such a way that English language learners do not lose their first language as they learn English. In addition, it emphasizes biliteracy. According to this model, there are four levels of bilingual education. At the first level, English language learners attend English language classes in subjects such as art, music, and physical education; ESL classes for English literacy; and all other academic subjects in their first languages. This gradually shifts so that more and more classes are in English. The second level has students still in art, music, and physical education classes conducted in English and in ESL classes, while they move to mainstream math and science classes that provide them with structured help, and language arts and social studies are in their primary languages. At the third level, math and science are now conducted in English, and students move to mainstream language arts and social studies classes with structured help. Finally, all subjects are conducted in English, and, as throughout, there is an emphasis on the continued upkeep of the students' primary languages. Until the students can understand English well enough to receive instruction in it for academic subjects, they will not have lost any content knowledge (Krashen, 1996). This is the main advantage of such a compromise transitional program. English language learners receive good and appropriate instruction, and their education serves to foster the development of self-determination.

FEDERAL BILINGUAL EDUCATION POLICY SUBVERTS LOCALLY CONTROLLED SCHOOLING

In a liberal democratic society such as ours, one of the strengths is that communities have local control over a variety of important systems. Public education is one such system. Gutmann (1987) sees federal bilingual education policy as too intrusive into local control because it places a value on bilingual instruction as a specific pedagogical approach. Local educators instead of the federal government should make pedagogical decisions and local cultural and community groups "should be empowered to decide whether and how they wish to preserve their culture through bilingual education" (Gutmann, 1987, p. 86).

I agree with Gutmann that in general local democratic control of schooling is the preferred system. However, when we are dealing with racially and ethnically charged issues (e.g., segregation and discrimination), history has shown us that it is the obligation of the federal government to intervene for the sake of justice. In fact, Gutmann herself makes a similar argument in reference to federal policy regarding students with disabilities. "The federal government," she says, "must not let states and local school districts neglect the educational needs of any children" (Gutmann, 1987, p. 159). In the case of the needs of English language learners, many local school districts were simply not doing the right thing. Consider the state of California. California has the largest language population of students of color of all the states, yet in the 95 years before bilingual education policy came into play, instruction was in English only. The dropout rate for Latino students in 1967 was 70 percent. Even then-Governor Ronald Reagan endorsed bilingual education at that point. After over 3 decades of federal bilingual education policy, California now has an approximate dropout rate of 20 percent for Latino youth, which is still too high, but immensely better than before the Bilingual Education Act of 1968 was passed (Lyons, 1998). Of course, the dropout rate is affected by multiple factors, not only by the availability of bilingual education. Federal bilingual education policy ensures that school districts properly attend to the various needs of English language learners. While Gutmann objects to such policy on the grounds that it endorses bilingual instruction of some sort over other pedagogical approaches such as English-only instruction and thereby takes away some local control, without it comes the significant danger of unequal, oppressive education for English language learners. Surely complete local control is not worth such an outcome.

In general, public support for bilingual education is strong[5] (Krashen, 1996). As such, it makes even more sense for the federal government to be involved with policies that support and promote it. A substantial amount of local control over the nature and implementation of bilingual programs can be preserved by educators and community groups.

BILINGUAL EDUCATION UNDERCUTS THE COMMON U.S. CULTURE

Language policy is closely connected with personal identity, cultural identity, and sense of belonging and place. Those worried about the status of our common culture claim that bilingual education policy undermines the assimilation of immigrants and English language learners into the mainstream culture (Hirsch, 1987; Ravitch, 1983). This argument seems rooted in fear and racism. Many Americans are afraid of immigration, especially when the immigrants are people of color such as Latinos and Asians. By complaining about non-English languages, these critics can avoid highlighting issues of race and ethnicity, but still attempt to exclude others on the basis of language. For instance, E. D. Hirsch argues that one national language is important to our "national culture," safety, and internal peace; "the encouragement of multilingualism is contrary to our traditions and extremely unrealistic" (Hirsch, 1987, p. 93). Bilingual education, then, wrongly encourages multilingualism, in Hirsch's opinion. He maintains that he is not opposed to biliteracy, but is concerned that students first learn English before worrying about other languages. The problem with Hirsch's thinking here is that before English language learners can become fully literate in English, they need to become literate in their primary languages. It is only then that biliteracy can be achieved.

K. Howe (1997) makes a good point about the danger of heeding Hirsch's warnings about multilingualism. Problems tend to occur, Howe notes, in nations where nondominant languages are suppressed, such as in the former Soviet Union, not where they are recognized and valued. Following Hirsch on this point, then, would lead us toward conflict, which is likely opposite of what he intends. In addition, if the primary concern is that English language learners learn English as quickly as possible in order to have meaningful access to educational opportunity structures, then bilingual education is what is, in fact, in order. Research has consistently shown that students of color (whose primary language is not English) have most success in acquiring proficiency in English if they receive instruction in their first language (Andersson & Boyer, 1976; Crawford, 1991; Cummins, 1981; Hakuta, 1986; Krashen, 1996; McKenna & Ortiz, 1988; Miramontes et al., 1997).

Regardless of this evidence, opponents of bilingual instruction underscore the idea that when immigrants arrive in the United States, it is their own responsibility to learn English. They make the point that no one forces non-English-speaking immigrants to come to the United States.[6] Immigrants should just have to deal with English as the country's dominant language without any special, expensive help. Although it is true that immigration is often voluntary, it is also true that many immigrants who come to the United States fill the need for low-wage labor and help to keep the capitalist economy moving. In addition, what is often forgotten within this debate is that by and large immigrants to the United States want to learn English as soon as possible. They are often desperate to do so, because they recognize as well as anyone that knowing English will provide them with many more opportunities.

Regardless of the immigration situation, though, schooling in the United States is compulsory, and equal educational opportunity is required for all students. As the *Lau* opinion emphasized, when a student cannot understand the language of instruction and no help is given to that student so that she or he might begin to understand, that cannot rightly be called education. And it is certainly not a *meaningful* opportunity by anyone's standards. Relevant, too, in this argument is that not all English language learners are recent immigrants. We cannot forget that Native Americans, Puerto Ricans, and portions of the Mexican American population lived in what is now the United States long before it became an English-dominant nation.

The fear that bilingualism and bilingual education will degrade American culture resulted in a call for English to be made into the official language of the United States.

The English-Only Movement

The English-only movement gained prominence in the 1980s with a proposed constitutional amendment and various state initiatives to designate English as the official language of government. Although it has broad implications for issues of race and ethnicity in the United States, bilingual education policy in particular is one of its targets. Supporters contend that official English is necessary in order to preserve the unity of American culture, immigrant traditions of assimilation, and the full participation of immigrants in mainstream society (Chavez, 1991). In contrast, opponents of the English-only movement maintain that legislating official English is unnecessary and unjust because English is the de facto public language of the United States. In addition, the law promotes ethnocentrism and xenophobia, is unconstitutional, and harms rather than helps English language learners (Crawford, 1991). Similar to the debates surrounding other race-conscious education policies, people on both sides of the issue claim to be interested in social justice. However, they propose vastly different ways to achieve it.

In 1981, an English Language Amendment to the Constitution of the United States was proposed by California Republican Senator S. I.

Hayakawa. Even though it did not pass, it did spawn a movement within some states for official English (Crawford, 1991). In 1986, Californians voted in Proposition 63 by a 3-to-1 margin, establishing English as the official language of the state. As a result, government business, legislation, and instruction all had to be conducted in English only. Other states with official English laws to date are Alabama, Alaska, Arkansas, Colorado, Florida, Georgia, Illinois, Indiana, Kentucky, Mississippi, Missouri, Montana, Nebraska, New Hampshire, North Carolina, North Dakota, South Carolina, South Dakota, Tennessee, Virginia, and Wyoming (Crawford, 1991, 1998; King, 1997). Arizona's official English law was ruled unconstitutional by the Arizona Supreme Court in 1998 (Crawford, 1998).

Despite the English-only movement's successes in many states, it has been difficult to gain widespread bipartisan support for a national official-English amendment to the constitution, as politicians from all parties seem reluctant to alienate the growing number of Latino voters. One example is President George W. Bush, who came out in public opposition to official English proposals in his state when he was Governor of Texas (King, 1997). In addition, English is widely seen as the de facto national language, with little chance of being displaced by any other. The 1990 census showed that 94 percent of all American residents speak English (King, 1997).

Nevertheless, the national group, U.S. English, has been supported by well-known people such as celebrity Arnold Schwarzenegger, philanthropist Walter Annenberg, and Linda Chavez, former staff director of the U.S. Commission on Civil Rights under President Reagan (Chavez, 1991; Crawford, 1991; King, 1997). Supporters of the English-only movement have a variety of reasons and arguments why they think that there need to be laws making English the official language of the United States. First and foremost is that because of increased immigration, the status of English as our common, unifying language is threatened. Moreover, they maintain that one official language would be the glue that holds this immigrant nation together. Public bilingualism is seen as divisive and a threat to cultural unity (Chavez, 1991; Crawford, 1991). In addition, Chavez contends that Latino immigrants' allegiance to their ethnic group over and above allegiance to being an American is one of the problems contributing to a society polarized along language lines. Official English would thus serve to curb the ethnic polarization that would inevitably arise from the prominent use of more than one language within the United States.

Opponents of an official-English law do not dispute that English is the common language in the United States and that it is important that everyone in the United States learn English. For this reason it is simply unnecessary to legislate an official language. The end result of an English-only law would inevitably be an increase in xenophobia, ethnocentrism, and racism. In essence, an English-only law would give people tacit permission to discriminate against others, including students, because of their native language. So, even though English-only supporters claim that legislating an official language will reduce divisiveness and interethnic conflicts, in reality, a law conceived from a fear of immigrants and of difference will cause the opposite effects of alienation and discrimination (Crawford, 1991; Torres, 1986). For example, Torres (1986) writes about Fillmore, California, where the political campaign for English-only centered on the Latino community. The community was so filled with antagonism that Latino residents boycotted businesses whose owners supported the English-only ordinance. In addition, Stanley Sue and Amado Padilla (1986) suggest that an English-only policy in the school system only serves to affirm "the superiority of the dominant group" (p. 57). A law that makes English language learners feel ashamed and inferior does nothing to promote cultural unity in the United States. Rather, it stigmatizes English language learners and hinders their abilities to learn and receive an equal education.

Another important part of the argument for official English is that such a law would help to preserve the time-honored tradition of the immigrant assimilation process. Supporters of official English maintain that earlier immigrants successfully learned English soon after arriving in the United States, usually through total submersion in the language and culture, so today's immigrant groups should function in the same way. The English-only movement works under the assumption that total assimilation into mainstream U.S. society is beneficial and desirable for language minority peoples. Under this assumption, it is total assimilation that opens the doors of opportunity for education, employment, and success (Chavez, 1991; Phillips, 1987).

Critics of using only English in the classroom contend that, as the prevailing research suggests, the English-only approach actually limits English language learners' learning potential and negatively affects their academic achievement (Heath, 1986; Reyes, 1992; Wong Fillmore, 1991). Shirley Brice Heath (1986), for one, points out that English language learners are best prepared to learn English in school when they have a solid foundation in their native language. Moreover, the alienation caused by monolingual English instruction serves to decrease student participation and opportunities to learn. Much like a domino effect, students' limited participation in academic activities often results in poorer performance and lower student achievement (Trueba, Jacobs, &

Kirton, 1990). Therefore, the claim by English-only supporters that monolingual English instruction speeds the processes of language acquisition
and cultural assimilation, thus solving the so-called problem of bilingual
education, is incorrect (Halcón & Reyes, 1991). How can students be
invested in learning if they cannot understand the language of instruction? As Arnoldo Torres (1986) observes "it would be far more helpful
if those concerned with this issue would support efforts to improve
bilingual education" (p. 19).

Finally, English-only supporters maintain that English language learners are better off learning English quickly, in English (Chavez, 1991; Philips, 1987). Bilingual education gives the message that English is not necessarily the preeminent language, which serves to confuse students' loyalties
and priorities. English-only supporters maintain that they are not opposed
to the learning of other languages, but are concerned that instruction in
English language learners' native languages causes them to remain illiter-
ate in English. Thus their opportunity for educational and economic success is compromised because they will be left out of the mainstream culture (Chavez, 1991; Crawford, 1991; Philips, 1987). This argument sounds
well intentioned, but it conveniently overlooks the important fact that
English language learners' civil rights are violated if the only acceptable
language to use in school is English. The *Lau v. Nichols* decision is very
clear on that point. Therefore, instead of enhancing students' opportunities, as English-only supporters claim, an official-English law actually creates problems by taking opportunities away.

For good or ill, the reality in the United States is that English is
already the predominant language in our society. It is important to learn
English in order to have access to mainstream power and status. English
language learners know this better than anyone. When all is said and
done, the English-only movement seems to be wasting energy. The lion's
share of English language learners and their families *want* to learn English as quickly as possible (Oboler, 1995). They want to succeed within
mainstream society. I maintain that our educational system has an obligation to help them do so, without forcing them to forfeit their particular
cultural identities. Through bilingual education, English language learners can maintain their cultural identities and expand their contexts of
choice, both of which lead them to a greater sense of self-determination.

BILINGUAL EDUCATION'S ROLE IN THE
PROMOTION OF SELF-DETERMINATION

In this section, I put forth my argument for bilingual education based
on the self-determination framework developed in Chapter 2. This philo-

sophical perspective is missing from the current debate and could add a great deal of foundational support for bilingual education policy. Recall that I posited that the development of self-determination among students is a key aim of a good and just education. Race-conscious education policies such as bilingual education contribute significantly to students' development of self-determination. In this case it is English language learners who derive the primary benefit. I theorized that two factors most influence self-determination. When students have a secure sense of authenticity in their cultural identity and a favorable social context within which to make important life choices, they then have the best chance of becoming self-determining. Bilingual education policy supports both of these factors. First, it supports the maintenance of English language learners' cultural identities by publicly recognizing the importance and equal worth of the students' native language and culture. Second, bilingual education policy contributes to a favorable social context within which English language learners have knowledge of and the ability to pursue meaningful life options. Ultimately, authenticity and good contexts of choice move students towards the ideal of self-determination.

FOSTERING ENGLISH LANGUAGE LEARNERS' AUTHENTIC CULTURAL IDENTITIES

The debate over bilingual education policy centers primarily on language, but also touches significantly on culture. More often than not, English language learners are also students of color, inasmuch as the lion's share of English language learners are Latino or Asian American. English language learners' identities are bound to change and shift as they learn English and adjust to the dominant culture of U.S. schools and society. That is an expected developmental outcome. However, their schooling should not jeopardize their feelings about the worth of their language, culture, and concomitant cultural identity. It is bilingual-bicultural education that can stave off such a negative effect of schooling. The issue of cultural identity plays a significant role in the overall equation for educational equality for English language learners. Kymlicka (1995) puts it well: "Cultural membership has a 'high social profile,' in the sense that it affects how others perceive and respond to us, which in turn shapes our self-identity" (p. 7). Indeed, culture has been characterized as the "hidden dimension" of bilingual education efforts (Tennant, 1992, p. 279). In addition, issues of race, ethnicity, and racism enter into people's passions surrounding bilingual education policy.

Without bilingual education, English language learners of color are not only denied the opportunity to advance academically in their native language and in English, but they are given the message that their native culture is unworthy of preservation. This has two main effects. First, English language learners are forced to assimilate fully into the dominant culture if they want to succeed within the educational system. Partly through the educational system they learn that their native culture is less worthy than the mainstream in general, and less worthy of maintenance in particular. Educational opportunities thus come at a high personal and cultural price. Now, one's cultural identity will not necessarily be lost if one's primary language is lost. Many Native American persons in the United States, for example, have lost their native languages, yet retain close connection and identification with their culture. How and why this occurs is complicated and beyond the scope of this work. Suffice it to say that for students who need bilingual education, entering into an educational system that allows (forces) them to lose their primary language would likely result in, at the very least, a shift in their cultural identity. Persons' identities are fluid and inevitably will change, regardless of whether or not bilingual education is available. However, English language learners need not experience total loss of their native language due to their pursuit of education.

The second effect of not receiving a bilingual education is that students' self-determination is often diminished. When English language learners are *forced* to neglect their native language and culture in order to participate meaningfully in the educational system, they may lose the ability to be who they authentically are. Rather, they must change themselves fundamentally in order to receive an adequate education. When this happens, their ability to determine how their lives will go is severely restricted. Meaningful self-determination is often lost. Although some English language learners may choose not to pursue bilingual programs in school, the key point here is that it ought to be a meaningful option.

When we pay serious attention to the arguments against bilingual education, we see a discernible pattern. Opponents of bilingual education are not only concerned about the potential loss of the primacy of the English language, although that is the most publicized complaint. They are also fearful of criticism and disdain for the dominant culture, which could result in conscious nonassimilation by English language learners. By affirming English language learners' native languages and cultures, bilingual education challenges the myth of the necessity of minority assimilation into the mainstream culture in order to succeed in America. It also encourages English language learners' self-determination and furthers the goals of social justice.

Therefore, the absence of maintenance or even good transitional bilingual programs in favor of simple immersion or ESL programs lessens significantly the opportunity for English language learners to become self-determining. Students may end up learning English to the detriment of their home language, which causes them to lose valuable connections to their families and communities, and, consequently, an important link to authentic identity. As Salomone (1986) says,

> For proponents of transitional bilingual-bicultural education, the most difficult obstacle to overcome is a growing national trend away from the conventional conception of this method toward alternative approaches that give only ancillary recognition at best, and no recognition at worst, to the child's home language and culture. (p. 105)

Similarly, Lily Wong Fillmore (1991) points out that losing their native language forces students and their families to pay a significant price, especially when the parents do not speak English well. Take, for example, the case of a young Latino boy, whose family immigrated to the United States from Bolivia before he was born. He grew up speaking primarily Spanish at home with his parents and grandmother. When he entered public school in New York City, there was no bilingual program to speak of. He ended up having a very difficult time with both Spanish and English, so much so, that his family switched him into a private Catholic school. Almost immediately, the school's nuns visited his home and instructed his family that they were not to speak to him in Spanish under any circumstances. English, they advised, had to become their language of choice. However, his grandmother did not speak any English, so this posed a big dilemma for the family. Of course, they felt compelled to do what the nuns asked since they thought it would be in his best interests. He soon lost the ability to communicate effectively in Spanish, but he never really became proficient in English either, and school was forever a chore. At 16, he left school. His case is an instance of what Crawford (1991) describes as "instruction that strives to change students into something else," which "inevitably discourages academic achievement" (p. 27). Even worse than his academic troubles, though, was the rift this caused within the family. He became ashamed of Spanish; the language of intimacy was lost. Hirsch (1987) maintains that "multilingualism enormously increases cultural fragmentation, civil antagonism, illiteracy, and economic-technological ineffectualness" (p. 92). However, in this boy's case, a push toward monolingualism threatened his literacy, and did not help him embrace the dominant (common) culture. This story is meant simply to be illustrative.[7] It provides a good example of the dismal consequences that a lack of bilingual education can have for one student, as it can have for countless other English language learners like him.

Bilingual education researchers find that excellent competence in their native languages helps students to reach what Krashen (1996) calls a "healthy sense of biculturalism" (p. 5; see also Wong Fillmore, 1991). Too often English language learners learn English at the price of their native language. Josué González, former director of the federal Office of Bilingual Education and Minority Language Affairs, points out that instruction should not aim to "change students into something else. . . . When children are painfully ashamed of who they are, they are not going to do very well in school, whether they be taught monolingually, bilingually, or trilingually" (quoted in Crawford, 1991, p. 27).

As the above case illustrated, assimilation into English speaking came at a high price: The English language learner could no longer communicate with his family on an intimate level. Heath (1986) found that parents should speak to their children in their native language so that the children receive the best opportunities to use language in myriad settings and for many different purposes. The children will then be best able to learn English effectively in school. There is no reason to place English language learners in the either-or bind of choosing between school success, on the one hand, and authentic cultural identity and family life, on the other. Such a choice characterizes an education that comes at too high a price.

When critics such as Diane Ravitch (1983) and Hirsch (1987) call for a common culture, they are promoting an oppressive idea, because it requires that people of color change their identities in order to successfully participate in the dominant culture. Iris Marion Young (1990a) criticizes this and calls attention to the fact that "self-annihilation is an unreasonable and unjust requirement of citizenship" (p. 179). In Suzanne Oboler's study of urban Latinos, Young's sentiment was an underlying theme in their experiences. One Colombian American woman commented, "How could we leave our customs and culture aside? We're not machines to be programmed! We are human beings born into a culture and educated with love for our home" (quoted in Oboler, 1995, p. 144). Without a federal policy requiring bilingual education for English language learners, they will be subject to an education that will likely result in forced assimilation and injustice.

Critics like Ravitch (1983) do not believe that this type of education is unreasonable. She notes that bilingual education was intended to help English language learners achieve better academically, drop out less, and have better self-respect. "Real as those problems were," she says, "there was no evidence to demonstrate that they were caused by the absence of bilingual education" (p. 279). Maybe not. However, the absence of bilingual education does cause English language learners to be placed in English-only classrooms, in which they cannot understand the instruction. The absence of bilingual education, then, perpetuates the problems of low achievement, leaving school, and feelings of low self-worth, which is inexcusable due to the fact that schools have access to effective bilingual programs for English language learners. The *Lau* case in particular demonstrated this commonsense point. Students cannot learn anything if they do not understand the language of instruction. If they cannot learn, then they clearly cannot be high academic achievers. It is no big leap to conclude that this would have a negative effect on school persistence and self-respect. I agree with Kymlicka's (1995) contention that "people's self-respect is bound up with the esteem in which their national group is held. If a culture is not generally respected, then the dignity and self-respect of its members will also be threatened" (p. 7). Federal bilingual education policy promotes the respect and recognition of language and culture that is necessary if English language learners are to be guaranteed the right to develop their sense of a bicultural or multicultural identity. In this way, English language learners can feel connected to their cultural communities as well as feel that their cultures are worthy of respect.

HOW BILINGUAL EDUCATION AFFECTS STUDENTS' CONTEXTS OF CHOICE

Along with having an authentic sense of cultural identity, English language learners need to be able to make meaningful life choices in order to become self-determining. Meaningful choices can most readily be made when students are operating within a social context of choice that is expansive rather than restrictive (discussed in more depth in Chapter 2). Education either can serve as an empowering institution in English language learners' lives or a further disempowering one.

The pivotal question is whether or not schools will provide bilingual-bicultural programs that allow English language learners genuinely to pursue every possible educational advantage. If schools do provide such programs, then the students' education would be contributing to a more favorable context of choice rather than a more constrained one. If, however, schools do not provide adequate bilingual programs, English language learners would probably still learn English, but too often would fail to reach their intellectual potential and would lose their secure cultural identity in the process as well. That is why federal bilingual education policy is a necessity. Ideally, it ensures that individual school districts will provide English language learners with a just educational experience. Otherwise, inadequate education would likely cause feelings of linguistic and cultural inferiority that would serve to limit English language learners' social contexts of choice. Andersson & Boyer (1976) make a good point:

> To the extent that English is the only medium of communication and the child's language is banned from the classroom and playground, he inevitably feels himself to be a stranger. Only as he succeeds in suppressing his language . . . does he feel the warmth of approval. In subtle or not so subtle ways he is made to think that his language is inferior to English, that he is inferior to the English-speaking children in school, and that his parents are inferior to English-speakers in the community. (p. 44)

Such an education ends up limiting English language learners' range of options. If they feel that they do not belong, that their primary language and culture invites disapproval, and that they cannot take pride in their heritage and home knowledge, it should not be surprising when English language learners are unable to envision academic success or educational opportunity. And even when they can envision such success, they may refuse to conform to dominant norms in order to achieve it, as John Ogbu and Margaret Gibson (1991) have documented. The point is that English language learners' education should not serve as a limiting factor within their educational opportunities or life choices. Consider the findings of Maryann Jacobi Gray, Elizabeth Rolph, and Elan Melamid (1996). In their study of immigrant and first-generation students pursuing higher education, they found that inadequate English language skills are the largest barrier to admission to and graduation from higher education (Gray, Rolph, & Melamid, 1996). Most of these students did not have access to bilingual-bicultural education. This provides an example of a tangible negative outcome of inadequate educational opportunities for English language learners.

Unfortunately, it seems that those opportunities may be kept willfully from students. For example, in the late 1950s and early 1960s after Sputnik, the study of foreign languages was encouraged, and even became a requirement for admission into competitive colleges and universities. Still, the native languages that English language learners brought to school were usually not given credit. To make matters worse, some school systems required all students to have a minimum grade of B or C in English before they could take a foreign language class. This often precluded many learners of English as a second language from taking a course in their home languages, and thus from qualifying for college admission (Castellanos, 1985). Too often educators and the public tend to believe that English language learners are actually deficient in some way because English is not their native language. Consider Zeynep Beykont's (2000) perspective. She points out that "language minority students face . . . academic challenges within a political context that defines their bilingualism as 'problematic,' 'deficient,' and 'a sign of inferior intellectual and academic abilities'" (p. vii). Bilingual education is viewed only as a compensatory (rather than enriching) program. This is a problem because it is simply not a deficiency to have a native language other than English (Fránquiz & Reyes, 1998). If it were, the majority of people in the world would be considered deficient. What is true is that as a resident of the United States it is critical to learn English. Hardly anyone disputes that. Consider what an immigrant from the Dominican Republic has to say:

> I want to get a good profession, a good job and I want to know more about the culture of this country, and I have to relate to people who speak English. It's the language you have to use in this country. (Oboler, 1995, p. 145)

Indeed, Oboler found that this exemplified the feelings of the vast majority of the Latinos she studied. However, it is also important to nurture one's first language while learning English. Schooling is compulsory and, therefore, school districts have a distinct responsibility to educate students whose native language is not English, especially in order to provide them with opportunities to improve their contexts of choice and, consequently, foster their self-determination as well. Not only is this just, but the Supreme Court supported the idea in *Lau v. Nichols*. Nonetheless, English language learners often get the detrimental message in school that "foreign language" study is valued, but a language other than English that students already know is not. How can this kind of message and educational constraint *not* serve to harm students' cultural identities and their contexts of choice?

To view English language learners as having a cognitive deficiency just because their native language is not English is to treat them unjustly. They may find themselves in a disadvantaged situation due to their lack of proficiency in English within a country where knowledge of English is critical for mainstream success, but this does not mean that English language learners are in any way unintelligent or unable to excel academically. A good and just education, as such, would serve to help English language learners maintain their first language, thus expanding their social contexts of choice. Indeed, in her study of academically and professionally successful Chicanos, Patricia Gándara (1995) found that the majority (84 percent) came from Spanish-speaking homes. This provides evidence that refutes the belief that coming from a Spanish-speaking home is somehow detrimental for students. This, per se, does not constrain English language learners' social context of choice; it is the way that the educational system treats English language learners that does so.

Good bilingual education will help students learn English and at the same time provide native language instruction in other academic subjects, along with affirmation of students' cultural identities. English language learners will gain access to the dominant language, keep up with their learning of other subjects, and have their native language and culture publicly recognized by the educational system. The decisions they then make for their lives are much more likely to be chosen from among meaningful options. Thus English language learners will be operating within a favorable social context of choice, and their education will foster their self-determination.

BILINGUAL EDUCATION POLICY AND SELF-DETERMINATION

Through the civil rights history of the United States, we have learned that it often takes federal intervention in states and localities to ensure that social justice is served by the educational system. Unfortunately, as discussed above, federal bilingual education policy has been the subject of intense debate. What seems to be good *prima facie*—bilingual education policy to ensure that English language learners are well served by education—is often seen as actually harmful to English language learners. Of course, bilingual education and the federal policies that support it have been defended from a variety of perspectives. Still, relatively little attention has been paid to the role bilingual education policy has in fostering English language learners' self-determination.

In this chapter I have thus far made the case that bilingual education and its concomitant federal policy have two major effects on English language learners. First, they provide the students with public recognition and support of their native language and culture and, consequently, their authentic cultural identity. Second, they enhance the social context within which English language learners make important decisions about the way their lives will go. Laws that ban bilingual instruction are oppressive in that they serve to suppress English language learners' cultures and constrain their contexts of choice. As such, they are antithetical to the ideal of self-determination, and they degrade social justice.

In contrast, policies that support bilingual education also support the development of students' self-determination. They help English language learners gain access to what Lisa Delpit (1993) calls the "culture of power" without harming their personal and cultural identities (p.

121). As a result, English language learners have the tools to understand and participate in the dominant culture without sacrificing themselves in the process. They can then develop the healthy balance within their personal and cultural identity that I described in the last chapter.

Bilingualism rather than monolingualism in English has been cited as more conducive to students' academic success. In their 1998 study of 700 Latino students, ages 12 to 14, Russell Rumberger and Katherine Larson found that Latino students gain academic success (as defined by grades, retention, and high school graduation credits) through bilingualism more than through fluency in English alone. They concluded that proficiency in both Spanish and English led students to better academic achievement than monolingual Spanish or English speakers ("Knowledge of English," 1998). Consider the experience of Richard Rodriguez. His case is an interesting and illustrative one in that he comes from a Spanish-speaking home and laments the way that learning English and gaining academic success made him lose his proficiency in Spanish and the close connection with his family. To succeed in the dominant culture he felt that he had to—literally and figuratively—change who he was. He says, "The social and political advantages I enjoy as a man result from the day that I came to believe that my name, indeed, is *Rich-heard Road-ree-guess*" (Rodriguez, 1982, p. 27). Throughout his autobiography, Rodriguez insists that this was necessary, and ultimately good for him. But couldn't he have made the same gains and still have been *Ricardo*? And still have been able to talk to his parents—*Mamá and Papá*? I am compelled to answer a qualified yes, *if* the education he had received had helped him to develop self-determination rather than forcing him down a path leading to internalized oppression and full assimilation. It seems to me that if Rodriguez had had the opportunity to experience good bilingual-bicultural education, he would have been able to maintain his native language, family intimacy, and respect for his ethnicity and culture, while still learning English and achieving academically. He would not have felt as though he *had* to choose between his family and mainstream society. Some assimilation is inevitable, necessary even, for non-English speakers in contemporary U.S. society. However, in the process, English language learners should not lose the right to maintain their native language as the price of learning English. The goal of one common culture, or a homogeneous public, championed by assimilationists, does not lead necessarily to a harmonious society (Young, 1990a). Conflicts are inevitably caused, not by multiculturalism and multilingualism, but by the racism and oppression exemplified by forced assimilation.

What this all means for bilingual education policy is that, ultimately, instruction that is not understood because of a language barrier is meaningless and limits students' freedom and self-determination. Such education is profoundly miseducative in a Deweyan sense: Students collaterally learn that their home language and culture are inferior to English and the dominant culture. What they should learn instead is that while their native language and culture may be different from the U.S. mainstream, both are deserving of respect and recognition. Their schooling should teach them, both explicitly and implicitly, that being bilingual and bicultural are assets. A federal policy of bilingual education supports that lesson and thus aids students in their crucial development of self-determination. Consequently, it fosters social justice as well.

THE POLITICAL CLIMATE

Carlos Cortés (1986) writes about a young Mexican American student who is forced to write "I will not speak Spanish at school" on the blackboard 50 times during "Spanish Detention" after he was caught speaking Spanish with his classmates during recess (p. 3). Although this type of school policy is no longer tolerated, we can imagine it occurring again, especially in light of the passage of laws like Propositions 203 and 227. Laws such as these could foster a rapid regression back to such shameful, discriminatory practices.

CALIFORNIA'S DUBIOUS LEADERSHIP

As with other political issues related to race and ethnicity, the state of California took the lead in legislation against bilingual education and languages other than English. California was the first state where, in 1994, voters passed Proposition 187, an initiative widely seen as anti-immigrant. Four years later, voters passed Proposition 227, also called the Unz Initiative, which virtually abolished bilingual education in favor of immersion and ESL programs for English language learners. A full 42 percent of all English language learners in the United States reside in California. Politicians in California seem to try to capitalize on wedge issues such as immigration policy, bilingual education policy, and affirmative action policy in order to anger Anglo voters into supporting them. The recent passage of initiatives opposing these policies, in conjunction with an earlier vote for English as the state's official language, place California in the dubious position of leading the nation toward voter referenda that undo some of the greatest gains of the civil rights movement. Taken together, California's three propositions—187, 209, and 227—send a strong message that is anti-people of color in general, and anti-Latino and anti-immigrant in particular. Due to the success of

Proposition 227, its supporters pledged to end bilingual education in other states, most notably Arizona.

Proposition 227

In June 1998, voters in California passed Proposition 227, an initiative called "English Language Education for Children in Public Schools" (1998, p. 12). The initiative virtually bans bilingual instruction in public schools. It marks the first time an initiative process has had a hand in determining public school curricula, as it calls for English language learners to be put into English-only immersion classes for one year before being transferred to mainstream classrooms. This ignores well-respected research that has found such limited, English-based types of instruction for English language learners to be counterproductive to their academic learning and achievement (Andersson & Boyer, 1976; Cummins, 1981; Hakuta, 1986; Heath, 1986; Krashen, 1996; "Knowledge of English," 1998; Wong Fillmore, 1991). In addition, school personnel may be legally liable if they choose to circumvent the proposition (Rodriguez, 1998). Thus some politics of intimidation were at play—with threats that teachers and administrators could be held personally and financially liable and potentially lose their homes for resisting Proposition 227 (Crawford, 1999).

Not only does Proposition 227 go against research-supported bilingual pedagogy, but it flies in the face of what *Lau v. Nichols* outlawed in 1974—educational approaches for English language learners that limit their equal opportunities. For how can English language learners receive equal educational opportunities when they have only one (school)year to learn English with enough fluency to enter mainstream classrooms? When in so doing, they lose a year of instruction in other academic subjects? When no one would even suggest that anyone else could easily learn a second language in 180 days? In essence, Proposition 227 advocates what Reyes calls a "one size fits all" approach to education for English language learners, who come to school with varying levels of literacy and English-language proficiency (Reyes, 1992, p. 427). With 25 percent, or 1.4 million, of all students in California categorized as ELL, this has an adverse affect on quite a large number of students, many of whom are Latinos (Crawford, 1999). How did this seemingly senseless proposition manage to get passed?

Ron Unz and the "English for the Children" campaign. Ron Unz, coauthor and sponsor of the "English for the Children" campaign for Proposition 227, is a millionaire businessman in California's computer industry. Single, with no children, Unz is a member of the board of the Center for Educational Opportunity, which is led by Linda Chavez, a long-time opponent of bilingual education and other race-conscious policies (Chavez, 1991, 2000; Miner, 1999). In 1994, he attempted a bid for the Republican nomination for Governor, but lost to Pete Wilson, so he seems to have some aspiration to elected office. Proposition 227—the Unz Initiative—is one way he was able to get name recognition, political clout, and a reputation as a political player. Unz's political strategy was, as Crawford (1999) words it, to "attack bilingual education *on behalf* of the groups it was designed to benefit, as a 'well-intentioned' program that was failing to teach English" (p. 5). Interestingly, some 63 percent of Latinos voted against the initiative, despite press coverage beforehand that claimed widespread Latino support (Crawford, 1999). With seemingly unlimited funds and advertisement, Unz was able to get the initiative on the ballot, even though most Anglos in the United States as a whole feel generally supportive of bilingual education (Huddy & Sears, 1990; Krashen, 1996). Of those who do not support it, most also have negative attitudes toward people of color and immigrants. Unz contends that Proposition 227 is not anti-immigrant or anti-Latino, but anti–bilingual education, which he views as a failed education policy largely responsible for the high dropout rate among Latino youth. However, as James Lyons (1998) points out, only 30 percent of California's English language learners received actual bilingual instruction; the rest received instruction in English only. So, if education has failed English language learners, it is likely due to the fact that most of their instruction has been conducted monolingually in English (Lyons, 1998). Nevertheless, the Unz Initiative mandates that "all children in California's public schools shall be taught English by being taught in English" ("English Language Education," 1998). Perhaps Unz and his coauthor, Gloria Matta Tuchman, truly believe that English-only instruction is the best way to provide equal education for English language learners. Whether or not this initiative was in fact well intentioned is unimportant. What is important is the fact that the initiative was conceived of at all, and that a majority of voters thought it was a good idea. Proposition 227 passed with 61 percent of the vote (Crawford, 1999). If nothing else, these facts underscore the strong need for federal bilingual education policy. There is just too much ignorance and misinformation about bilingual education, second language acquisition, and the cultural needs of English language learners. Dennis Baron (1990) makes the point that

> it is painful to realize that American public schools refused to cater to the needs of nonanglophone children until recently, when court rulings and federal legislation forced them to deal with the issue, and it is discouraging

to observe that even after the need for formal language instruction has become clear to educationists, many schools continue to resent and resist providing their clients—the students—with what those clients need and want, an education. (p. 175)

Federal policy in support of bilingual instruction provides school districts with at least some guidelines regarding the needs and rights of English language learners. This is crucial if the educational system is to contribute to English language learners' development of self-determination.

After Proposition 227 passed, opponents attempted to get a court injunction against it, but a judge turned them down because they could not yet show irreparable harm to students due to the proposition (Crawford, 1999). There is, however, one way for parents to try to bypass the restrictions of Proposition 227. The initiative stipulates that after 30 days,[8] families may request a waiver of the law, with students under age 10 classified as having "special needs" in order to receive bilingual instruction (Crawford, 1999, p. 1). By using this exception, opponents of Proposition 227 have been able to organize some positive counteractions to the initiative. One example of this in use is Starlight Elementary School in Watsonville, California. Approximately 80 percent of its students are Latino, many of whom are new immigrants or migrants with limited proficiency in English. Starlight parents signed the allowed waivers and the school's bilingual-bicultural programs survived. It is important to note that there is also leadership from the top, in that the superintendent in Starlight's district supports bilingual education in spite of Proposition 227 (Miner, 1999). Cases like Starlight, however, are in the minority.

OTHER CHALLENGES TO BILINGUAL EDUCATION

It is not uncommon for the federal government to follow California's political mood. For example, after Proposition 187 passed in 1994, Congress passed legislation in 1996 to curtail illegal immigration to the United States, which resulted in the deportation of nearly 300,000 immigrants, double the deportations of 1994. In 98 percent of these deportations, the immigrants were sent back to Latin American, Spanish-speaking countries (Miner, 1999). In fact, the federal government has tried to follow California's lead, and immediately after Proposition 227 passed in the summer of 1998, the House of Representatives passed a bill aimed at stopping federal funding for bilingual education and mandating that all English language learners be mainstreamed within 2 years. If not for the intervention of the Clinton administration, bilingual education policy would have been annihilated (Crawford, 1999).

Proposition 203

Proposition 203, Arizona's more restrictive version of Proposition 227, passed in November 2000 with 63 percent of the vote (Crawford, 2000). The Arizona initiative, also known as "English for the Children of Arizona," was funded in large part by Unz. It restricts instruction to English only, and holds that English language learners must receive instruction in English immersion programs for a maximum of one year. Though it leaves the possibility for schools to provide bilingual education, a school would need to receive 20 parental requests for such a program. Perhaps the most difficult circumstance brought on by Proposition 203 is that the Arizona legislature is not allowed to repeal it. The only way it can be reversed is by the passage of another ballot initiative (Crawford, 2000). And yet, studies of bilingual education in Arizona show that it is effective and worthwhile (Krashen, Park, & Seldin, 2000). Regardless of such findings in Arizona and other states, Unz told reporters that he hopes to target the states of Massachusetts, Colorado, and New York as well (McCloy, 1999).

Still, there is some hope to be found. Supporters of bilingual education in other states have reacted against the threat of anti-bilingual education ballot initiatives. Colorado successfully staved off having such an initiative on their November 2000 ballot. Bilingual education supporters brought suit against the Unz-proposed initiative, citing its deceptive wording. Four months before the election, the Colorado Supreme Court ruled against the initiative because it misled the public by inadequately explaining that the law would restrict schools' ability to choose between a variety of different programs for heritage language learners (Weber, 2000). In Florida, the Miami–Dade County School Board unanimously voted to reaffirm the district's commitment to bilingual education programs. In Texas, another state with a large proportion of heritage language learners, 72 percent of Texans recently polled said that they thought bilingual education was an important program (Miner, 1999).

CONCLUSION

It seems that a key issue within the debate over bilingual education is that bilingual programs often are based on a weak compensatory model where, as Sonia Nieto (1992) contends, students' "knowledge of another language is not considered an asset but at best a crutch to use until they master the 'real' language of schooling. This is at best a patronizing and at worst a racist position" (p. 164). She goes on to cite examples of children who will no longer speak Spanish because they think that it is the language of the "dumb kids." These students obviously have received a negative message about languages other than English. If Spanish is the language their families speak, what must they be thinking about their parents? If opponents of bilingual education meet their objectives, English language learners will not only end up suffering within the school system, but in their homes and communities as well.

In this chapter I have aimed to make the case that bilingual education is a valuable and necessary approach to the education of English language learners. As such, it plays a positive role in enhancing the educational opportunity structure for English language learners. I argued that bilingual education fosters students' self-determination in two main ways. First, instruction in English language learners' native languages and recognition of their cultures serve to create an atmosphere that supports and values their cultural identities. Second, when educational programs give English language learners the opportunity to learn English while maintaining their primary language and moving forward in other academic subjects, those programs serve to enhance the context from which the students make their life choices. Consequently, English language learners receive an education that helps them develop their self-determination. As I posited in the last chapter, the development of self-determination is crucial for a just education in that it enables students to participate in our democracy and lead good lives. Self-determination, then, is characterized by the ability to make meaningful choices about opportunities, rather than merely empty or forced choices. For English language learners, this would mean access to good bilingual instruction that leads them toward a "real" opportunity to learn both English and other academic content (K. Howe, 1997, p. 18). As K. Howe (1997) observes, educational opportunities are not "equally worth wanting solely because they are there for the taking" (p. 53). For example, when an English language learner is placed in an English-only instructional situation, that student has only a "bare" (Dennett, 1984, p. 116) opportunity to learn and, subsequently, to advance academically. The opportunity exists, but it is a hollow one, or one not worth wanting, because the student would have to overcome nearly insurmountable obstacles in order to take advantage of it (Dennett, 1984; K. Howe, 1997). In addition, the English language learner would end up paying a high "opportunity cost" (K. Howe, 1997, p. 53) for the educational opportunity, as it likely would come at the expense of her or his cultural identity and community connection.

The dismantling of bilingual education policy would have the effect of closing the very doors of opportunity that opponents of bilingual instruction like Unz claim they wish to open. To offset the negative societal messages fostered by laws like Proposition 203 and Proposition 227, educators and policymakers have a responsibility to find a way to reconceptualize the language issue in schools. Languages other than English must not continue to be perceived as deficiencies, but as assets that significantly enhance a student's knowledge base (Fránquiz & Reyes, 1998). Educators should never contribute to the further alienation of already dominated groups (Nieto, 1992). Policymakers have the ability to help schools change in order to accommodate the present and future diversity of students, instead of forcing the students to change fundamentally in order to adapt themselves into the dominant structures. As discussed earlier, the process of assimilation can be painful and counterproductive for English language learners. The research supporting native language instruction and nonassimilationist models of education can help students only if educators and policymakers take heed and change their practices accordingly.

Because bilingual education makes such a positive contribution to the cause of social justice in education, it is incumbent upon the federal government to at least support existing policy that requires school districts to offer bilingual education programs in the name of treating English language learners as equals and providing them with equal educational opportunities. The lion's share of bilingual programs fall into the early-exit transitional category. It would be wise for the federal government to expand bilingual education policies such as the Bilingual Education Act so that bilingual programs would be required to follow the philosophy of a maintenance program or a late-exit transitional program, which are more likely to help English language learners gain the skills necessary to excel academically (Ramírez, 1992).

Of course, there are still critics who maintain that English language learners should only be taught in English. The anti–bilingual education ballot measures underscore that point. These critics are endorsing an education that can really only be described as oppressive to English language learners. In summary, then, bilingual education fights oppression by supporting the development of self-determination through its support of students' feelings of authenticity as well as through its important contribution to expanded contexts of choice. Without it, there is the significant danger that for English language learners to succeed in mainstream education, they will be forced to change who they are fundamentally (in a negative way). As educational history shows us, without bilingual education, English language learners either languished in class-rooms where they could not learn, or they achieved academically but lost a valuable piece of themselves in the process. In order to support justice, the dominant culture manifest within schools ought to adjust to the diversity of students, rather than assume that it is the English language learners—often students of color as well—who must change who they are in order to fit themselves into the existing structures.

David Berliner and Bruce Biddle (1995) observe that "some of those who oppose bilingual programs seem to be xenophobic, racist, and just plain mean-spirited" (pp. 206–207). Xenophobia comes into play because of a fear of non-English languages and cultures, and racism because most English language learners are Latino. While all are deplorable, the mean-spiritedness is perhaps the most difficult with which to contend. When we get down to it, bilingual education is about the students—students who, through circumstances beyond their control, come to school speaking primarily Spanish or Vietnamese or Laotian. They also come to school ready to learn and ready to embrace the opportunities promised by education in the United States. Policies that will strongly support bilingual education are needed so that we can provide the students with an education that feeds their hearts as well as their minds.

NOTES

1. I should point out that although bilingual education is not in itself a program that is either explicitly race-conscious or beneficial for students of color only, I include it here as part of a group of policies that are (officially or not) conscious of race and ethnicity. The reason that I believe bilingual education is a race-conscious policy, and the major reason that it is in need of philosophical defense, is because it is under political attack due to the fact that the vast majority of students who are in need of and who participate in bilingual programs are Latino students whose primary language is Spanish. Of the students receiving bilingual instruction who are not Latino, the majority are Native American or Asian American. This makes bilingual education a policy that disproportionately benefits three groups of people of color. As I note later in the chapter, racism and ethnocentrism often motivate the harshest criticisms of bilingual education. Issues of race and ethnicity play a significant role in the development of bilingual education policy in U.S. public schools. Similar points may be made for remedial education, which will be examined in Chapter 6.

2. There are a variety of different terms used to describe the students who either do not know or have little knowledge of English because their native or primary language is a language other than English. These terms include *limited English proficient, second language learner, linguistically different, linguistically diverse, linguistic minority, language minority, heritage language*

learner, and *English language learner*. Herein I mainly refer to such students as English language learners (ELL) because it seems to me to be both the clearest and most descriptive term in this context, even though I do not think of these students as only concerned with learning English.

3. Bilingual education benefits many different racial and ethnic groups, speaking a variety of different languages. The most prominent of these are Latino Spanish speakers. In 1996, over 91 percent of the Bilingual Education Act program proposals were for Latino English language learners (Valdés, 1997). Hakuta (1986) observes that there is a "strong identification of 'bilingual' with 'Hispanic'" (p. 226).

4. Bilingual Education Act, 81 Stat. 816 (1968).

5. What is not strongly supported is the maintenance of the primary language *at the expense of* the learning of English (Krashen, 1996).

6. The cases of refugees and political exiles would perhaps be exceptions.

7. It is based on the experience of one of my relatives.

8. As stipulated by Proposition 227, 30 days is the minimum amount of time that every student must be in English-only instruction (Crawford, 1999).

4

Multicultural Curricula

In November 1998 a group of students at Cornell University protested against the College of Arts and Sciences by occupying the lobby outside of the office of a dean. At issue was a report commissioned by the dean that suggested that Cornell's Ethnic Studies programs should operate in greater cooperation with its American Studies programs. More than 500 student protesters feared that the hard-won Ethnic Studies programs would then be overshadowed and ultimately subsumed by American Studies (*The Chronicle of Higher Education*, 1998c).

As the protest at Cornell underscores, the classroom still represents possibility. Perhaps because of this, we can begin to understand why the issue of multicultural curriculum policy is so controversial, an issue that invites rancorous debate on college campuses and within both the educational literature and the popular press. While the debate is certainly lively enough, as with bilingual education, it generally lacks attention to the philosophical underpinnings for multicultural curriculum policy and practice. This chapter focuses on an important philosophical justification for multicultural curricula, in relation to the framework I sketched in Chapter 2. In particular, I argue that a broad policy of multicultural education, at both the K–12 public school and college levels, is necessary in order for students to be able to develop self-determination.

Early research on multicultural education highlighted the need for curricula that would somehow help deal with "minority"[1] students (Mogdil, Verma, Mallick, & Mogdil, 1986). It is still often portrayed that way, even though it has been suggested that good multicultural education is essential for democracy and social justice (Ladson-Billings, 1998; Sleeter & Grant, 1987). Multicultural curriculum policies emphasize the importance of a nonoppressive education and thus aim to enrich the quality of students' educational experiences and their sense of authentic cultural identity. The debate over multiculturalism within education in the United States concerns not only the quality of academic life and persons' identities, but the very aims of education. Hot debates about multicultural curricula occurred during the late 1980s and early 1990s. Many were satisfied with the gains made in diversifying curricula. As a result, there is perhaps more complacency surrounding the need for multicultural education now. This complacency gives rise to the need for clear education policies that support multiculturalism in curricula.[2]

Multicultural curricula are not a panacea for the ills of the educational system, yet like bilingual education, they are one important piece of an overall educational picture that strives for nonoppression. Antimulticulturalists, or essentialists, as Gutmann (1994) calls them, argue that the curriculum should focus on the time-tested traditional canon of great works from Western civilization. This canon does not include more current works by multiethnic or multinational authors. On the other side, multiculturalists call for the inclusion of the perspectives of more women and people of color, and for the integration of these perspectives within all subject areas. This way, students can learn varied perspectives and perhaps begin to think critically about dominant societal norms.

This chapter addresses the following question: What do multicultural curricula have to offer students seeking a self-affirming education? I begin by looking at the historical background for the current debate over multicultural education. Next, I explore the various assumptions and principles that underlie multicultural curriculum policies. Finally, I outline just how multicultural curricula contribute to students' feelings of authenticity and expanded contexts of choice. Within this discussion, I examine specific debates over multicultural curricula from K–12 schooling and higher education.

FRAMING THE DEBATE OVER MULTICULTURALISM

America has always been a multicultural nation. In spite of this (or maybe because of it), early in its history, the United States' educational system showed a propensity toward assimilationist education. This is exemplified most clearly by the efforts of the European colonists to "civilize" Native American people and, in essence, replace native cultures with Anglo, Protestant culture. For example, the Naturalization Act of 1790 officially excluded Native Americans from citizenship because they were considered domestic foreigners. Later, during the common school movement of the 1830s, the designers openly hoped to use education to support and advance the Protestant-based Anglo culture as the one best culture for America (Spring, 1997). This attitude was pervasive in the treatment (specifically within the educational system) of many different minority groups—from white ethnic cultures to African Americans and Latinos. After the Civil War, more attention was focused on the education of black students and other students of color. Yet, this education continued to be assimilationist in nature, with the inferiority of these students and their cultures taken for granted (J. Anderson, 1988; Gonzalez, 1990).

Around the beginning of the twentieth century until World War I, there was an increase in immigration to the United States from southern, central, and eastern Europe. In 1908, English-Jewish playwright Israel Zangwill's play *The Melting-Pot* opened in Washington, D.C., with President Theodore Roosevelt in attendance. It put a name to the assimilationist philosophy that dominated that time period. Zangwill called America a "great melting-pot where all the races of Europe are re-forming," implying that immigrants and non-Anglos would lose their particular cultures as they became part of the common American culture. Even then, however, there were those who felt uncomfortable with the melting pot metaphor. Sociologist Horace Kallen contested the idea of the melting pot, saying that it was harmful for immigrants to feel as though they had to abandon their cultures in order to fit into American society (Salins, 1997). Instead, he advised, we should celebrate America's "cultural pluralism" and encourage the various immigrant cultures to preserve their diverse traditions (Kallen, 1924). Kallen's ideas were really the precursor for the multiculturalism movement during the rest of the twentieth century. Despite Kallen's emerging idea of cultural pluralism, at that time in the United States there was still a general distrust of foreigners, especially those who spoke languages other than English, as I mentioned in Chapter 3. The Immigration Acts of 1917 and 1924 supported the anti-immigration sentiments. First, the 1917 Act attempted to limit immigration from countries such as Italy and Poland by forcing potential immigrants to pass a reading test before they could come into the United States. When that measure failed to result in decreased immigration, the 1924 Act went further and specifically limited immigration from areas of Europe other than the north and the west (Banks, 1994). It is perhaps no surprise that the public educational system served as the primary mechanism of assimilation for the non-Anglo immigrants that did manage to enter the United States. Assimilationist efforts that attempt to minimize, or even ignore, all differences parallel these early efforts at what Joel Spring (1997) calls "deculturalization."

In the 1930s and 1940s, some educators of color attempted to respond to such deculturalization through educational reform (Noffke, 1998). There were curricular reform efforts aimed at African American schoolchildren in the southern United States. These efforts centered on

revising standard curricula to include the life of black people in the
United States. In addition, notables such as Horace Mann Bond, a scholar
published in the *Journal of Negro Education*; Carter G. Woodson, a
managing editor of *The Negro History Bulletin*; and W. E. B. DuBois,
founder of *The Crisis*, carried on substantive discussions of curriculum
theory and policy in the 1930s (Noffke, 1998). During and after World
War II, there was increased U.S. attention to intolerance, resulting in
some emphasis on intercultural education and on respecting individual
others despite differences (Noffke, 1998). These were the roots of the
contemporary movement for multicultural education, which emerged in
the late 1950s and the 1960s within the context of the national civil
rights movement.

As with the civil rights movement, calls for multicultural education
and access to higher education for students of color were led primarily
by people of color (Ogbu, 1992). The civil rights movement continued
into what William Watkins (1994) calls "the subsequent period of post-
civil rights cultural pluralism" (p. 101). During this period of the 1970s,
multiculturalists called for the inclusion of the voices of people of color
and women specifically within the curriculum. By doing so, they attacked the sacredness of the Western canon (Botstein, 1991). A controversy over the core curriculum at Stanford University provides a prime
example of what came to be known as the culture wars, as discussed
in more detail below. The proponents of multicultural curriculum policy
called for the public recognition of diverse cultures within education.
This recognition is sought still, as Protestant cultural values continue to
pervade today's educational system. Taking a cue from early-twentieth-
century assimilationists, proponents of the current efforts implicitly condone a belief in the superiority of Anglo, Protestant culture.

Hirsch's *Cultural Literacy* (1987), Bloom's *The Closing of the American Mind* (1987), and D'Souza's *Illiberal Education* (1991) attempted
to refute the value of both multicultural education and the importance
of expanding the literary canon to include works by women and authors
of color. In Hirsch's later book, *The Schools We Need and Why We
Don't Have Them* (1996), he continues to assert that conservative education policies, presumably those that are nonmulticulturalist, are "the
only practical way to achieve liberalism's aim of greater social justice"
(p. 6). Works such as these contributed to the most heated portion of
the contemporary multiculturalism debate during the late 1980s and the
early 1990s.

In 1998, the Modern Language Association (MLA) issued a list of the
"100 best" novels written in English during the twentieth century.
Again, the multiculturalism controversy reared its head as people from

all sides of the political spectrum criticized "The List." It was condemned most for lacking writers of color, women writers, modern (read
"living") authors, and authors from places other than Britain and the
United States (Dettmar, 1998). Still, lists such as this one, especially from
an association as prestigious as the MLA, have an impact on which
works are perceived as "great" and, consequently, which ones are
taught within the educational system.

Amidst the well-publicized attacks on multicultural curriculum policy at both the K–12 and higher education levels, multiculturalism nonetheless has seemed to gain some ground as an important educational
concept. For example, the Carnegie Foundation reports that as of 1990,
20 percent of all 4-year colleges and universities required undergraduate
students to take one course at minimum that displayed clear racial/
ethnic content. Indeed, as of 1992, one third of all institutions of higher
education had some sort of multicultural requirement within their curriculum (Springer, Palmer, Terenzini, Pascarella, & Nora, 1997). Even
a noted (former) antimulticulturalist such as Nathan Glazer (1997) has
supported the need for multicultural education because of one of its
important intellectual aims: to help students gain a better understanding
of all the different groups that make up America.

Of what should such understanding consist? To answer this question, I turn to the underlying principles of an education that is multicultural and consider how multicultural curricula serve the aim of fostering
students' self-determination.

UNDERLYING PRINCIPLES OF MULTICULTURAL CURRICULA

Leading proponents of multicultural education like James Banks (1994)
assert that "a major goal of multicultural education—as stated by special-
ists in the field—is to reform the school and other educational institutions so that students from diverse racial, ethnic, and social-class groups
will experience educational equality" (p. 3). In addition, multicultural
education should have an impact on students' educational success and
social mobility.

According to Eduardo Duarte (1998), "multicultural education represents a policy that insures nondominant cultures a space within the curricula, but also provides *all* students with a meaningful context of
choice in which they can choose to incorporate, critique, modify, etc.,
their lifestyle" (p. 11). I agree with Duarte on this main point, but his
interpretation is incomplete. It seems that we agree on the important
role that multicultural curricula play in expanding a student's context

of choice; however, we provide different philosophical justifications for that argument. The way Duarte describes it, multicultural education seems to be primarily a compensatory measure, that is, a policy that aims to rectify "minority" students' disadvantages. This view does little work in helping multicultural education gain wider acceptance. Intended or not, the notion of students of color as disadvantaged in the sense of a cognitive deficiency or an inherent inferiority because they are not part of the dominant culture is unjust. Multicultural curricula benefit *all* students by providing more accurate pictures of the world and of the cultures that make up that world. As such, an education that is multicultural provides students with the intellectual and cultural tools to be able to evaluate and negotiate the various life choices they need to make. By publicly recognizing the worth of different cultures, balanced multicultural curricula allow students to make their educational and life choices from a strong social and cultural foundation. The curriculum plays the largest part in an education that is multicultural. According to traditional multiculturalists, multiculturalism should be integrated into all subject areas and courses (Banks, 1994; Nieto, 1992). Banks (1994) points out that a teacher's commitment to pedagogy concerned with equity issues, and students' awareness of how knowledge is constructed in the dominant culture are also both important parts of multicultural education.

Critical multiculturalists such as Christine Sleeter and Peter McLaren (1995) maintain that multicultural education cannot really be transformative unless it is combined with critical pedagogy. In their opinion, both multicultural education and critical pedagogy "refer to a particular ethico-political attitude or ideological stance that one constructs in order to confront and engage the world critically and challenge power relations" (p. 7). Also coming out of the critical theory perspective, Cameron McCarthy (1994) tries to conceptualize multicultural education beyond what he considers merely "adding more content to the dominant curriculum" (p. 81). He believes mainstream multicultural education focuses on understanding, sensitivity, and tolerance. This, McCarthy suggests, results in only superficial change that overshadows the need for deep curricular and pedagogical change. Instead, he supports a "critical multiculturalism," which goes beyond the content of the curriculum to address issues of power and of the distribution of wealth and resources within society (p. 83).

Traditional multiculturalists like Banks and Nieto and critical multiculturalists like Sleeter, McCarthy, and others stake out their particular positions about what are the most essential goals for multicultural education. At times, they are at odds with one another, with the more mainstream camp focusing on inclusion and equality (Banks, 1994; Gay, 1983; Nieto, 1992) and the more radical, or critical, camp focusing on structural inequalities and power relations (Leistyna, 1999; McLaren & Muñoz, 2000; Ovando & McLaren, 2000). I draw from both views in staking out a different position. The very fact that I am coming from within the liberal political tradition, albeit the contemporary version, places me somewhat at odds philosophically with critical multiculturalists. However, at the same time, the contemporary liberalism that I endorse places me beyond traditional multiculturalism. As a result, I am forging new ground; I contend that not only is the ideal of multicultural education that I advance the most complete, but that it is the most reasonable as well.

While multicultural education takes myriad forms, I begin with the following conceptualization: multicultural education is a broad educational approach in which students learn what is necessary in order for them to live and prosper in a multicultural society. They learn that different cultures deserve public recognition, understanding, and respect; that coercive assimilation into the dominant culture should not be endorsed; and that unjust societal structures ought to be questioned (Fullinwider, 1991b; Moses, 1997).

Accordingly, the three most critical goals for the ideal of multicultural education are (1) shaping attitudes that not only honor multiculturalism, but also embody the disposition to evaluate, challenge, and end racism and oppression; (2) creating social contexts where students—regardless of culture, ethnicity, religion, gender, ability, sexual orientation, and social class—are treated and treat others with equal respect; and (3) fostering empowered, self-determining students (Banks, 1992; Fullinwider, 1991b). These goals lead students to a favorable context of choice and to a sense of authenticity in their social and cultural identities. In so doing, multicultural curricula serve the aim of developing self-determining students and thus, the goals of democracy and social justice.

CHARACTERIZING OPPRESSION

Since I describe the reduction of oppression as paramount within the goals of multicultural education, it is important to characterize oppression. Here I make use of Young's (1990a) taxonomy of oppression, one of the clearest accounts I have seen of what oppression means. The "five faces of oppression" she describes—marginalization, exploitation, powerlessness, cultural imperialism, and violence—are helpful in distinguishing between people's different historical and political situations, for different cultures are related to the five faces of oppression in different ways (p. 39). Different oppressed groups are not oppressed in the same ways or at the same levels. Still, being African American, Latino, Native American, Asian American, or multiethnic are important social identities, even if they are not based on common cultures. And there are some significant commonalities between specific groups. As Young asserts, "in the most general sense, all oppressed people suffer some inhibition of their ability to develop and exercise their capacities and express their needs, thoughts, and feelings. In that abstract sense all oppressed people face a common condition" (p. 40).

Young's faces, or conditions, of oppression deserve closer attention. First, *exploitation* occurs when the fruits of one social group's labor consistently benefit another social group. Examples of this include the enslavement of African Americans in the United States, the menial labor of migrant farm workers, and the unpaid labor of many women. Second, *marginalization* results from the inability to earn a decent living within the system of labor. In this sense, older people, single mothers, and people of color in inner cities are often marginalized. Young (1990a) points out that marginalization is unjust because it "blocks the opportunity to exercise capacities in socially defined and recognized ways" (p. 54). Third, *powerlessness* is found when people lack the respect, authority, or status to give direction (or orders) to others. This is often the case for people who are not employed as professionals. Fourth, *violence* occurs when people are attacked randomly, for no reason other than to embarrass, harass, or harm them. One example is the random beating and sometimes killing of gay people (e.g., the 1998 murder of Matthew Shepard in Wyoming). Fifth, *cultural imperialism* comes when "the dominant meanings of a society render the particular perspective of one's own group invisible at the same time as they stereotype one's group and mark it out as the Other" (p. 58). In this case, the experiences and perspectives of members of the dominant culture are taken as the norm. It is this particular condition of oppression, cultural imperialism, that is diminished most by multicultural curriculum policy (as well as by bilingual education policy), which combats students' forced assimilation into the dominant culture.

Appiah (1996) helpfully defines this dominant culture as being English-speaking, Christian, and European-oriented (mainly Anglo). In terms of education, the dominant culture has historically led young people of the dominant class to the best educational opportunities. Thus, a good multicultural education would address the relationship between the cultures of people of color and the dominant culture and its educational institutions. Ogbu (1992) argues that sufficient attention to these relationships positively affects students' academic achievement. Mainstream incarnations of multicultural education that focus primarily on the content of the curriculum, tend to overlook the importance of the academic learning and achievement of students of color. To be sure, good multicultural curricula concentrate not only on nonoppression but also on preparing students for informed participation in a democracy.

MULTICULTURAL CURRICULA AND STUDENTS' SELF-DETERMINATION

The main claims I make in this chapter are that the nature of the curriculum contributes to the quality of a student's context of choice, and that curricula can positively or negatively affect students' feelings of authentic identity within the dominant culture. Thus, the availability or the absence of good multicultural curriculum policies and practices at the K–12 and college levels have a complex impact on whether or not students develop self-determination, which, as I argued in Chapter 2, should be an all-important aim of a just education. Curricula that are multicultural in nature are crucial in this regard because, as Bikhu Parekh (1986) points out, they represent education for freedom. Students gain freedom from biases, as well as freedom to be open to other cultures and to develop a full awareness of available alternatives. This full awareness is part and parcel of self-determination.

Critics of the implementation of multicultural curricula maintain that an education policy that serves to bolster people's respect for their own cultural identity (as well as that of others), ends up promoting particularity over unity. They believe that an education based in multiculturalism tends to create separation and fragmentation, rather than a shared culture (Bernstein, 1994; Bloom, 1987; Hirsch, 1987, 1996; Ravitch, 1995; Schlesinger, 1992). Some of their criticisms may at first appear to be sound. They do make a good point when they maintain that our educational system should not foster separation and opposition between students.

Nonetheless, I argue that overall their claims are not sound. These critics are more likely to assert their worries than actually prove that fragmentation is a real problem for multicultural education. They nostalgically romanticize an educational system that never really worked for students from marginalized societal groups. The monocultural curricula Bloom and Schlesinger champion are at odds with key liberal democratic principles like freedom and equal respect. Needed instead are curricula that help all students, not just those from within the dominant culture, make meaningful choices about their own lives and respect and recognize their own diverse cultures and identities and those of others.

EXPANDING CONTEXTS OF CHOICE

As I discussed in Chapter 2, a social context of choice is framed by a society's historical and social environment in conjunction with a person's membership in a particular culture (Kymlicka, 1991). I posited that education plays an important role in shaping the context within which students make decisions about their lives. A good education would contribute to the public recognition of diverse cultures. It would also help students become aware of options for the future and be able to pursue those options in a meaningful way. An education that is bad, or unjust, on the other hand, would serve to deny the worth of nondominant cultures and provide students with only limited knowledge of their options. Students' contexts of choice would thereby be constrained rather than expanded.

A good, multicultural education, then, contributes to an expansion of students' social context of choice by affirming the diverse cultural conditions from which they come, which helps students to be able to imagine themselves pursuing educational opportunities. To be clear, moving toward an expanded context of choice does not imply that the student will need to move toward the dominant culture. Rather, an expanded context of choice for students of color means just the opposite. Because multicultural curricula foster the recognition of various particular cultural identities, students of color are more likely to remain or become secure in their identity. Thus they will feel confident in their capacity for success without feeling as though they must fully assimilate into the dominant culture. As Raz (1986) points out, we should "secure natural and social conditions which enable individuals to develop an autonomous life" (p. 156). The goals of multicultural education include fostering such secure social conditions, as well as equal concern and respect for people. They contribute to a general education that challenges unjust societal structures and systems and thus improves the social context of choice of students of color. Leon Botstein (1991) claims that through the curriculum, "not only can racism be combated directly and profoundly, but the horizons of students can be broadened in a way that can retard the spread of prejudice" (p. 89). Because of this broadening of horizons, multicultural curricula play a significant role in furthering social justice goals. Dominant, exclusionary curricula, on the other hand, thwart a student's "capacity to enact and/or to choose a particular form of life" (Duarte, 1998, p. 11). Monocultural curricula thus serve to constrain students' contexts of choice.

Equal Concern and Respect

"Government must not only treat people with concern and respect, but with equal concern and respect. It must not distribute goods or opportunities unequally on the ground that some citizens are entitled to more because they are worthy of more concern" (R. Dworkin, 1978, pp. 272–273). In our case, "government" includes public education. The notion of equal concern and respect encompasses concern for the welfare of others and respect for the autonomy of others. Students who engage in a multicultural education as defined above—one that helps them value multiculturalism and combat oppression—hopefully learn to treat others with equal concern and respect. They learn to be fair, nonracist, and nonoppressive in their conduct towards diverse others. Accordingly, these students, who treat others with dignity, are also themselves treated in this way. They thus develop a sense of reciprocity, which is critical for justice, as Rawls (1971) has argued. He points out that "the successes and enjoyments of others are necessary for and complimentary to our own good" (p. 523). The principle of reciprocity requires that we treat others with consideration and respect, particularly those who are different from ourselves. This sense of equality and respect for themselves and others leads students to value diverse cultures and cultural identities. When students feel valued and worthwhile, they are more likely to have a sense of possibility for their lives.

By contrast, a monocultural education gives students the message that only one culture is worthy of respect and, as a result, one race is superior to others (Parekh, 1986). For example, a Latino college student attending a traditional, predominantly white university may feel unwelcome as a "minority" student. This could have a variety of effects on him or her, including a feeling of inferiority that might serve to limit the choices he or she makes. If a monocultural education leads some students to feel inferior, then they become less able to conceive of good choices and options for their lives, to imagine themselves as worthy of success. Hence, they would not gain a sense of self-determination. And students from the dominant culture would gain a sense of false superiority, causing them to have a distorted understanding of society and equality.

Having equal concern and respect for others entails that one learn that all cultures are worthy of respect.[3] Kymlicka (1991) argues that in order to display equal consideration of every person's interests, people must *recognize* that cultural membership is an important part of pursuing a good life. I see this recognition as grounded in Taylor's (1994) politics of recognition, which are characterized by a recognition of people's cultures in a way that transcends mere toleration, and reaches toward understanding and equal dignity. This idea is found within K. Howe's (1997) principle of nonoppression.

K. Howe refashions the principle of nonoppression from Gutmann's (1987) principle of "nonrepression" (p. 44), which Howe sees as "too weak to adequately protect marginalized and oppressed groups" (1997, p. 67). Briefly, nonoppression, within education, requires that schools identify which groups are oppressed and then work to eliminate the oppression through multicultural education. As Howe conceives of it, the principle of nonoppression assumes that since schools play "such a crucial role in forming democratic character," they are responsible for educating students to recognize and respect diverse cultures in order to eliminate oppression (p. 72). The main form of oppression on which I will concentrate here is cultural imperialism, which takes the form of forced assimilation within education.

An educational experience in which students are not oppressed and in which they learn the importance of eliminating oppression is essential within multicultural education. One important part of that is ensuring that education does not subscribe to assimilationist ideals.

FEELINGS OF AUTHENTIC IDENTITY

Recall that earlier I characterized cultural identity as involving three important facets: one's racial and ethnic heritage, a connection to one's cultural community, and a sense of the worth and dignity of one's race and culture. Historically, the assimilation of diverse cultures into mainstream culture has been the goal of public education. However, instead of blending into the United States' grand melting pot, many students of color either are forced to give up their cultural identities in order to fit into the educational system or to give up on a school system from which they feel alienated (K. Howe, 1997). This is not acceptable within an educational system that claims to subscribe to a public ideology of fairness and equality. An education concerned with nonoppression and recognition demonstrates a concern for equal dignity and cultural difference. These concerns take into account the grievous harms that can be inflicted upon people when their identities are either not recognized or misrecognized. Consider again the experience of Richard Rodriguez. In his autobiography, he shows how schools force students of color to assimilate: "What preoccupies me is immediate: the separation I endure with my parents in loss . . . it is education that has altered my life. Carried me far" (1982, p. 5). He goes on to explain that while students obtain "a diminished sense of *private* individuality by becoming assimilated into public society, such assimilation makes possible the achievement of *public* individuality . . . the loss implies the gain" (pp. 26–27).

In like fashion, Nieto (1992) has observed the following bind in her research on students of color:

> If they choose to identify with their culture and background, they may feel alienated from this society; on the other hand, if they identify with the United States (generally meaning European American) culture, they feel like traitors to their family and community. The choices are still heartbreaking ones for many students. . . . As they currently exist, these choices are quite clear-cut and rigid: One is either true to oneself and family or one is American. (p. 271)

The choices about which Nieto writes can hardly be considered adequate or just. There needs to be a balance between students' American and particular cultural identities. This point hearkens back to the third alternative I posited in Chapter 2. That is, rather than having a dualistic choice to identify with their particular cultures or to eschew their cultures and identify as American, students ought to be able to choose a third option. In identifying with their cultural background, students need not feel alienated from the educational system. Students can somehow reconcile their particular identity with dominant norms. This does not mean they would succumb to the dominant norms, but that they would still be able to take advantage of educational opportunities without denying their own culture. It does mean that, in essence, they would find a satisfactory balance between their private and public contexts. Multicultural curricula that educate for nonoppression teach students to be aware of themselves and to treat others with equal respect. Neither will students of color feel forced to assimilate into the dominant culture, nor will members of the dominant culture feel falsely superior to others. Each will then have the knowledge and adequate range of options needed to lead autonomous lives.

It is important to note that some students may decide to assimilate fully or partially[4] (Delpit, 1993). In fact, it may be conducive to their development of self-determination for students to separate somewhat from their family and culture. Author Eric Liu (1998) is one example of someone who felt the need to choose to separate himself from his parents and what he views as *their* culture. The son of Taiwanese immigrants, Liu contends that the loss of culture inherent in assimilation is not the loss of anything sacred, especially for Americans of Asian descent. It is, instead, a necessity for mainstream success. Still, for all his assertions regarding the necessity of assimilation, Liu remains conflicted about his choices as he calls for neither monoculturalism nor multiculturalism, but omniculturalism. Perhaps he is just begging the question. Perhaps his success within the dominant culture has made him blind to the struggles of others, even other Asian Americans, who have not assimilated as easily as him.

At this point, I must emphasize that although it is of critical importance, culture is but one aspect of individual identity, as Liu observes. I have identified it as especially critical in the argument for multicultural curricula because, as Robert Rhoads (1994) insightfully observes, education plays a pivotal role in "legitimizing certain cultures and identities, while marginalizing others" (p. 256). When an education is multicultural it instead honors differences in culture and identity. It is important to note that there is much variety within people of color. Ogbu (1992) has supplied one perspective on what he calls "minority status" (p. 8). He has identified three types of "minority groups," each of which have different experiences of oppression within the dominant culture: (1) autonomous minorities, which are self-sufficient groups that function independent of mainstream society, such as the Amish; (2) immigrant, or voluntary minorities, which have chosen to move to the United States for various reasons (e.g., economic opportunities), such as Japanese people; and (3) castelike, or involuntary minorities, which were somehow forced to be in the United States, such as Native American peoples or many African Americans.

Because of the different histories and current experiences of these diverse groups, multicultural education will serve each group, as well as the dominant one, in different ways. What each group does share is the need to have its culture respected and recognized by others, and to be free from oppression. It is, quite simply, oppressive for many students for the dominant culture to be imposed upon them regardless of their cultural membership. According to Taylor (1994), without multicultural curricula to combat this imposition, the educational system condones the assumed superiority of the dominant culture. Unlike Hirsch (1987), Taylor downplays the specific content of a multicultural curriculum, playing up instead the idea that multicultural curricula enhance students' knowledge of self and their feelings of authenticity. In this regard, the public recognition of hitherto excluded cultural groups is one of the most important reasons to support multicultural curriculum policies. And, as Susan Wolf (1994) points out, justice simply requires such recognition.

Still, how can any education policy claim to be able to provide recognition of the hundreds of cultural groups represented in the United States (not to mention other countries)? The concern here is that in theory, multicultural education sounds good, but it would be very difficult to reach its goals without excluding someone (e.g., smaller cultural groups). Along with this critique is the charge that multicultural education in the United States places an unfair emphasis on the experiences of African Americans and Latinos.

I agree that it will be complicated to avoid bias against smaller cultural groups. However, this problem does not provide justification for dismissing multicultural education just because it is not a perfect policy. Educators must begin somewhere in the significant task of creating multicultural curricula. Perhaps some remedy can be found if school systems act locally to make sure that in addition to the predominant national minorities, smaller, locally represented cultural groups are included (K. Howe, 1997). Robert Fullinwider (1994) provides another good response to this problem. He argues that multicultural education should characterize its basic project as "instilling an open mind" in students (p. 9). This would entail including as many cultural groups as possible in the curriculum, where ranking certain groups as more or less important does not come into play.

As I have conceptualized it, an ideal of multicultural education instills in students an open mind. It is true that it would be impossible to study the histories of every minority group. However, if students are able to develop the multicultural attitudes and understandings that would lead them to develop personal autonomy, then they will likely treat themselves and others with equal respect, regardless of the exact content of the curriculum. Such criticism is resolved when the overall goals of multicultural education are taken into account.

Good multicultural curricula combat nonrecognition and misrecognition of the cultures of people of color. With adequate recognition of cultural particularity, people of color will not be obliged to succumb to cultural imperialism by denying their cultures and assimilating into the dominant culture in order to be able to pursue the good life. The educational system, then, would avoid contributing to the internalized oppression of many students of color. Students of color, in turn, would be much less likely to have an impoverished or distorted sense of cultural identity. In addition, there would not be an assumption of superiority by members of the dominant group.

The claim that multicultural education must be explicitly nonassimilationist is criticized in some quarters for being too political an aim and for focusing too much on self-esteem issues and not enough on academic content (e.g., D'Souza, 1991; Hirsch, 1987, 1996). However, since the educational system is responsible for fostering self-determination among students, curricula clearly should focus on such so-called self-esteem issues. In fact, issues of self-esteem and academic content are really inseparable and neither necessarily excludes the other (Noddings, 1992). The bottom line is that a just education should provide the possibility for all students to learn about and understand themselves, their lives, and their cultures. Anything less is only a part of a good education.

SCHOOL AND COLLEGE CURRICULUM CONTROVERSIES

Curriculum controversies are quite complicated. A recent study by the Ford Foundation (1997) illustrates the confusion that members of the public display around the issue of multicultural education. When asked whether diversity education overemphasizes our differences and ends up creating more division and conflict, 52 percent of the respondents agreed. Yet, 85 percent of the respondents supported multicultural course offerings. These types of conflicting findings show that people may support curricula that emphasize differences if these curricula also help students "develop a balanced understanding and appreciation for their own and other cultures" (p. 7). The public recognition of individual cultures within the educational system is in direct opposition to an educational atmosphere in which students feel they have few, if any, real options for choice. Thus, by gaining understanding and appreciation for diverse cultures, students would make a great deal of progress toward the goal of self-determination.

PUBLIC SCHOOL CURRICULA: MOVING FROM MONOCULTURAL TO MULTICULTURAL

Debbie Maddux (1997), a high school social studies teacher, asserts that from her experience,

> high school social studies curricula leave much to be desired. African American students rarely see themselves in the curricula, and when they do, it is usually in instances where they are portrayed as subservient, or second-class citizens. This phenomenon is strongly characteristic of the Eurocentric curriculum. (p. 65)

Maddux's description of the high school curriculum portrays it as largely monocultural. Because students are not receiving an education that is multicultural, they are being *mis*educated. This miseducation leads students to an incomplete view of themselves and of the world. Thus their sense of possibility in life is limited in such a way that they cannot accurately envision the options available to them.

Proponents of the more traditional Western-based education (what Maddux above calls "Eurocentric") claim that curricula in U.S. public schools ought to focus on a common U.S. culture rather than on myriad immigrant and ethnic cultures. In doing so, they are (perhaps unwittingly) calling for schools to continue the process of systematic denial of the importance of cultures other than the dominant one. Ravitch (1995), for one, continuously laments the loss of common culture and American community because of political campaigns within education. She characterizes the multicultural education movement as "interest groups [that] politicize the curriculum and attempt to impose their views on teachers, school officials, and textbook publishers" (p. 458).

Nevertheless, the call for integration of multicultural perspectives and voices into the curriculum is not, as naysayers such as Ravitch maintain, merely a way to use education to further leftist political ends and foster separations between students. While I readily acknowledge that this is a political issue, it is important to note that politics is not at all new to education, or to debates about what constitutes the proper content of curricula. Because of the complicated social history of the United States and, by extension, its educational system, the curriculum has always been political. Think back to the founders of the common school. Their explicit agenda was to bring people together to support Anglo, Protestant values. Even Schlesinger (1992) notes that Anglo, Protestant males provided the standard to which others had to conform and assimilate. In partial response to the charges of separationism and particularism, Appiah (1996) notes that

> teaching young people to respect those with other identities is not the same as teaching them some of the central practices and beliefs of a different subculture. When we teach Toni Morrison to children with serious attention, we are demonstrating respect for the cultural work of a black person in a culture where there is still pressure not to respect black people. We are showing that respect to black children; we are modeling that respect for other children. (p. 68)

Indeed, in striving for nonoppression through multicultural curricula, the aim is for all students to be educated so that they may examine and deconstruct oppression, and work to eliminate it (K. Howe, 1997).

Still, Hirsch (1987, 1996) maintains that it is the more traditional curriculum with its emphasis on the memorization of facts important to Western culture that leads to decreased marginalization of students of color, and hence to decreased educational disadvantages. For him, cultural literacy is paramount. Many children remain disadvantaged educationally and economically, Hirsch contends, because public schools are failing them by subscribing to progressive educational theories. Barbara Herrnstein Smith (1990) challenges Hirsch's seemingly noble aims by pointing out that his preferred curriculum would actually help perpetuate the very social ills he claims it would combat. She cautions that even though many may find Hirsch's reform ideas ridiculous, we still must be wary of the anti-multiculturalist position, because

> we must remember, the fact that the arguments for a proposal are vague and muddled, that its recommendations are patently absurd, and that the possibility of its success rejected by all of the most eminent people in the field does not mean that it won't become national policy. (p. 84)

In fact, there are plenty of official education policies that are detrimental to the neediest students. School funding disparities provide one salient example (Kozol, 1991). Hirsch (1987) actually states that it is important for students to learn the information related to Western culture that most Americans know, so that they will know what those in power know, regardless of its inherent merit. Thus society will be unified in shared knowledge and our political-economic structure will be upheld, insofar as it is based on shared knowledge and standards. This implies that it is more important to learn about the contributions of Anglo, Protestant males (since most Americans know about them already), than it is to learn about people of color and women. What Hirsch does not acknowledge is that he is calling for a continuation of the status quo, which is inherently exclusive, racist, and sexist, as only white males had a hand in formulating that shared knowledge and those universal standards. From his point of view, then, issues of student identity and cultural recognition should not be taken into account in designing curricula (Hirsch, 1987, 1996). It is just this type of traditional, assimilationist viewpoint about education that may cause students to feel as if they have no choice but to give up their most cherished social identities in order to succeed in their educations. Some are unwilling to do so. Scott Fletcher (2000) perceptively points out that the argument put forth by scholars such as Hirsch and Ravitch is "destructive of an education for autonomy; it excludes or diminishes aspects of identity that are essential for developing the capacity to make informed, uncoerced choices about present interests and future plans" (pp. 24–25).

If, as I argue, personal autonomy as self-determination is a critical goal of schooling, antimulticulturalist arguments actually serve to thwart the development of all American students. Schlesinger (1992) maintains that the values of Americanization and assimilation within schooling will remain important because students want to achieve traditional success. It may be true that many students outside of the dominant culture desire educational achievement and success within the educational system as it stands. But history has shown that a monocultural curriculum that helps to force assimilation is not the way to best assist students to attain their educational goals. Helping them to achieve true self-determination within a secure cultural identity and a favorable context of choice is.

The San Francisco School District Diversity Requirement

For a long time, the only texts that San Francisco high school English teachers were required to use were *Romeo and Juliet*, *The Adventures of Huckleberry Finn*, and *The Canterbury Tales*. But in March 1998, two school board members suggested a change in these requirements so that students would get to read a more diverse selection of authors. A huge controversy was born. Much of the uproar had to do with one part of their proposal that called for 70 percent of the literature assigned in each class be written by authors of color. The board eventually passed a resolution in favor of the proposition, leaving out the specific percentages. The end result is that each year high school students in San Francisco must choose at least one work by an ethnic author (not necessarily an author of color) (Harris, 1998).

This case is an example of the immense controversy that often follows changes in favor of multicultural curricula. Even in the late 1990s, within an atmosphere of relative complacency regarding issues of multicultural education (as compared with the late 1980s), these issues pushed hot buttons among educators and other members of the community. Even when the change is a minor one, as in San Francisco, multicultural curriculum policies get people's ire up and prompt debates about politics and academic standards. The controversies at the K–12 level are paralleled by controversies at the college level.

CANON DEBATES WITHIN HIGHER EDUCATION

Campus protests, such as the one at Cornell University discussed early in this chapter, remind us that students are still endeavoring to support multicultural curricula initiatives in order to create for themselves a better higher education experience and an academy that is welcoming, inclusive, and nonoppressive. Take, for example, a protest staged by Latino students at Michigan State University. They held 5,000 books from the library in a demand for the creation of a Latino Studies major (*The Chronicle of Higher Education*, 1999). Regardless of efforts such as these, critics of multicultural curriculum policies contend that such curricula infringe upon the autonomy of students because of the nature of mandatory courses. Interestingly, a study aiming to determine (1) whether or not people are supportive of multicultural curricula and (2) whether or not multicultural curricula are really effective in changing attitudes about diversity on campus, found that a large majority of the respondents supported a curricular emphasis on multiculturalism and diverse perspectives, and that such courses had positive effects on students (Springer et al., 1997). The researchers found that both ethnic and women's studies courses have statistically significant positive effects on students' attitudes about diversity on campus. Still, while these results are encouraging, these researchers also found that white students in their sample enrolled in ethnic and women's studies courses in much lower numbers than students of color, and that half of the respondents believed that a focus on oppression and particular cultures created conflict and division.

Antimulticulturalists try to capitalize on this type of ambivalence over multicultural education. They argue that curricula focusing on multicultural issues or integrating multicultural authors and topics will result in relativism, trendiness, and, at worst, a loss of universal standards by which to judge educational worth (Bork, 1996; D'Souza, 1991; Kimball, 1990; Schlesinger, 1992). They worry that instead of having high intellectual rigor and academic merit, courses featuring an expanded canon make up a watered-down curriculum where political ideology reigns supreme. Robert Bork (1996) takes this argument even further by suggesting that Eurocentrism is necessary because Western culture is far superior to any other cultures. Multiculturalism, he says, invites chaos, meaninglessness, and barbarism.

Taking a less extreme position, Irving Howe (1991) argues that we should want students to read the classics (e.g., works by William Shakespeare and Jane Austen) for their own sake, and not for a political reason. He says, "we should want students to read such writers so that they may learn to enjoy the activity of the mind, the pleasure of forms, the beauty of language—in short, the arts in their own right" (p. 9). It is true that the traditional great works should be read for whatever light they may shed on essential questions about justice and truth. Although that is a worthy educational goal, it is not the only purpose of education, and for most students, gaining an appreciation of the beauty of art is not enough of an educational aim. Curricular reliance solely on the literary works included within the traditional canon promotes the dominance of the societal status quo. Henry Louis Gates (1990) writes that antimulticulturalists like Bloom and Bork

> symbolize for us the nostalgic return to what I think of as the "antebellum aesthetic position," when men were men, and men were white, when scholar-critics were white men, and when women and persons of color were voiceless, faceless servants and laborers pouring tea and filling brandy snifters in the boardrooms of old boys' clubs. (p. 89)

What they also fail to recognize is that the infusion of multiculturalism into college curricula enhances the quality of all students' educational experiences. It does so by combating racism and oppression, promoting equal respect for diverse cultures, and thereby diminishing the institutionalized racism inherent in most, if not all, predominantly white colleges and universities.

The Culture Wars at Stanford University

In 1986, students in the Black Student Union at Stanford University complained about the Western Culture requirement, a yearlong sequence of courses focusing on Western civilization that first-year students were required to take. They charged that the core curriculum was both racist and sexist because it excluded the experiences of and works by women and people of color (Pratt, 1992). By the spring of 1988, the Faculty Senate had voted to do away with that course sequence in favor of a new group of courses called "Culture, Ideas, and Values" (CIV) (Kimball, 1990). The new three-course CIV requirement called for every course in the program to include works by women and people of color. That a top institution like Stanford heeded student demands for the diversification of the curriculum resulted in a heated controversy about the nature of the college curriculum, as the debate about multicultural education went from the theoretical to the practical. The debate and subsequent core curriculum change at Stanford affected the rest of the nation. Students protested and called for change at many other schools including Columbia University and the University of Vermont (D'Souza, 1991).

Then-Secretary of Education William Bennett publicly criticized the Stanford change, calling it "education by intimidation," even though the president of Stanford maintained that the change was primarily called for by members of the faculty (Kimball, 1990, p. 29). The requirement's emphasis on multiculturalism was called self-righteous by critics such as Richard Kimball (1990). In fact, he cites it as the most prominent example of how liberal education has been corrupted by politics. But isn't any decision on what is deemed important to know political? As Watkins (1994) observes, "educating people of color has always been a political proposition" (p. 104). And, I would add, educating white people has always been a political endeavor as well. It is important to note that a move such as Stanford's toward the curricular inclusion of diverse perspectives does not support a claim that nondominant cultures are all perfect and thus worthy replacements of Western civilization, as is suggested by critic D'Souza (1991). On the contrary, nondominant cultures and works by people of color can and should be looked at critically also. One example is the machista tradition in Latino culture. In any case, the complete replacement of Western civilization curricula was never a goal (Lindenberger, 1989; Pratt, 1992).

Stanford graduate Raoul Mowatt (1992), a student during the height of the CIV debate, points out that little really changed with the advent of CIV. The reading lists remained virtually unchanged; students still read the traditional great works, with what Mowatt calls a tip of the hat to writers of color like Toni Morrison.

Ultimately, CIV did not last. In 1997, the Stanford faculty once again voted for a change in their core curriculum, after only an hour of discussion. This time, CIV was replaced by a new course entitled, "Introduction to the Humanities" (*The Chronicle of Higher Education*, 1997a). Different from CIV, this course focuses explicitly on critical thinking rather than on a prescribed canon of literary works. Therefore, there is no mandatory reading list, though at least one work must still come from outside of the traditional Western canon (Schneider, 1997). Critics of the new requirement worry that it erases the Stanford commitment to multicultural education that CIV supported.

While this change caused debate on the Stanford campus, there was little attention paid to it within the rest of academe, unlike the 1988 change from Western Culture to CIV. Interestingly, similar issues on other campuses also received little popular attention. For example, at the University of Washington, the faculty rejected the 1996 proposal that required undergraduates to take at least five credits worth of courses dealing with multicultural issues (Cage, 1996). And at Wellesley College, the Academic Council revised their 1990 multicultural requirement so that students would have more choice. Since few faculty members disagreed that students should be educated in diversity, there was little debate on campus. Beginning in 1997, Wellesley students were required to take at least one course focusing on either African, Asian, Pacific Island, Caribbean, Latin American, or Native American cultures; or a U.S. minority culture; or the processes of racism, discrimination, or cross-cultural interaction (Magner, 1996).

Regardless of the relative complacency that characterizes recent changes in multicultural curricula, it is still essential for schools and colleges to make sure to have at least some multicultural education requirement, especially because of what most college and university faculties look like. In 1995, over 85 percent of full-time college faculty members were white. Only 12.6 percent were American people of color (Stewart, 1998). If white faculty members do not take it upon themselves to infuse multiculturalism into their courses, multicultural curriculum policies serve to ensure a practical curricular focus on multiculturalism and nonoppression.

CONCLUSION

I have set out to argue that a contemporary liberal ideal of multicultural education leads students to satisfy the conditions for the development of self-determination. Taking into consideration that a broad policy of multicultural education allows students to expand their social contexts of choice, gain a sense of equal concern and respect for themselves and others, and learn the importance of eliminating oppression and coercive assimilation into the dominant culture, it is fair to contend that multicultural curricula help students develop self-determination. Although the objections to this idea contain truth and insight, they do not pose enough of a threat to negate the argument for multicultural education.

Hirsch (1996), for instance, asserts that U.S. schools overall are not good, demanding, or fair, and that they have actually gotten worse due to reforms like multicultural education. Progressive educational ideas, he maintains, have neither made practical gains in educational achievement, nor led to greater social equality; "the only practical way to achieve liberalism's aim of greater social justice is to pursue conservative educational policies" (p. 6). What a disaster that would be! As Kimball (1990) notes,

> what is at stake in these difficult questions is more than an academic squabble over book lists and pedagogy; what is at stake is nothing less than the traditional liberal understanding of democratic society and the place of education and high culture within it. (p. 2)

While I agree with Kimball on this point, I do not agree with the conservative approach he would take to answer these difficult questions. Instead, I advocate a contemporary liberal agenda for social justice. Social justice requires that institutions foster respect for differences as well as create mechanisms with which to combat oppression (Young, 1990a). Education, both at the K–12 and postsecondary levels, should promote the development of self-determination of all students.

Recently, Duke University managed to change its core curriculum policy with little to no controversy (Schneider, 1997). In an effort to update their undergraduate requirements, Duke's faculty voted to change their general education curriculum to one that is more rigorous and more diverse. For example, students must take two required courses in "Cross-Cultural Inquiry" as well as in "Science, Technology, and Society" (Schneider, 1997, p. A14). Duke's Curriculum 2000, as it is called, may not include the sweeping multicultural infusion of Stanford's CIV curriculum, but two of the main areas it emphasizes are cross-culturalism and foreign languages. In addition, it enjoys widespread faculty support. There are two main lessons to be learned from Duke's success. First, the faculty and administration were proactive in pursuing curriculum change; they did not wait until disgruntled students and faculty demanded change. Second, those on the curriculum committee treated their task as part of a very visible political process and, as such, included as many voices as possible in formulating the new requirements. As a result, various, often-opposing constituencies ended up agreeing on the curricular changes. School districts and other institutions of higher education would do well to follow Duke's example in creating curricula with an emphasis on multiculturalism in the process as well as the product.

The curriculum is at the heart of the educational experience. Indeed, Nussbaum (1997) contends that the classical (Socratic) imperative to examine our lives *requires* that students study those who are different from themselves as well. Multicultural curriculum policy ensures that this will take place. Historically, white students have been given an education that fosters self-determination. In the best of situations, educational institutions will undergo fundamental curricular changes that will serve to foster the development of self-determination in students of color as well.

Students of color at the University of Vermont demanded such changes when they protested in favor of more multicultural curricula and ethnic studies courses in both 1988 and 1991.[5] Through a series of campus protests, students aired their criticisms of the university administration and the too-slow process of change at the predominantly white institution. The debates on campus were angry and acrimonious, and the 1991 protest ended with students being arrested after they took over the main administration building. These events have had a lasting impact on the university and helped create a conflicted campus atmosphere for many students. It remains difficult for the University of Vermont to recruit students and faculty of color. Just as the issue of multicultural curriculum policy is difficult, issues concerning the recruitment and enrollment of students of color into prestigious, predominantly white institutions of higher education are difficult as well. This is especially so in light of the many recent attacks on affirmative action policy.

NOTES

1. I use scare quotes around the term "minority" because of its negative connotations. Many people of color (myself included), prefer not to be referred to as a "minority," but as a person (especially because when we add up the world's population, people of color are not in the minority).

2. Consider that some colleges are dropping multicultural curricula requirements with little notice or complaint (see Leatherman, 2000).

3. It is important that students learn this, even though certain cultures may seem morally repugnant (e.g., peoples who engage in ethnic cleansing), and they may later, after learning a great deal more about a certain culture, come to believe that it is perhaps not as worthwhile as some others.

4. Delpit (1993) discusses the need for a balance for African Americans between black culture and dominant culture in order for them to succeed within dominant society.

5. I was a Master's student and employee of the University of Vermont during the 1991 protests. Because of my work with undergraduate students of color on campus, I was involved in the conflict. I was also in support of the students' demands.

5

Affirmative Action

Affirmative action has emerged as the most contentious of all race-conscious education policies. It is also the one policy I examine that is officially intended to be conscious of race and ethnicity. Whether one supports or opposes the concept, it seems that affirmative action and its implications for equality, justice, and democracy strike a tender chord in the lives of Americans, who are "arguably the most 'race-conscious' people on earth" (Marable, 1995, p. 185). When the Clinton administration conducted an evaluation of all federal affirmative action programs, he came out in public support of affirmative action, echoing the feelings of many supporters, by saying mend it, but don't end it.[1] Christopher Edley (1996), one of Clinton's advisors on affirmative action, observes that the ongoing controversy surrounding affirmative action is primarily concerned with people's competing ethical values and moral vision. One well-received book on race in America argues that the racial climate in the United States was actually better before the civil rights movement brought the widespread implementation of programs like affirmative action (Thernstrom & Thernstrom, 1997). Affirmative action accordingly is seen as a wedge issue. According to Sandel (1997), affirmative action causes a "conflicted public mind" (p. 13). People have competing intuitions about the issue of nondiscrimination and the role that race and gender should play in the awarding of educational and employment opportunities.

College and university campuses across the nation are embroiled in the controversy over affirmative action. Students who support the policy have protested against the scaling back or abolishment of affirmative action programs. For example, students at Florida International University staged a protest at Governor Jeb Bush's office in response to his plan to end affirmative action in admissions to Florida's public universities (Selingo, 2000). Students at the University of New Hampshire occupied the president's office demanding increased numbers of students and faculty of color (*The Chronicle of Higher Education*, 1998b). University of California at Los Angeles students were arrested because they refused to vacate an academic building as they demanded their university's noncompliance with California's ban on affirmative action (Basinger, 1998). And at the University of Massachusetts at Amherst, students gathered in protest when their chancellor announced that the university's affirmative action policy would change to place less emphasis on race in the admissions process (Healy, 1999b). These protests exemplify a continued passion for affirmative action policies and the democratic ideals that they represent. Students are likely driven to protest because they believe that abolishing affirmative action in college and university admissions will result in deep losses not only for campus communities, but for individual students as well.

This chapter frames the debate on affirmative action in higher education admissions within the historical context of the policy's origin. It addresses two central questions: (1) How does affirmative action foster self-determination among students? (2) In light of the many critiques of affirmative action, can a defense of affirmative action hinging on the educational aim of developing students' self-determination take us beyond the standard arguments toward a place where critics and supporters might actually agree? In answering these questions, I begin with a sketch of the history of affirmative action policy. In order to understand the current debates, it is important to approach them with a picture of affirmative action policy that is grounded in historical perspective. Next I undertake a detailed examination of the most common criticisms of affirmative action policy. It is with an understanding of these dominant themes of the debate that I then offer a new defense of affirmative action in relation to the contemporary liberal framework I developed earlier. I use the concept of self-determination to augment the qualifications argument for affirmative action put forth by R. Dworkin (1978, 1998) and Gutmann (1987). I argue that affirmative action is necessary because it fosters students' self-determination by playing a crucial role in expanding their social contexts of choice,[2] both while they are students and afterwards. The chapter ends with a discussion of the status of affirmative action policy in the United States as of this writing.

The range of affirmative action programs is broad, from federal contracts to employment and promotion, to college and university admissions. This examination specifically targets affirmative action policy for students of color in higher education admissions because, as Gutmann (1987) writes, colleges and universities "serve as gatekeepers to many social offices; they have a virtual monopoly on the education necessary for many of the most valued jobs in our society" (p. 180). Higher education's gatekeeping role puts the selection of students for college and university places at the heart of the struggle for equal opportunity and social justice in education.

THE MEANING AND HISTORY OF AFFIRMATIVE ACTION

It is important to discuss the complicated issue of defining the concept of affirmative action. This will help frame the discussion of how affirmative action was begun, how it became controversial, and how it has had different meanings and connotations, depending on the political climate.

Although it had been utilized before, the phrase *affirmative action* came into the language of governmental policy in 1961 with President John F. Kennedy's Executive Order No. 10925, which required that all government agencies and agencies receiving federal funds take "affirmative action" to be nondiscriminatory in their hiring practices. Exactly what was meant by "affirmative action" was not defined, but according to historian Hugh Davis Graham (1990), the meaning of affirmative action simply "seemed self-defined to require more aggressive recruitment in hiring" in order to facilitate the inclusion and advancement of people of color (p. 42).

The phrase was used again in President Lyndon B. Johnson's 1965 Executive Order No. 11246, a revision and reaffirmation of Executive Order No. 10925. Once again, the meaning of affirmative action was not officially outlined. In 1968, the Department of Labor, which was responsible for enforcing the policy, publicly explained that affirmative action was a program emphasizing expanded applicant pools, active recruiting strategies, and opportunity rather than proportional representation (Ravitch, 1983). The issues of proportional representation (also known as quotas) and historical discrimination would come to be quite controversial as the implications of affirmative action policy unfolded. For the purposes of institutions of higher education, the significance of affirmative action policy was unclear from its inception. Since public institutions received federal funding, affirmative action was required in employment practices. At issue was how to treat college and university admissions. Stanley Pottinger (1972), Director of the Office of Civil Rights under President Richard Nixon, clearly stated that Title VI of the Civil Rights Act of 1964 mandated that no federally assisted programs and activities (e.g., public higher education) could discriminate against people of color. The Office of Civil Rights supported the interpretation that Title VI, in conjunction with the Executive Orders requiring affirmative action, applied specifically to college and university admissions procedures.

Although one specific program may be a little bit different from another, affirmative action in higher education admissions is a policy that aims to take an applicant's race, ethnicity, and sex into account in making selection decisions. Generally, this means that if an applicant is African American, Latino, Asian American, Native American, or female, this fact is taken as one qualifying factor among many considered in the admissions process. Of course, just who is considered under affirmative action varies regionally according to specific populations. Massachusetts, for example, includes Portuguese immigrants (Tierney, 1997).

THE WAGNER ACT

The first officially documented use of the term *affirmative action* came in the Wagner Act, also known as the National Labor Relations Act of 1935. The term *affirmative action* was used in explaining the role of the National Labor Relations Board in its dealings with biased labor practices. An offending group was required to "cease and desist from such unfair labor practice, and to take such affirmative action as will effectuate the policies of this Act" (National Labor Relations Act, 1935, p. 454). There was seemingly little to no controversy regarding the language of the Wagner Act. The term was even used again in New York's 1945 Law Against Discrimination, as a policy to be used to protect victims of discrimination (Graham, 1990). Of course, the 1930s and 1940s civil rights climate in the United States was quite different from the 1960s and 1970s, when the phrase affirmative action and its policy implications did take hold and cause much controversy.

EXECUTIVE ORDER NO. 10925

Many believe that affirmative action policy began with President Johnson.[3] In actuality, affirmative action policy as we have come to know it started in 1961 when President Kennedy issued Executive No. 10925 (1961), known best for creating the President's Commission on Equal Employment Opportunity. Johnson's Executive Order No. 11246 (1965) later solidified affirmative action policy. Executive Order No. 10925 required more of employers than merely passive nondiscrimination in all employment practices. It required that employers act affirmatively to hire and treat employees fairly regardless of their race, creed, color, or national origin (Sovern, 1966).

The actual phrase *affirmative action* was used only once in Executive Order No. 10925, in conjunction with other, similar terms like *affirmative steps* and *positive measures*. Interestingly, the policy did not cause much of a stir (Graham, 1990). Perhaps that was because affirmative action was not explicitly defined; it simply connoted more than the passive nondiscrimination to which most employers professed to adhere. Still, the intent was significant. In fact, Kennedy can be credited with beginning much of the civil rights legislation in the United States. That said, it is also important to point out that Kennedy approached civil rights policy as it behooved him politically. For most of his term as president, Kennedy resisted enacting civil rights legislation for fear of losing what he thought of as crucial white southern votes. When he finally proposed civil rights legislation, it was due to the many race-related protests that were occurring in the South in 1963, about which he had to make some statement (Carmines & Stimson, 1989). Regardless of his motives, he paved the way toward the passage of a meaningful civil rights bill.

THE CIVIL RIGHTS ACT OF 1964

After Kennedy was assassinated, Johnson assumed the presidency and then won a landslide victory in 1964. Before his reelection, Johnson worked for the passage of the Civil Rights Act of 1964. Still, Johnson was not a righteous supporter of civil rights policy. In fact, as a Texas senator, he had openly opposed civil rights policies such as poll tax repeals and antilynching laws (Carmines & Stimson, 1989). However, his political support of civil rights issues had swung with the political climate. By February 1964, the bill had passed the House of Representatives and 4 months later the Senate passed an amended version (Sovern, 1966). The Civil Rights Act of 1964 was part of a substantial group of 1964–65 legislation known as Johnson's Great Society and War on Poverty programs. This group included the Civil Rights Act of 1964, Economic Opportunity Act of 1964, Voting Rights Act of 1965, Elementary and Secondary Education Act of 1965, and the Higher Education Act of 1965. These new programs had the following goals: helping low-income people through education and health programs, stimulating the economy for new jobs, and removing race and sex barriers to educational and employment opportunity.

Most significant for affirmative action policy was the Civil Rights Act, specifically its Titles VI and VII. Title VI "bars discrimination under any federally assisted activity" and Title VII bars employment discrimination according to "race, color, religion, sex, or national origin" (Sobel,

1980, pp. 1-2). Although the focus seemed to be on employment discrimination, Title VI also applied to colleges and university admissions, and was interpreted as such by the Office of Civil Rights. Any educational institutions that received active financial assistance risked losing their aid if they did not comply with the federal requirements. After the passage of the Civil Rights Act, Johnson added Executive Order No. 11246 to the civil rights legislation.

EXECUTIVE ORDER NO. 11246

Executive Order No. 11246 formally encompassed and overrode Executive Order No. 10925, so it is widely seen as the source of federal affirmative action policy, even though it is best known for creating enforcement of federal contract compliance. Since Executive Order No. 11246 used much of the language of Executive Order No. 10925, affirmative action is still only mentioned once (Graham, 1990). As in Executive Order No. 10925, all agencies had to "take affirmative action to ensure that applicants are employed, and the employees are treated during employment, without regard to their race, creed, color, or national origin" (Sovern, 1966, p. 104). A few months before issuing this executive order, Johnson gave a celebrated speech at Howard University's graduation ceremony. Foreshadowing the coming policy, he made the now well-known statement that it is not possible to "take a person who, for years, has been hobbled by chains and liberate him, bring him up to the starting line of a race and then say, 'you are free to compete with all others,' and still justly believe that you have been completely fair"[4] (quoted in Kull, 1992, pp. 186-187). This thought is often cited in justifications for affirmative action in college and university admissions.

INITIAL IMPLEMENTATION

Resting on the affirmative action policies in Executive Order No. 11246 and Title VI of the Civil Rights Act of 1964, many colleges and universities began to revise their admissions policies so that a broader pool of students could have an increased opportunity to attend college and graduate school.

The 1960s and the 1970s

The concept of affirmative action did not enter into the public consciousness until the late 1960s and the 1970s. After the Johnson administration mandated affirmative action and issued its regulations, colleges and universities began designing compliance procedures. By 1969, awareness of racial and ethnic affiliation was increasing so much that the U.S. census began to record the racial and ethnic origins of the population. As this awareness increased so did the activities of minority group organizations on campus and beyond. Pottinger commented that Executive Order No. 11246 had gone unnoticed in relation to higher education until minority group organizations called for colleges and universities to comply (Bennett & Eastland, 1979). Politically, it became in Nixon's best interest to support affirmative action policies, though he did not always do so.

When Jimmy Carter was elected, he became the first president to appoint a meaningful number of people of color and white women to positions in government and the courts where they could take part in enforcing civil rights policies. Another significant change for affirmative action under Carter was a reorganization of the Department of Health, Education, and Welfare's Office of Education. Ernest Boyer, Commissioner of Education, directed a reorganization that included the creation of a special affirmative action office to integrate and organize the affirmative action programs that had been spread across several other offices. The special affirmative action office was slated to deal with programs for women, people of color, and people with disabilities (Sobel, 1980).

Once people started to see affirmative action policies in practice, especially in higher education, debates about affirmative action and its role in achieving equal educational opportunity began to surface. Even with the support of President Carter and his administration, affirmative action controversy gained momentum. The seemingly irreconcilable dilemma surrounding affirmative action is that those in favor of affirmative action want people of color and white women to enjoy opportunities to allow them to become educated and successful within a society historically and presently dominated by white men, whereas those who oppose affirmative action want everyone to be treated as individuals, judged solely by quantifiable standards of merit, without regard to race, ethnicity, or sex. Historically, these debates have set the stage for affirmative action policies in higher education admissions to be tested by the courts. Since the backlash against affirmative action built up steam in the 1970s, the way was paved for the landmark Supreme Court case, *Regents of the University of California v. Bakke* (1978).

BACKLASH

Americans shared little agreement over affirmative action in higher education admissions. Nevertheless, people did not think about the issues too much unless they somehow directly touched their lives; they were reminded only upon filling out a college application and having to check a race/ethnicity category, going through job searches, competing for coveted graduate school slots. So, even as politicians and educators debated affirmative action policies, most people accepted the policies — either with passive chagrin or passive approval. In the presidential elections between 1964 and 1976 all the winners, Democrat and Republican alike, were in support of affirmative action programs. Yet, during the 1976 election campaign, candidate Ronald Reagan came out strongly opposed to federal affirmative action policy (Sobel, 1980). He would win in 1980 with just such attitudes. Reagan had taken note of the changing national mood on affirmative action because of court challenges to University of Washington and University of California at Davis affirmative action policies. That change in national mood has been characterized as "a spreading mania within American society, a mania increasingly adamant against governmental and societal efforts to help blacks, other minorities and the poor" (Gill, 1980, p. 1). It is seen as a change in the spirit that led up to the Great Society and War on Poverty programs.

University admissions and affirmative action programs were scrutinized and put to the test by two major court cases in the 1970s, *DeFunis v. Odegaard* (1974) and *Regents of the University of California v. Bakke* (1978). Some 18 years later, *Hopwood v. Texas* (1996) would begin a new wave of court challenges to college and university affirmative action policies.

Early Court Challenges

Some supporters of affirmative action felt that institutional diversity and equal opportunity goals could be served by an affirmative action program centering on race awareness and the use of racial/ethnic status as one factor in university admissions. Others thought affirmative action needed to remedy historical discrimination by making changes to admissions standards accordingly, and still others wanted affirmative action programs to outline quotas for proportional representation of all minority groups.

Among opponents, there were those who condemned affirmative action as inherently discriminatory because of what they called reverse discrimination. Others thought affirmative action perpetuated racial stereotypes and negatively stigmatized all students of color, while still others believed that to maintain fairness and quality, higher education admissions should be judged completely on objective academic qualifications, which did not include race or sex (Belz, 1991; Bennett & Eastland, 1979; R. Smith, 1978; Turner & Pratkanis, 1994). Although the issues of quotas and reverse discrimination were raised from the outset, they did not become huge controversies until the Supreme Court encountered *DeFunis v. Odegaard* and, a bit later, *Regents of the University of California v. Bakke*. Suddenly, the entire nation found itself wondering how the Supreme Court would rule.

DeFunis: Precursor to Bakke (1974). Marco DeFunis, a white male, applied to the University of Washington Law School in 1971 and was denied admission, so he sued the University on the grounds of reverse discrimination. Eventually, his case made it to the Supreme Court. This case became especially important because it was a precursor to *Bakke*. In the time between when DeFunis first brought his case to court and when it reached the Supreme Court in 1974, one of the lower courts had ordered him admitted to the law school; so, by the time the Supreme Court heard the case, DeFunis was just a few months away from graduation. The Supreme Court declined to rule on the case because a majority of the justices held that the case was moot because of DeFunis's law student status (Sobel, 1980). It seemed to many observers that the Supreme Court justices were simply attempting to avoid judgment on such a volatile issue. Nonetheless, they would be forced to address the matter a few years later when the *Bakke* case reached the high court.

Regents of the University of California v. Bakke (1978). It was widely believed that no other court case, not even *Brown v. Board of Education* (1954), had attracted such immense media attention as the *Bakke* case. As such, there was much speculation about the outcome before the case was reviewed by the Supreme Court.

Allan Bakke was born in Minnesota of Norwegian ancestry and graduated from the University of Minnesota as an engineer. He served with the Marines in the Vietnam War and upon his return, became a mechanical engineer for NASA in California (O'Neill, 1985). His experiences in Vietnam had prompted him to want to become a medical doctor; subsequently, in 1972 at the age of 32, he applied to 12 medical schools, including the University of California at Davis School of Medicine. His application to Davis had been late because of family illness, so by the time he applied, many of the spots in the class had already been filled. He was rejected by all of the schools, which surprised him since he thought he had excellent qualifications. When he learned that a special admissions program at Davis held 16 out of 100 spaces for students of color, Bakke wrote to the Davis admissions office in polite protest. An admissions officer responded to Bakke's letter and agreed that the admissions procedures seemed unfair. Many believe that this admissions officer tacitly urged Bakke to file a lawsuit (Sobel, 1980).

Bakke decided to apply again the following year before he filed a lawsuit. When he applied in 1973, he was again rejected. University files noted that his age had been a factor weighing against his acceptance, and that the second time, his earlier complaints had weighed against him as well. This time, Bakke sued on the grounds of reverse discrimination that put the Davis School of Medicine in violation of the 14th amendment and Title VI of the Civil Rights Act. *Bakke v. Regents of the University of California* was adjudicated in California Superior Court, which ruled in favor of Bakke on both counts. On appeal by Davis, the California Supreme Court also ruled 6 to 1 in favor of Bakke, but this time only on one count—the 14th amendment, not Title VI (Bennett & Eastland, 1979; Sobel, 1980). In the majority opinion, the justices ruled that the Davis School of Medicine admissions program was unconstitutional because it was a type of quota system, which was in violation of the 14th amendment (Ravitch, 1983).

The California Supreme Court decision brought out some other interesting facts and opinions about the case. Bakke had been rejected by 11 other medical schools—even his alma mater. It also became apparent that white applicants with lower scores than Bakke had been admitted each year he applied. Some of these students had been admitted due to their family wealth or other connections. Although Bakke claimed he was superbly qualified, the admissions numbers indicated that Bakke would not have been admitted even if the 16 special admissions spaces did not exist. In both years there were 30 or so other students who would have been admitted before Bakke. Many found it curious that Bakke only chose to contest the minority students admitted rather than the "special" white students admitted. Similar charges had been made against DeFunis. In addition, Bakke did not choose to fight against possible discrimination due to his over-30 age, which he had specifically been told was a liability (R. Smith, 1978). Amidst the controversy, the Davis School of Medicine decided to appeal the decision of the California Supreme Court to the Supreme Court of the United States.

In June 1978, the Supreme Court announced its decision. They held 4-1-4 that "(a) the minority-admissions program of the University of California Medical School in Davis had discriminated illegally against a white male applicant, but (b) that universities could legally consider race as a factor in admissions" (Sobel, 1980, p. 145). Justices Warren Burger, John Paul Stevens, Potter Stewart, and William Rehnquist decided in favor of Bakke on both counts, Justices William Brennan, Byron

White, Thurgood Marshall, and Harry Blackmun decided in favor of Davis on both counts, and, in the swing vote, Justice Lewis Powell decided *against* the quota part of the Davis policy, but *in favor of* using race as a factor in admissions. Powell's became the court's majority opinion, since he was the deciding vote for both sides. This type of split decision showed that the justices were as divided as the nation.

The Carter administration praised the decision because it supported affirmative action programs. Prominent minority leaders had mixed reactions. Vernon Jordan, Urban League director, and Benjamin Hooks, executive director of the NAACP, were both disappointed that the ruling had ordered Bakke's admission to the medical school, but were pleased with what they considered to be a hopeful affirmative action ruling. In a more critical reaction, the Reverend Jesse Jackson saw the decision as part of a national move toward conservatism and against civil rights (Sobel, 1980).

Despite the *Bakke* ruling, institutions of higher education in the 1980s and 1990s struggled with their affirmative action admissions policies and diversity goals. The 1980s Republican presidential era provided fertile ground for the 1990s challenges to affirmative action.

The Reagan–Bush Years

Just after Ronald Reagan was elected president in 1980, Republican senator Orrin Hatch pledged support for a constitutional amendment outlawing affirmative action programs in education and employment. In 1983, Mary Francis Berry of the Commission of Civil Rights testified before the House Subcommittee on Postsecondary Education and Civil and Constitutional Rights. She testified that she believed that "since this administration took office, the commission has been concerned by efforts to reverse longstanding federal civil rights enforcement policies." She pointed out that the laws designed to prevent discrimination against people of color in higher education admissions, such as Title VI of the Civil Rights Act, were "not being fully enforced" (Berry, 1983, p. 2). Soon thereafter, Reagan appointed Linda Chavez as staff director of the Civil Rights Commission. Almost immediately, she spoke out against federal affirmative action policies.

Despite Reagan's opposition to affirmative action, educators and policymakers in some arenas were still trying to use affirmative action to do what they believed to be the right thing. For example, in 1989 the California legislature introduced a bill to require all California colleges and universities to have by 2000 a student body as diverse as California's high school graduates (Kull, 1992). This bill is especially interesting when we note that it is in California where the most stringent legislation against affirmative action, Proposition 209, is now in effect.

The 1990s

In the 1992 case concerning historically segregated universities, *United States v. Fordice*, the Supreme Court underscored states' affirmative duty to actively overcome the lingering effects of past discrimination against people of color, saying that race-neutral policies do not do enough to meet that goal (Kauffman & Gonzalez, 1997). While President Clinton was a supporter of race-conscious policies in general, and affirmative action in particular, he did not aggressively champion this portion of the civil rights agenda. The first 2½ years of his first term as president passed with nary a mention of affirmative action. In June 1995, he spoke on affirmative action and solidified his support for the policy even though he said that it needed reform. "When affirmative action is done right," he said, "it is flexible, it is fair, and it works" (quoted in Purdum, 1995, p. B10). By 1997, he made efforts to create a public dialogue about the issue of race in America. Still, it was during Clinton's tenure in office that affirmative action policy faced the strongest attacks yet.

California led the way in the backlash against affirmative action. Spurred on by regent Ward Connerly, the regents of the University of California in 1995 voted to bar the consideration of race and ethnicity in admissions decisions. Then, in the 1996 elections, affirmative action was seen as a pivotal issue, one that Republicans used to alienate white male voters from liberal Democrats (Chávez, 1998). This led Robert Dole, the Republican candidate for president, to support California's Proposition 209, a ballot initiative entitled the California Civil Rights Initiative (CCRI). This constitutional amendment, written by two conservative academics, abolished all "preferences" based on race, ethnicity, and sex, but never specifically mentioned affirmative action. It was passed by 54 percent of California's voters. During the campaign, Clinton stayed out of the affirmative action debate, fearing that it would negatively affect his ability to get the white vote (Chávez, 1998). Opponents of the amendment challenged its constitutionality in court, but in 1997 the Supreme Court affirmed the ruling by the Ninth Circuit Court of Appeals that upheld Proposition 209 (Lederman, 1997). The impact on California's college student population was felt almost immediately. In fall of 1998, the most prestigious University of California campus, Berkeley, reported a 52 percent decrease in the number of African American and Latino first-year students for the first class admitted without affirmative action. Because of this, African American and Latino students made up only 9.9 percent of the first-year class, in comparison with 20.7 percent the previous year (Healy, 1998a). At Berkeley's law school, there was only one African American student in the first-year class of 1997–98. In partial response to the negative attention given to the University of California system, in 2001 the regents voted to rescind their ban on affirmative action (Schevitz, 2001). Nevertheless, the sentiments in California spread to other states as well. The most significant developments have been in Texas, Washington, Georgia, and Michigan.

In deciding the *Hopwood v. Texas* case in March 1996, the Court of Appeals for the 5th Circuit ruled against race-conscious affirmative action policies in higher education admissions, thus nullifying the Supreme Court's *Bakke* ruling in all 5th Circuit states: Texas, Louisiana, and Mississippi. The three-judge panel prohibited the use of race-based admissions criteria to achieve diversity at the University of Texas Law School. They found for Hopwood based on the notion that a state's interest in acquiring a diverse student body was not compelling enough to justify a program like that of the University of Texas Law School. The 5th Circuit also held that race preferences would be allowed only if they were used as a remedy for the present effects of past discrimination (Greve, 1999).

There are some inconsistencies about the case. While plaintiff Cheryl Hopwood's attorneys argued that she would have added diversity to the school, little has been reported of Hopwood's application. As a single mother of a disabled child, she may indeed have brought a unique perspective to the University of Texas Law School. However, the admissions committee had no way of knowing that, because she did not provide a personal statement or any letters of recommendation to support her qualifications. In addition, the ruling does permit certain preferential criteria for selection such as geographic area, athletic talent, special talents, and alumni status (Kauffman & Gonzalez, 1997). Texas appealed the case to the U.S. Supreme Court. In declining to review the case, the Supreme Court both upheld the ruling and limited its applicability to only the 5th Circuit states.

In Washington State, 59 percent of the voters approved Initiative 200 in 1998, a CCRI-like referendum banning race and sex preferences in public employment, contracts, and university admissions. It is in this political context that white applicants to the University of Washington Law School contested their rejection in the *Smith v. University of Washington* (2000) case. In other cases, the University of Georgia, the University of Michigan, and the University of Michigan Law School also were sued by white applicants who were rejected for admission. (These cases will be examined in more detail later in this chapter.) At issue in these cases was the constitutionality of the *Bakke* ruling that colleges and universities seeking diversity may use race as a factor in admissions in order to meet that goal.

As these legislative challenges to affirmative action take center stage, the theoretical and ideological debates about whether the policy is right or wrong continue to rage.

THE MAJOR ARGUMENTS AGAINST AFFIRMATIVE ACTION

In order to propose an innovative defense of affirmative action policy in higher education admissions based on the key educational aim of developing self-determination among students, it is important first to grapple with the major arguments both against and for affirmative action policy in higher education. In this section I will respond to the five most prominent criticisms of affirmative action. First among these is the argument that affirmative action amounts to reverse discrimination and that it actually violates key civil rights legislation such as the 14th Amendment and Title VI of the Civil Rights Act. I maintain that affirmative action is quite different from the types of discrimination outlawed by the 14th Amendment and Title VI in that it aims to diminish a significant social injustice: the oppression faced by women and people of color. Second is the notion that affirmative action degrades the standards of merit at selective colleges and universities, resulting in the acceptance of students who are unqualified for the rigors of selective higher education. The concept of merit itself is a thorny one, but I contend that taking race into account is in keeping with higher education's socially conscious mission. A third criticism, often movingly brought to the fore by critics of color, is that students of color admitted under affirmative action policies end up feeling inferior to their white classmates. While I understand that some people of color genuinely do feel harmed by the presumption that they did not earn their admittance, I believe that the overall benefits of affirmative action surpass that potential harm. Fourth is the argument that affirmative action should shift to being class-conscious rather than race-conscious. This way, the neediest members of all races, ethnicities, and sexes would benefit. I agree that class should be taken into account, but not to the exclusion of race and ethnicity, for racial and ethnic oppression, although correlated with class, continues to be a problem over and above it. Finally, a fifth claim made by opponents of affirmative action is that it ends up causing racial division on campus rather than enhancing a healthy climate of diversity.

They argue that the years of affirmative action have been enough and that it is no longer needed; college and university admissions should thus be color-blind. I argue that affirmative action, insofar as it helps enroll students of color in predominantly white institutions, makes a positive difference in the composition of the student body at selective colleges and universities. There is empirical evidence that a more integrated student body enhances social and intellectual diversity. Although in some respects it would be nice if race-neutrality could do the trick, the United States has not yet reached that point. Color-blindness will not do any work in reducing oppression just because we wish that it could.

DISCRIMINATION IN REVERSE?

One of the most common criticisms of affirmative action is that it violates the idea of equal rights for all. Critics argue that when colleges and universities take an applicant's race or ethnicity into consideration in the admissions process, it is tantamount to discrimination against white students. Shelby Steele (1990) maintains that affirmative action policies "have reburdened society with the very marriage of color and preference (in reverse) that we set out to eradicate. The old sin is reaffirmed in a new guise" (p. 115). According to critics such as Steele, this is an odious practice that results in the rejection of some applicants simply because they are white, which is just as objectionable as the rejection of applicants because they are people of color. However, supporters of affirmative action agree with Nicholas Katzenbach and Burke Marshall (1998):

> To speak of . . . [affirmative action] efforts as though they were racially biased against whites and to equate them with the discriminatory practices of the past against African Americans is to steal the rhetoric of civil rights and turn it upside down. For racial bias to be a problem, it must be accompanied by power. (p. 45)

Nonetheless, charges of reverse discrimination abound in the public debate over affirmative action. Although the 14th Amendment to the Constitution of the United States guarantees equal protection to all under the law, nowhere does it preclude the consideration of race, ethnicity, or sex. In fact, sometimes in order to treat people fairly, it is necessary to be conscious of race, ethnicity, and sex in education policies (Appiah & Gutmann, 1996). Yet, when it comes to the challenges that affirmative action has faced in court, the chief complaint against it is that it amounts to reverse discrimination.

The civil rights legislation of the 1960s championed nondiscrimination. At the time, it went unquestioned that the nondiscrimination principle banned discrimination against people of color or women, because white men were not in danger of being discriminated against for educational or employment opportunities because of their color or gender. In fact, both sides of the affirmative action debate usually agree that race, ethnicity, and sex should not be used to discriminate against people of color or women.[5] The concept of nondiscrimination has evolved in such a way that policies that view a person's race, ethnicity, or gender as a qualification for selection are still considered legal. An applicant's race is a relevant qualification because the social purposes of (selective) colleges and universities include educating professionals and community leaders that can serve all types of communities (Gutmann, 1987). The notion of affirmative action was conceived as an active expansion of opportunities for people of color and women, not just as freedom from discriminatory practices. Given the past and present racism entrenched in American society, mere nondiscrimination can actually perpetuate the oppressive status quo. Young (1990a) argues that it is precisely affirmative action's challenge to passive nondiscrimination that makes its case stronger, because it aims to combat the oppression and domination of marginalized groups. Oppression is the major wrong endured by people of color and women in U.S. society. Young points out that "if discrimination serves the purpose of undermining the oppression of a group, it may be not only permitted, but morally required" (p. 197).

Young's assertion underscores another important point: affirmative action policies take nothing away from white men that they actually earned or deserve to keep. Because of societal inequality, they enjoy many unearned privileges (McIntosh, 1989). Affirmative action, in part, attempts to remedy that situation. Studies have shown that increases in the numbers of students of color in higher education, although positive, have been small and "have been made without causing undue personal or financial hardship to white males" (Ethridge, 1997, p. 70). Of the approximately 1,800 4-year institutions of higher education in the United States, about 120 of the most selective schools practice "serious affirmative action" because the other schools have much less competitive or noncompetitive admissions processes (Chenoweth, 1997, p. 10). A recent study by the College Fund/UNCF found that between 1984 and 1995, the lion's share of the top 120 institutions seemed to accommodate the increase of African American and Latino students by expanding their first-year cohorts in toto. For example, at the University of Virginia, the entire 1995 first-year class included a total of 292 more students, while the number of African American and Latino students increased by 237 (Chenoweth, 1997). Regardless of education, on average, white males still had higher wages than women and people of color. White students usually attend their first choice of college, whereas African American and Asian American students are more likely than whites to have to attend a second or third choice college (Hurtado & Navia, 1997). Interestingly, following the 5th Circuit's decision in favor of Hopwood and two other white students, a lower court charged with awarding damages to the plaintiffs considered it so unlikely that any of them would have actually been admitted to the law school, even under a race-blind policy, that they were each only awarded one dollar (R. Dworkin, 1998). In 1995, the Department of Labor found that out of 3,000 discrimination cases filed, fewer than 100 involved reverse discrimination; of these, only 6 were actually validated (American Council on Education, 1996). Still, the widespread impression is that white people unjustly lose out because of affirmative action. In a 1995 *USA Today*/CNN/Gallup Poll, 15 percent of the white males believed that "they've lost a job because of affirmative action policies" (Marable, 1995, p. 85). Whether or not this perception is based in reality does not change the fact that a good portion of white people feel cheated by civil rights gains in the United States. These feelings may provoke questions about the fairness of affirmative action. This leads to another argument often raised by affirmative action's critics, that some students of color are less deserving of college and university admissions than some white students with higher standardized test scores or grade-point averages.

WHO MERITS ADMISSION?

The idea that affirmative action is discriminatory is a misconception that stems from the myth of meritocracy. Those who make this argument never consider how much privilege, often afforded by skin color and the arbitrary circumstances of birth, influences one's ability to meet traditional, quantifiable standards of merit. Without this deep understanding of the meritocratic myth, many white students become resentful. All they see is that the rules of the game that privileged their fathers have changed; they cannot now always count on having the favored position.

Affirmative action causes people to question whether or not the students admitted under such policies were qualified enough, or worthy of admission. Many white students believe that affirmative action policies came at the expense of their fair educational opportunities, at the expense of merit-based selection. Representative S. I. Hayakawa (R-CA)

protested affirmative action policies in 1979, even though he had supported initial affirmative action efforts to draw attention to the problems
of discrimination (Sobel, 1980). He was wary of opportunities that may
have gone to people who did not merit them. This is the crux of the
merit objection to affirmative action, perhaps the most prominent of all
the opposing arguments. A main part of the contention that affirmative
action desecrates merit-based admissions processes is that it reinforces
the idea of white superiority by tacitly confirming that applicants of
color cannot meet the traditional admissions standards, which is exactly
the idea that the Civil Rights Act tries to overcome (Belz, 1991). A recent
study by two researchers at the University of California at Davis Medical
School examined the career paths of 356 medical school students who
were admitted to Davis under affirmative action policies. They compared the affirmative action beneficiaries with a matched sample of students who were not admitted under affirmative action. Their findings
directly challenge the idea that students admitted under affirmative action policies are necessarily less qualified and less able to compete and
succeed in higher education. The graduation rates of both groups were
quite similar: 94 percent of the affirmative action students graduated
compared with 97 percent of the matched sample. In addition, after
graduation, both groups performed equally well in their residencies, as
evidenced by their evaluations and rates of completion (Davidson &
Lewis, 1997). Medicine is arguably one of the most challenging career
paths one could undertake. This study makes it clear that although the
affirmative action policy at Davis Medical School helped some students
of color gain entry, it was their qualifications and abilities that enabled
them to graduate and gain success as physicians.

An affirmative action policy such as the one at Davis Medical School
is justifiable mainly because it makes up for biased and oppressive structural and institutional factors, rather than compensating for the supposed deficiencies of students of color.[6] Students of color may perceive
what Claude Steele (1999) calls a stereotype threat when confronted
with standardized and other tests on which their college admissions and
self-concept may hinge. In addition, it is not uncommon for students of
color to receive little to no encouragement from school officials to attend college. Consider the experience of a well-respected Chicano scientist: "I was in an accelerated class, I was in the top 10% of my high
school graduating class. I wasn't dumb; I was pretty good, I thought. She
[the counselor] told me, 'Well, you should go into vocational school'"
(Gándara, 1995, p. 62). But encouragement can make a positive difference. Take, for example, the case of a Chicano physician. He says, "I
remember going to an Open House and my [public school] instructor

told my parents that I was 'college material' . . . and it seems from then on, I was their son: 'college material' " (Gándara, 1995, p. 60). Structural factors such as the attitudes of K–12 educators have an impact on students' perceived future options. Affirmative action tries to offset some of the structural inequities suffered by students of color within their K–12 educations. As Susan Sturm and Lani Guinier (1996) contend, the "tests and informal criteria making up our 'meritocracy' tell us more about past opportunity than about future accomplishments on the job or in the classroom" (p. 957). Of course, the argument is made that students need better schools, college preparation, and encouragement from educators, not admittance to a college for which they are likely not qualified. Although this is certainly true, students of color should not suffer due to the inferior quality of their public schools. It is not right to assume that most students of color do not have superior academic achievement. Indeed, in the fall of 1998, Berkeley rejected 800 African American and Latino students who had perfect 4.0 grade point averages (Takaki, 1998).

Still, critics will wonder why white students should suffer due to arbitrary circumstances of race, but students of color should not. This raises an emotion-laden point. To be sure, white students should not suffer because of their race. However, the issue is far more complex than the answer intimates. Affirmative action policy does not entail that students be rejected because they are white. It also does not entail that students be accepted because they are Latino or Asian American or African American or Native American. It does entail that admissions officers select those students who have the most to offer in accordance with the institution's mission and goals. When one of those goals is to educate students who will serve as leaders for all portions of U.S. society, then an applicant's race or ethnicity is indeed a relevant qualification for admission (R. Dworkin, 1998; Gutmann, 1987).

Using race and ethnicity as a factor in admissions is somehow seen as being in opposition to "regular" or "objective" admissions criteria. What is perhaps more likely is that it is the thorniest criterion. Race is one qualifying factor, not a sufficient qualification to guarantee admission. Other factors taken into consideration go relatively unquestioned. College and university admissions procedures have always taken special circumstances into account when selecting students. It is rather ironic that the practice of taking race and ethnicity into consideration raises such ire; the reliance on quantifiable scores to determine merit became standard practice only when more women and people of color began gaining access to college (Rodriguez, 1996). There is little public outcry against other factors such as being children of alumni (legacies), being friends or children of large donors, having athletic ability, having veteran status, or coming from an underrepresented geographic area. University of California admissions records from 1991 to 1996 show that influential people such as regents, politicians, and businesspeople often try to use their community standing to affect particular admissions decisions at the most selective institutions (Rodriguez, 1996). In fact, in 1997, nine students were admitted to the University of California at Berkeley due to their connections to wealthy donors. None of these students would have been admitted otherwise (*The Chronicle of Higher Education*, 1997b). At Harvard, student legacies admitted in 1989 outnumbered all the African American, Mexican American, Native American, and Puerto Rican students combined (Karen, 1998). Opponents of affirmative action nevertheless balk at the idea that selection criteria other than academic ability (as measured primarily by tests and grade-point averages) should matter in the admissions process. Although academic ability is certainly very important, it is hardly the only, or even the most, important factor in deciding who should attend competitive institutions of higher education. As Gutmann (1987) notes, "Academic ability is, by the best accounts, a very poor predictor of social contribution, however it is measured" (p. 197). This is especially so because an important institutional aim of selective colleges is for their graduates to benefit society in some way. And qualifications are not separable from the "social function" of the institution (Gutmann & Thompson, 1996, p. 324).

Interestingly, a study of affirmative action shows that within selective schools' admissions records, some 90 percent of African American applicants have higher standardized test scores than the national African American average and some 75 percent had higher scores than the national white average (Bowen & Bok, 1998). According to this measure, their level of qualification was quite high. Even so, the African American students at these schools had lower mean scores than the white students. Facts such as these cause affirmative action critics to argue that college-minded students of color should simply attend less selective institutions. This way, the argument goes, they have a better chance of succeeding academically and graduating from college. Here again, the evidence from the William Bowen and Derek Bok (1998) study is relevant. African American students were more likely to obtain graduate or professional degrees when their undergraduate college was more selective, even if their grade-point average was lower than it might have been at a less selective institution.

A FAUSTIAN BARGAIN?

Do students of color lose more than they gain from affirmative action policies? Some scholars of color would answer yes to this question (Chavez, 1991; D'Souza, 1991; McWhorter, 2000; Rodriguez, 1982; Sowell, 1981, 1993; S. Steele, 1990). They argue that affirmative action further victimizes students of color who end up feeling inferior, first because they begin to doubt that their own qualifications earned their admission, and second because they cannot compete with other students at selective institutions. According to S. Steele (1990), disclosing one's race or ethnicity on a college application amounts to a Faustian bargain. If students of color do disclose their race or ethnicity, they risk presenting themselves as victims in need of special help, which may be damaging to their self-worth and confidence. Along these lines, Belz (1991) contends that "as long as legal rights and social benefits are conditioned on racial victimization, . . . it appears to be impossible for the beneficiaries of preferential treatment to achieve full equality" (p. 263). Indeed, these critics believe that affirmative action forces students of color to sell their souls to gain educational opportunity.

Although this line of argument is undoubtedly heartfelt, and despite the possibility that some students of color may have feelings of self-doubt, it is not affirmative action policies that cause those feelings. It is racism that causes people to doubt the abilities of students of color and it is oppression that causes these students to doubt themselves. Unfortunately, people of color who achieve in the educational realm are often questioned, whether or not affirmative action is at issue. Their qualifications and abilities are called into question despite the evidence of educational achievement and success. Consider what this Chicano student has to say:

> I took my eighth grade diploma which was straight A's, and I was valedictorian of my eighth grade. . . . And I told him [the counselor] I would like to go to college and could he fit me into college-prep classes? And he . . . said, well, he wasn't sure I could handle it. (Gándara, 1995, p. 61)

This type of incident is all too common and had nothing to do with affirmative action.

The fact is that college students at selective institutions whose race or ethnicity was taken into account in the admissions process are largely successful (Bowen & Bok, 1998). From 1960 to 1995, when affirmative action policies were implemented, the percentage of African American college graduates (ages 25–29) and law school graduates increased, according to Bowen and Bok (1998). Bowen and Bok also found that the 6-year graduation rate for students of color at selective institutions was similar to that of white students. White students had a 94 percent graduation rate, whereas the graduation rate was 96 percent for Asian American students, 90 percent for Latino students, and 79 percent for African American students. The more selective the college, the higher the graduation rates for all groups. These statistics refute the notion that affirmative action should be abolished so that students of color would attend less selective schools where they would have a better chance of success. They also reject the idea that affirmative action harms its beneficiaries. The Bowen and Bok study also found that students of color at selective institutions that considered race and ethnicity in admitting students had high levels of success and satisfaction, as measured by their graduate and professional school success, satisfaction with their college experience, and perceived intellectual benefit of attending a selective school. Far from damaging its beneficiaries, affirmative action policy does what it is supposed to do—it allows admissions officers to view a student's race and ethnicity as a relevant qualification for admission, and thus provides students with the real opportunity to attend a selective institution of higher education. From most accounts, then, affirmative action programs do not cause students of color to suffer as Faust. Instead, they gain knowledge and success through their own abilities.

ARE THE NEEDIEST OVERLOOKED?

Many believe that affirmative action in higher education admissions primarily benefits students of color who need it least (Connerly, 2000; D'Souza, 1991; S. Steele, 1990). It may be true that affirmative action disproportionately benefits students of color from middle or higher income families rather than students from lower income families, because those from higher income families are likely to have better college preparation and more family assets. That said, it is important to realize that in admitting students of color from any wealth background, colleges and universities are fulfilling their social purposes of, for instance, educating officeholders and enabling graduates to choose from among good lives (Gutmann, 1987). It would be difficult to argue that only students of color from working-class and poor backgrounds will offer something new to the diversity on campus or to post-graduate positions of leadership. Middle-class students of color bring relevant experiences to the campus related to their race and ethnicity. Through his research on the black middle class, Ellis Cose (1993) observes that "America is filled with attitudes, assumptions, stereotypes, and behaviors that make it virtually impossible for blacks to believe that the nation is serious about its promise of equality—even (perhaps especially) for those who have been blessed with material success" (p. 5). These are compelling reasons for the continued emphasis on race-consciousness in affirmative action programs, even if students from middle-class families benefit the most. So, if the question is whether affirmative action policies should benefit a middle-class Latino child of an attorney or a poor child of a rural white farmer,[7] I would say the answer is both. We are, in essence, comparing apples to oranges. However, if we compare a Latino child of an attorney with a similarly situated white child, it is fair to say that the Latino student will have a different experience in that she or he will always have to deal with the issue of race and ethnicity (Edley, 1996).

There are those on both sides of the affirmative action issue who would solve the controversy by simply replacing race and ethnicity with socioeconomic class (D'Souza, 1991; West, 1993). They argue that the neediest Native Americans, Asian Americans, African Americans, and Latinos would benefit most from increased access to college. Middle-class students of color would then compete in the same way that white students do now. We must remember, however, that when affirmative action is done right, students of color do compete in the same way as white students. The only difference is that being white is not seen as a relevant qualification for admission, whereas being, say, Native American is. One major concern is that viewing class as a proxy for race would dilute the unique importance of a focus on race and ethnicity. In her study of law school admissions, Linda Wightman (1997) found that using an admissions model focused on class rather than race does not help identify a racially and ethnically diverse group of applicants. Similarly, Thomas Kane (1998) found that substituting class for race as an admissions factor in California would favor low-income white and Asian students instead of African American and Latino students. Even though Cornel West (1993) favors class-conscious affirmative action, he acknowledges that race-based policy has been necessary, given U.S. history. Another concern is that it seems dishonest to substitute class for race in the admissions process when the policy is still intended to benefit students of color. It is as if we are somehow pretending that race and ethnicity are no longer the central issue.

While using class as a proxy for race is neither an honest nor an effective solution, I think it is important to take class into consideration within the college admissions process because poor and working-class students would benefit from affirmative action in similar ways as students of color. Walter Feinberg (1998) maintains that there is a significant difference between racial injustice and injustices based on socioeconomic class, and I agree. However, he goes on to argue that as a result, poor people may sometimes be more to blame for their economic misfortunes than people of color are ever to blame for the misfortunes they face due to racial and ethnic considerations. This seems to be a wrongheaded way to resolve the question of whether or not class should be substituted for race in affirmative action policy. Class considerations fit appropriately into the socially conscious mission of selective colleges and universities. Students from poor families and depressed inner-city neighborhoods or those who are the first in their family to attend college have a background characteristic that is relevant in the admissions process. In addition, there are regional cases when it would be especially appropriate to take class issues into account (e.g., Appalachia). Nonetheless, I want to underscore the idea that a solely class-based system of affirmative action is not an effective solution to the lack of racial and ethnic diversity on college and university campuses. A class-conscious policy would likely benefit many poor white students, which is certainly good (Bernal, Cabrera, & Terenzini, 1999). But because poor white people outnumber poor people of color, there would be fewer students of color at selective institutions.

SHOULDN'T WE SEE PAST COLOR ALREADY?

In yet another argument against affirmative action, opponents such as D'Souza (1991) point to campus tensions surrounding issues of race as evidence that affirmative action policy augments racial divisions. Without a policy that admits students using race and ethnicity as a factor, students would not feel such a great separation due to race, or so the argument goes. Opponents argue that it is time to return to the ideal of color-blindness, that the divisiveness of affirmative action has been endured long enough. The separation that affirmative action policies create leads to racial conflicts between white students and students of color, often because of the resentment that white students feel. Incidents of racism and hate on campus may underscore this point. Nevertheless, proponents of this view appear to be overlooking the fact that conflicts related to racism and stereotyping are far more attributable to our past and present history of racial tension than they are to affirmative action policy. In addition, present racial oppression makes the ideal of genuine race-neutrality in education policy little more than a pipe dream. Sylvia Hurtado and Christine Navia (1997) make the excellent point that

> since social construction of inferiority and beliefs about cultural differences predate the implementation of affirmative action policies, the dismantling of these policies is not likely to eradicate the deeper problem of longstanding stereotypes or institutionalized racial, ethnic, gender, and class discrimination. (p. 114)

A study of college students shows that when a college or university has a strong emphasis on diversity, students gain more cultural awareness and a deeper commitment to promoting racial and ethnic understanding than they would have otherwise (Astin, 1993). Indeed, in reviewing the literature on the educational benefits of diversity, Jeffrey Milem and Kenji Hakuta (2000) found empirical evidence documenting that a diverse campus is beneficial for individual students, the campus as a whole, and society overall. More specifically, both the African American and white graduates in Bowen and Bok's (1998) study said they value the diversity to which they were exposed as undergraduates. One of the goals of affirmative action culled from the mission of selective institutions of higher education is to create a healthy campus climate, one in which students have a diversity of backgrounds, experiences, opinions, and knowledge so that they can learn from one another and bring their knowledge into the community as graduates.

"Diversity" has become an oft-cited justification for affirmative action (Chang, Witt, Jones, & Hakuta, 1999; Gurin, 1999; G. Liu, 1998; Marin, 2000; Milem & Hakuta, 2000). This is due in part to Justice Powell's *Bakke* opinion, in which he affirmed diversity as a worthy goal for which colleges and universities should strive. Recent research shows that campus diversity is beneficial for all students, as well as for institutions of higher education and society (Marin, 2000; Milem, 1999). Legal analysis by Goodwin Liu (1998) posits diversity as a constitutionally compelling interest, intimating that the diversity rationale for affirmative action could withstand court challenges. The judges who heard the University of Washington Law School and University of Michigan undergraduate cases agreed with this rationale (Schmidt, 2001). With the understanding that the diversity rationale is crucial to the defense of affirmative action policy in court, it should not stand alone. Admitting a few students of color in the hopes of increasing campus diversity does not necessarily ensure intellectual diversity or diversity of viewpoint. Similarly, because a student body is diverse does not mean that different perspectives will be heard.

Despite the fact that affirmative action cannot guarantee that a campus will have real and noticeable diversity of viewpoint, it can ensure that students of color will be represented in higher numbers. This, in turn, moves us toward the noble (and legal) goal of a diverse and rich campus environment; when diversity is strongly lacking, white males tend to dominate the classroom discourse (*The Chronicle of Higher Education*, 1998a). Because the ideal of color-blindness sits well with many of us does not mean that it is a good, or even decent, course of action for education policy. Genuine race-neutrality would be preferred if there were more doctors, lawyers, scientists, and teachers of color, but there have been small increases in these fields even with race-conscious policies. Reverting to so-called color-blindness and dismissing affirmative action will not solve this problem.

Color-blind policies cannot be championed in a society that is not color-blind. Consider these facts: 50 percent of African American and 44 percent of Latino children under the age of 6 years live below poverty level, as compared with 14.4 percent of white children (Edley, 1996); African Americans make up just 4.2 percent of all doctors, 5 percent of university teachers, and 3.3 percent of attorneys, even as they make up some 12 percent of the U.S. population (W. Feinberg, 1998); celebration broke out in the engineering community when 1998 yielded 3 African American Ph.D.s in engineering from just one school, representing a large portion of the total in the last few years (Wilson, 1998); among accomplished graduates of selective colleges, whites still earn much more than their African American counterparts (Bowen & Bok, 1998). As these statistics illustrate, race continues to matter in the United States. Consequently, education policies ought to take it into account. In addition, affirmative action is necessary and useful in our society as long as race and ethnicity continue to play a role in the awarding of social and educational opportunities.

Having now considered the most common arguments against affirmative action put forth in the debate, I would like to move on to a defense of affirmative action that is not considered within the current discourse. Because the development of a sense of self-determination is a crucial aim of a good and just education, a race-conscious education policy such as affirmative action is necessary because of its role in fostering more favorable societal contexts of choice for students of color.

AFFIRMATIVE ACTION AND THE ARGUMENT
FROM SELF-DETERMINATION

In this section I advance my own argument for affirmative action. Good affirmative action policies implemented by institutions of higher education do much more than merely help students of color to gain admittance. When race is used as a factor in the college and university admissions process, there are two main occurrences. First is the strongest outcome: The context from which students make choices in life is greatly expanded. The systemic oppression of people of color in the United States justifies policy that combats limiting societal structures. The second effect is more indirect: Students get the message that their race or ethnicity is considered important enough to be used as a qualifying factor for university admission. This public recognition of the exter-

nal worth of students' cultural background enhances students' ability to
be true to themselves. As I argued in Chapter 2, when these two factors
are fostered by education policies, students are better able to become
self-determining persons. Therein I claimed that the oppression of people of color in the United States warrants education policy that combats
the misrecognition of their cultural identities and the limitations on their
social contexts of choice. Because affirmative action policy places value
on nondominant races and ethnicities and expands access to the opportunity structure, it counteracts oppression. Affirmative action policy,
therefore, greatly contributes to the development of students' self-determination, especially students of color. It does this first and foremost by
contributing to the expansion of their contexts of choice. In a less direct
manner, it also supports students' authentic cultural identities.

EXPANDING THE SOCIAL CONTEXT OF CHOICE

A well-respected Chicano political scientist recounts how significant it
was for him to have a sibling who attended a top university. He explains:
"My sister was a tremendous influence on me. . . . I can remember, how
many times I used to tell people my sister was at Berkeley. That was sort
of a success image, a very important success image" (Gándara, 1995, p.
35). This political scientist is 1 of 50 Chicanos with Ph.D.s, M.D.s, or
J.D.s from selective institutions that Gándara studied in an effort to understand the factors that influenced their educational success and social
mobility. One common theme was that examples of family success like
a sister at Berkeley helped to expand the students' perceived options
for educational and career choices. Gándara found that having role models of intelligence, achievement, and success made a big difference for
these successful Chicanos. In addition, over half of the study's partici-
pants attributed their enrollment in college or graduate school to outreach and recruitment programs such as affirmative action for students
of color.

A higher education is widely viewed as crucial to the pursuit of
economic equality and upward mobility. When higher education in
America began, there was great concern with the role it would play for
equality and democracy (Institute for Higher Education Policy, 1998;
Tierney, 1997). On measures such as teacher quality, money spent per
student, and curriculum offerings, public schools with large numbers of
students of color enjoyed fewer resources than predominantly white
schools (Darling-Hammond, 1998; Kozol, 1991). Inasmuch as affirmative
action contributes to greater educational opportunities and possibilities
of highly valued positions in society for students of color, it significantly

enhances their ability to become self-determining in a meaningful way. In addition, it combats oppression and contributes toward a healthy democracy. Without people of color and women in positions of professional and community leadership, it is fair to say that there is a substantially reduced chance of eradicating institutionalized racism, sexism, and oppression. A corollary benefit is that when white people embrace the need to share power with all members of society, their humanity becomes more meaningful, a notion championed by Paulo Freire (1970). Diminishing racial injustice can be seen as a special obligation held by white people (Gutmann, 1987). Until the policies and programs we have that fight oppression are protected, those who have traditionally benefited from the oppressive and racist societal structures remain morally stunted and less than fully human (Freire, 1970). According to Edley (1996), "the diversity we experience enriches our lives in immeasurable material and immaterial ways, changes who we are and how we develop. This has little to do with instrumentalism and everything to do with wanting completeness in our humanity" (p. 130). To be sure, there are those who will disagree with this idea, arguing that their humanity feels complete enough just as it is, thank you very much. In spite of that, it is right and good to strive for a moral ideal where all people feel worthy of respect, can conceive of themselves in positions of power, and have an overall sense of possibility about their lives. Surely this is a humanity worth wanting by all.

When the dominant social structure places one at a disadvantage in competitive higher education admissions, thereby constraining one's context of choice, affirmative action policy adds to one's capacity for self-determination by taking that oppressive structure into account. By helping to expand the social context of choice of students of color, affirmative action takes a step closer to humanity worth wanting. The argument can be made that affirmative action programs restrict white students' contexts of choice. *Prima facie* this seems to be the case because as access is increased for students of color, white students may be displaced. However, that is not what has happened. Top institutions of higher education have chosen instead to make more room for increased numbers of students of color (Chenoweth, 1997). Admissions examples from court cases like *Bakke* and *Hopwood* dramatize this issue by making it seem like a zero-sum calculus. However, in both of those cases, the white plaintiffs would not have been admitted even if the university's affirmative action policy had not been in place. What is most important is that affirmative action policy serves the interests of justice for students of color. Through affirmative action, students of color enter into selective institutions of higher education in greater numbers than they would have otherwise been able to do. Graduation rates for white students and students of color are similar at such selective institutions (Bowen & Bok, 1998). Once students are accepted to college or graduate school, the context within which they make decisions grows much wider. Recent research measuring the value of a higher education proves this to be true. College-educated individuals enjoy higher rates of employment, improved health, better working conditions, higher salaries and benefits, greater personal status, and better overall quality of life (Institute for Higher Education Policy, 1998). They are not forced to rely on only a high school education for the skills and training needed for good employment opportunities. Consider the experience of Delbert Thunderwulf, a Native American student who had dropped out of college the first time around. Even though he entered a nonselective community college, Thunderwulf's experience provides us with a relevant lesson. He tells the story of what brought him back to higher education a second time:

> I started seeing a bunch of people around me with college educations and *they were going for what they wanted.* And me, I couldn't do that on $5.50 an hour. . . . At first I was afraid to come back to college. I was afraid I wouldn't make it. It took a lot to do it, and I'm glad I did. (Tierney, 1993, p. 310, emphasis added)

Thunderwulf recognizes how important a higher education is for people's ability to go "for what they wanted." He, too, seeks to enrich his context of choice to one in which he can pursue opportunities for better jobs with higher wages.[8] Thus, higher education will contribute to his present and long-term success. Within a more favorable context of choice, Thunderwulf can enjoy greater self-determination and go for what he wants in life. His experience shows us how, once students graduate from college, their social contexts of choice expand beyond just opening up educational opportunities to include widening career and other life opportunities as well. This has broad implications because that expansion leads not only to the development of self-determination and more worthwhile opportunities for individual students like Thunderwulf, but also to a more favorable social context of choice for other members of society who then interact with those college-educated role models of color.

Yet, critics can still challenge affirmative action, this time with the good of society in mind. If, as I contend, affirmative action helps create more favorable contexts of choice for students and hence leads them to positions in which they can most benefit the community, then couldn't the same effect occur by doing away with affirmative action and admitting only the students who score highest on standardized admissions examinations? It could be better for society as a whole if the highest-scoring students are given the most opportunities. They would gain in self-determination and society would benefit from their expertise, ingenuity, and new discoveries. Of course, this assumes that it is actually those with the highest test scores who will have the most to contribute to society. There is, however, no guarantee that the students who perform best on admissions examinations will be either the most likely to succeed in and after college or the most likely to provide leadership for society. In fact, there appears to be evidence for just the opposite situation. In Bowen and Bok's (1998) study, it was the graduates of color who spent more time working in and providing leadership to their communities. Often they did not have the highest test scores. Admitting the students with the best scores on admissions examinations would not serve the same social function as affirmative action.

Widening access to higher education through affirmative action contributes to justice (R. Dworkin, 1998; Lawrence & Matsuda, 1996). R. Dworkin (1998) notes that "we expect educational institutions to contribute to our physical and economic health, and we should expect them to do what they can for our social and moral health as well" (p. 100). Without college-educated role models of color in the positions of power to which affirmative action policies facilitate access, children receive unhealthy hidden messages. If they are white students or male students, they learn that people in power usually look like they do; if they are students of color or female students, they learn that those in power do not usually look like them. Whether or not affirmative action is in place, white people and males benefit from unearned race and sex privileges (McIntosh, 1989). With the implementation of affirmative action policies, we publicly recognize that people of color and women add something vital to college and university campuses and to society. It is this recognition that puts us on the road to fuller humanity. It is in everyone's best interest that all persons do as well as possible. The evidence shows that affirmative action expands the social contexts of choice and life possibilities of its beneficiaries. According to at least one researcher, there is little empirical evidence of white backlash against affirmative action. White persons with personal experience with affirmative action programs are more likely to support race-conscious policies (Winkler, 1995). Because of firsthand experience with the way affirmative action programs work, white people recognize the overall benefits of affirmative action.

Nevertheless, we cannot necessarily assume that if only white people *understood* why affirmative action is ultimately good, then they would support it in large numbers. It is predictable and even understandable that white people might not like affirmative action, since they have benefited, both directly and indirectly, from longstanding preferences. Affirmative action does not feel like it is beneficial for most white people, who see it as an unfair policy. Some scholars of color charge that this is indicative of a tendency to deny real racial and ethnic oppression, despite evidence to the contrary. Patricia Williams, an African American law professor, for one, recounts an incident in which she attempted to enter a Bennetton store. Even though it was obvious to her that the store was open for business, the employee refused to let her enter. Williams (1991) spoke out publicly about the incident and encountered a strong unwillingness to believe that things like this happen all too often for people of color. The catch is that not only do they happen, but they have a profound impact on the people to whom they happen. Incidents like this as well as more serious incidents cause people like Williams to question their inherent worth and place them in an impoverished context of choice. Those who refuse to believe that such incidents occur are also unlikely to support race-conscious policies like affirmative action. Accordingly, Edley (1996) notes that Americans have moral confusion over race-conscious policy.

One step toward clearing up this confusion is to use the principle of self-determination, in conjunction with Gutmann's (1987) qualifications argument, as the best philosophical justification for race-conscious policies like affirmative action. Because it advances the self-determination of students of color, critics and supporters can begin to view affirmative action as a fair and ethical policy. Affirmative action carries a moral cost (Edley, 1996). Whether Americans ultimately embrace or reject affirmative action, certain of us will likely feel worse off. Nonetheless, I do believe that if we can all step back, even briefly, from the emotions surrounding the issue of race-consciousness, we can begin to understand that social justice requires affirmative action and other such policies. The current oppression of people of color due to dominant institutional structures, systems, and ways of being is both undemocratic and unjust.

This portion of the argument is not very likely to convert the most die-hard of naysayers. It still will not feel good to many white critics to embrace affirmative action as a morally just policy when it continues to use what they see as arbitrary characteristics—race, ethnicity, and sex—as factors in awarding opportunities. What they seem to choose not to see is that race and sex have always been factors. This time, however, it is not their own race or sex that is viewed as an important qualification, and that is just not palatable. In the final analysis, affirmative action is justifiable because race and ethnicity ought to be seen as relevant qualifications for admission (Gutmann, 1987). An important addition to this is that affirmative action improves the self-determination of people of color, while it does not significantly diminish the self-determination of white students. In the cases where a white student's context of choice became more limited due to affirmative action, we must realize that it was a context of choice based on intolerable injustice in the first place. As a result, the bottom line is this: Regardless of its costs, affirmative action is morally justifiable because it plays a significant role in fostering marginalized students' development of self-determination, educating leaders and professionals, and reducing societal oppression. What is more, all told, it is the right and good thing to do.

Relevant Qualifications

When a campus practices affirmative action, both students of color and white students learn that the experiences, perspectives, ideas, and so forth that students of color bring to the campus environment are worth extra attention by admissions committees. It is important enough to a selective institution's mission for it to enroll students from a wide variety of different cultural backgrounds that they consider a minority racial and ethnic background a plus factor. In this way, being a person of color is seen as a qualification that is relevant to the mission and social function of a selective institution of higher education[9] (Gutmann, 1987).

As I noted earlier, the idea that race and ethnicity are relevant qualifications for admission to a selective college or university stems from the work of Amy Gutmann[10] (1987; Gutmann & Thompson, 1996). She presents a presentist defense of affirmative action policies designed to diminish structural and institutional repression and discrimination. Her argument relies on the main principle of nondiscrimination, which stipulates that qualifications for selection be relevant to the social function of the institution (or job, as the case may be). Nondiscrimination prevents repression and allows educational opportunities to be distributed on grounds that are relevant to legitimate social purposes. Nondiscrimination entails taking all relevant qualifications into account in admissions decisions and hiring practices. For example, within public schools, it is essential to view sex as a relevant qualification when hiring elementary school principals. If schools are to be nonrepressive and fulfill their social purpose of educating all students so that they can rationally deliberate about different conceptions of the good life, then being a woman is a relevant qualification for the position of elementary school principal.

Because most elementary school principals are men and most elementary school teachers are women, both boys and girls receive, implicitly through the hidden curriculum, an education in gender role stereotypes and power positions. According to Gutmann (1987),

> girls learn that it is normal for them to rule children, but abnormal for them to rule men. Boys learn the opposite lesson. The democratic problem lies not in the content of either lesson per se, but in its repressive nature: the lessons reinforce uncritical acceptance of an established set of sex stereotypes and unreflective rejection of reasonable (and otherwise available) alternatives. (p. 114)

In order to provide the children with a nonrepressive and nonoppressive[11] education, more women need to be hired as elementary school principals. A similar, albeit more controversial, argument can be made regarding the selection of elementary school teachers, but this time male teachers would have an extra qualification for the job. Gutmann argues that affirmative action provides students with the experiences necessary in order for them to be able to deliberate in a rational way about differing conceptions of the good life. It serves to diversify the people in positions of authority and status as role models to whom students can look for a sense of what is possible in life.

A parallel example can be constructed regarding college and university admissions. There is a clear need for more physicians of color, both as role models for students, and because they are more likely than white doctors to practice in generally underserved minority communities (Schroeder, 1996). As a result, race and ethnicity are relevant qualifications for admission into medical school. One of the functions of medical schools is to provide doctors for medical services in all types of communities. Fewer than 5 percent of all doctors in the United States are African American and Latino (American Council on Education, 1996). Due to the recent rollbacks in affirmative action, the number of students of color enrolling in medical school declined by 11 percent (Srinivasan, 1997). Because selective higher education is a privilege that one must earn, rather than a right that everyone has, qualifications matter (Gutmann, 1987). As part of their social function in a democracy, institutions of higher education serve as the gatekeepers to and educators for the highest status and highest power positions in our society. It is the exception rather than the rule that someone without at least a college degree could reach the highest levels of professional success and prestige in the United States.

Race is obviously not the only qualification considered by admissions committees. Academic ability, generally measured by standardized test scores and grades, is perhaps the most well-known and supported qualification for higher education. Opponents of affirmative action may consider it the only relevant qualification. In actuality, academic ability has always been one of many factors that admissions officers take into account in selecting students who they believe have the best chance to succeed in higher education. Test scores predict students' first-year grades, not overall college success. Therefore, admissions committees must also consider nonacademic qualifications. These qualifications need to be publicly defensible and related to the university's legitimate social functions (Gutmann, 1987). Nonacademic qualifications include intangibles such as creativity, motivation, maturity, and perseverance. It is within these categories that admissions committees can consider factors such as special talents, athletic ability, and hardships in life. It is often not the most academically gifted (at least as measured by standardized tests and grades) students who have the most to gain from and to contribute to higher education (Gutmann, 1987). Another relevant nonacademic qualification that is related to the university's social purposes is the ability to serve society and to help others. Insofar as a varied student body contributes to the robust exchange of ideas and to intellectual stimulation on campus, it is relevant to consider factors such as race, ethnicity, sex, ability, and religion. Of course, race and sex are also relevant because of how they serve the university's social functions of gatekeeping and educating officeholders. It is often students of color who have much to contribute in moving the university toward positive change.

In justifying affirmative action because it contributes to students' development of self-determination, I have been relying not only on Gutmann's qualifications argument, but on K. Howe's (1997) principle of nonoppression as well. Race and ethnicity are relevant qualifications for college and university admissions; in admitting more students of color, selective institutions of higher education are taking an important step toward the reduction of societal oppression. Affirmative action combats the primary wrong of oppression. By having a policy of affirmative action, institutions of higher education begin to address institutional oppression and domination. For example, one study found that if law schools abandon their affirmative action policies, there will be a striking decrease in the number of law students of color (Wightman, 1997) and, consequently, fewer lawyers of color available to serve communities of color. The increase in self-determination gained by college and professional school graduates and the concomitant contributions that they can make to society seem to be in the best interests of those on both sides of the affirmative action debate.

This is admittedly a forward-looking argument. Other arguments look more toward the past for a primary justification for affirmative action policy. Of these, the argument from historical debt is the most prominent. The argument from historical debt is based on the ethical need to redress the racist and sexist history of the United States. Generally, this defense only applies to those groups that were either brought to the United States against their will or were already living here and were either killed or treated extremely poorly by white people. As such, affirmative action would only apply to women, African Americans, Native Americans, and some Latinos. The argument, put forth by W. Feinberg (1998), goes something like this. We owe a special debt to women, African Americans, Native Americans, and some Latinos due to the outrageous violations of rights they suffered through our history of the subjugation of women, slavery, genocide, and cultural imperialism. Feinberg (1998) explains that

> the assault on a culture has real consequences for many people in terms of truncated expectations and opportunities both denied and overlooked and in terms of a general social attitude on the part of others that accepts as part of the natural state of affairs lower levels of material well-being. Affirmative action—that is, race-based, backward-looking affirmative action—can be part of a strategy for repairing the rupture. It attempts to reconstruct the opportunities to which intentions and expectations must be attached. (pp. 69–70)

Thus, according to the argument from historical debt, policies of affirmative action play one part in redressing our shameful history by providing the affected groups with increased educational opportunity to make up for the legacy of the opportunities missed in the past.

The idea that the sole, or most important, aim of affirmative action policy is to correct past wrongs against people of color is faulty for two reasons. First, it emphasizes the past to the detriment of the present. There is no small amount of current discrimination in need of remedy. Second, and more compelling, to think of affirmative action as justifiable only or mainly because of the need to compensate for past wrongs is a significant roadblock to wider acceptance because individual persons today do not feel responsible for these historical wrongs. They refuse to accept the blame and the guilt that inevitably accompany this argument. W. Feinberg (1998) acknowledges this problem, but argues that even though white people might not feel responsible for historical racism, they should still feel obligated to right past wrongs. Although the very real debt that is owed to people of color in our society should not be overlooked, a better way of defining the aim of affirmative action policy is to correct present *oppression*. As some contemporary liberals have pointed out, the principle of nonoppression rather than nondiscrimination would satisfy the spirit of civil rights policy and contribute to the cause of justice for people of color (K. Howe, 1997). It would also place affirmative action firmly within the project of fostering social justice now rather than addressing wrongs committed by people in the past with whom many white Americans feel no kinship. Appeals to a reduction of oppression and injustice will likely carry more weight with most Americans. The argument from historical debt is just not the most compelling, especially for white people who believe that they had no part in that racist and discriminatory history. A more compelling justification relies on the idea that affirmative action furthers social justice goals both by helping students develop self-determination and by fighting oppression.

THE RELATIONSHIP BETWEEN AFFIRMATIVE ACTION AND AUTHENTICITY

By virtue of the fact that affirmative action policy highlights the societal relevance of race, colleges and universities underscore the worth of nondominant cultures. This, in turn, shows students of color that an institution as well respected as higher education publicly recognizes the significance of minority cultural backgrounds. In addition, white students receive the same message. The impact of this recognition is a pivotal part of the relationship between affirmative action and students' authentic cultural identities. While it is an indirect relationship, it is nonetheless important. Given that, as I posited in Chapter 2, authentic identities are created both by inner reflection and in relation with other persons and society in general, the message sent by affirmative action does much to underscore the importance of authenticity in students' personal and cultural identities.

However, one could make the counterargument that affirmative action policies actually serve to harm students' authenticity due to the widespread *misrecognition* of their cultures by institutions of higher education. This point is best illustrated with an example. There is another side to Thunderwulf's story recounted above. He does not only see higher education as a way of expanding his life choices, he also sees it as pulling him and other Native Americans away from their roots. He remarks:

> I think white people think education is good, but Indian people often have a different view. I know what you're going to say—that education provides

jobs and skills. It's true. That's why I'm here. But a lot of these kids, their parents, they see education as something that draws students away from who they are. (Tierney, 1993, p. 311)

Unfortunately, higher education is sometimes seen by people of color as part of an overall educational system that functions to assimilate students into the dominant culture. In this way, affirmative action can be viewed as part of a racist system that challenges rather than supports students' cultural identities. True, affirmative action policies do not necessarily affirm students' sense of identity in a direct way. What they do is send a strong message to society that nondominant cultures are worthy of recognition and respect by affirming that race and ethnicity should be seen as qualifying factors for higher education.

A MUTUALLY AGREEABLE IDEAL

One of the attributes that makes the argument from affirmative action from self-determination especially appealing is that self-determination is a principle on which both proponents and critics of affirmative action can agree. Basing the argument for affirmative action on the ideal of self-determination, then, gives it a favorable starting point that other arguments do not enjoy. If we ask people whether or not all Americans ought to have an education that fosters their self-determination, we are likely to garner mostly positive responses. This makes the argument for affirmative action from self-determination more viable than other defenses. One significant criticism of affirmative action offered by conservatives is that it constrains the freedom and autonomy of individual Americans. Herman Belz's (1991) libertarian view exemplifies this opinion. He writes, "The chief historical significance of affirmative action . . . has been to promote statist intervention into the free market and weaken political and social institutions based on individual rights" (p. 265). Affirmative action is thus viewed disparagingly as a big-government policy concerned with the rights of groups to the exclusion of individuals, which is seen as undemocratic. What could be more democratic than the attempt to broaden people's social context of choice and, consequently, help them develop a meaningful sense of personal autonomy as self-determination? Self-determining citizens make contributions to a democracy because of their capacity to engage thoughtfully in democratic deliberation and participation. Our democracy was conceived with self-determining citizens in mind. Affirmative action policies deeply affect the lives and imaginations and, consequently, the self-determination of the individual students who benefit from them.

However, this argument could possibly be turned on its head. If one believes that affirmative action policies restrict the personal autonomy of white students, the ideal of self-determination would actually preclude the support of affirmative action. Using the example of Cheryl Hopwood, one could argue that because she could not attend the University of Texas Law School, her social context of choice was impoverished and, consequently, her self-determination restricted. Attending a less prestigious school would not afford her the same social capital as the highly selective flagship campus of the University of Texas. Although her individual context of choice was indeed limited by her Texas rejection, the contexts of choice of the students of color who benefited from the affirmative action program were expanded. The university's social purposes were fulfilled by educating a larger number of lawyers of color. I am not saying that there are no moral costs of affirmative action. I am saying that, on balance, affirmative action programs for students of color best serve the dual purposes of enhancing their individual development of self-determination and supporting the goals and functions of institutions of higher education. Unfortunately, there will be students like Hopwood who will not be selected because they lack some relevant qualification for admission. Of course, Hopwood would most likely not have been accepted to Yale Law School[12] either. The nature of highly selective universities is that there are many fewer places than students who would like to attend.

The argument from self-determination does not solve all of the possible problems with affirmative action perfectly. It cannot; no argument could. The substantive components of specific affirmative action policies need to be carefully considered and constructed. One aspect that makes this argument for affirmative action policy the most defensible of the arguments to date is that it is based on an ideal—self-determination—that has a good chance of mutual acceptance. Another is that it is centrally focused on resisting oppression and promoting social justice. In so doing, it reminds us about the lives of the individual students who are profoundly affected by a policy that is often formulated, changed, scaled back, or even abolished without their input.

THE STATUS OF AFFIRMATIVE ACTION IN
AMERICAN HIGHER EDUCATION

As of this writing, affirmative action in higher education admissions is still alive and well in most of the United States. However, the U.S. Supreme Court has not ruled on it directly since the *Bakke* case. In the

1990s, state initiatives abolished affirmative action in two states, and there were a number of court cases important to affirmative action's well-being. The legacy left by the *Bakke* case provides the legal guidelines for affirmative action policy.

BAKKE AS LAW

Justice Powell's deciding opinion in the *Bakke* split decision stated that universities should be allowed to admit any students who they believe will add most to the robust exchange of ideas on campus; the search for a diverse student body, Powell explained, is a constitutionally acceptable goal (O'Neill, 1985). Thus race could be a legitimate factor to consider in admissions decisions. The opinion of the justices who sided with Bakke, written by Justice Stevens, cited that Title VI could be interpreted as forbidding quotas, saying that "race cannot be the basis of excluding anyone from participation in a federally funded program" (Sindler, 1978, p. 294). This invalidated the University of California at Davis Medical School's admissions procedures because a specific number of spaces were set aside for students of color, which excluded Bakke presumably because of race. By contrast, the justices who sided with the regents and Davis Medical School argued that Title VI and the 14th Amendment justified the use of racial preferences in university admissions. Writing the opinion, Justice Brennan pointed out historical and current inequality and wrote, "we cannot let color-blindness become myopia which masks the reality that many 'created equal' have been treated within our lifetimes as inferior both by the law and by their fellow citizens" (Sindler, 1978, p. 296).

Justice Powell appended Harvard College's affirmative action program to his *Bakke* opinion, as a guide to the constitutionality of such admissions programs. Within the plan, diversity was held as the most important rationale for affirmative action. Harvard officials believed that a diversity of students enhanced their student body and the educational experience (Sindler, 1978). With this in mind, the admissions committee looked at myriad activities, heritages, talents, and career objectives in selecting students for admission. One might conclude that since the Supreme Court rated Harvard's program constitutionally permissible and fair, much of the debate over affirmative action in higher education admissions would have been squelched. However, that has not been the case, despite the fact that prominent legal scholars have also endorsed the *Bakke* idea that well-crafted race-conscious admissions policies are indeed constitutional. According to R. Dworkin (1998), "we have no reason to forbid university affirmative action as a weapon against our deplorable racial stratification, except our indifference to that problem, or our petulant anger that it has not gone away on its own" (p. 102). Nevertheless, there have been various legislative attempts to bar affirmative action policies and to establish their unconstitutionality despite the *Bakke* precedent.

THE POLITICS OF INTIMIDATION

Conservatives have led political campaigns against affirmative action in many states. The onslaught against affirmative action in the courts is led by the Center for Individual Rights (C.I.R.) in Washington, D.C. They are the leaders in the politics of intimidation that characterize the campaign against affirmative action. Attorneys for the nonprofit legal center represented the plaintiffs in *Hopwood v. Texas* (1996), and they represent the plaintiffs in *Smith v. University of Washington* (2000), and in the two University of Michigan cases, *Gratz v. Bollinger* (2000) and *Grutter v. Bollinger* (2001). However, their role has gone beyond just helping disgruntled students sue universities. They have been engaged in a crusade to intimidate administrators and officials of selective institutions of higher education. Their primary method is to spark fear of lawsuits and to recruit white students as plaintiffs against colleges and universities that have affirmative action programs. According to one C.I.R. attorney, the group's ultimate goal is to see affirmative action policies declared unconstitutional by the Supreme Court (Greve, 1999). To that end, they released two guidebooks, one for college and university trustees that focuses on how to avoid lawsuits over affirmative action in admissions, and one for students that explains how to review institutional policies and sue to change them. The book for trustees warns college officials that nearly every selective institution of higher education is violating the law with their affirmative action programs and that, if challenged in court, individual trustees can be held personally liable for those violations (Bronner, 1999; Healy, 1999a). Of course, those contentions are a matter of considerable public debate. The *Bakke* decision has not been overturned by the Supreme Court even though they have had the chance to do so, and there is no clear legal precedent for holding trustees personally liable for institutional policies (Hebel, 1999a). In fact, in 1999 and 2000, the *Bakke* standards were upheld in federal court during the *Smith* and *Gratz* cases.

THE CONSEQUENCES OF THE CONSERVATIVE CAMPAIGN

Those engaged in the politics of intimidation have made some headway. After seeing C.I.R.'s advertisement in their campus newspaper and receiving the trustee handbook, officials at the University of Virginia began to review their admissions policies. As a result, the policies were changed so that race was no longer a qualifying factor for African American applicants. Perhaps related to this change, the number of African American applicants seeking fall 2000 admission dropped by 25 percent (Hebel, 2000). Similarly, in the aftermath of California's Proposition 209, *Hopwood*, and Washington State's Initiative 200, there have been decreases in the numbers of students of color applying for admission to and enrolling in the selective institutions in these states. There had previously been steady (albeit slow) increases in the numbers of students of color in the ranks of undergraduate and graduate students. Between 1985 and 1993, for example, 36 percent more African Americans, 34 percent more Native Americans, 75 percent more Latinos, and 103 percent more Asian Americans graduated from college (American Council on Education, 1996). In 1994, these increases resulted in 7 percent of all college graduates being African American, 4 percent Latino, 0.5 percent Native American, and 4.4 percent Asian American. Although these are not high percentages, they are more substantial than they were before affirmative action policies were initiated. Between 1996 and 1998, while affirmative action was attracting negative publicity due to Proposition 209 and *Hopwood*, the percentages of students of color in the first-year classes at all colleges decreased by 1.8 percent (Geraghty, 1997; Reisberg, 1999). For the most prestigious University of California campuses, Berkeley and Los Angeles, the percentages of students of color accepted for admission to their first-year classes declined dramatically the first year that affirmative action was not used. At Berkeley, for example, 66 percent fewer African Americans, 60.9 percent fewer Native Americans, and 52.6 percent fewer Latinos were admitted. In 1999 the numbers of applicants of color to the University of Washington Law School declined significantly from the previous year. For Latinos the decline was 21 percent, for Filipinos, 26 percent, and for African Americans, a whopping 41 percent (Selingo, 1999). As for the University of Washington's undergraduate admissions, the number of Latino students in the 1999 first-year class decreased by 30 percent, African American students by 40 percent, and Native American students by 20 percent (Ma, 1999). No African American students were admitted to the University of California at San Diego's School of Medicine in 1997, even though 196 applied; only 4 Latino students out of 143 were accepted (Selingo, 1997). In the 1998–99 first-year class at Berkeley's Boalt Hall Law School, only 1 of 268 students was African American. At the University of Texas School of Law, only 4 of 468 were African Americans. These admissions and enrollment statistics only begin to demonstrate the impact that the legislation and court rulings against affirmative action have on people.

Court Challenges within Higher Education

Court cases challenging affirmative action were brought against the University of Washington Law School, the University of Georgia, the University of Michigan, and the University of Michigan Law School. It is likely that these cases will be the deciding factors regarding the status of affirmative action in higher education admissions. In *Smith v. University of Washington*, three white applicants who were not accepted to the University of Washington Law School sued the university with legal representation from C.I.R. Even though Initiative 200 caused the university to abandon the admissions program under question, the case moved forward. A victory came for affirmative action supporters in December 2000, when the 9th Circuit Court of Appeals ruled that the Law School's affirmative action program was constitutional. In 2001, the Supreme Court let stand the lower court's ruling in *Smith*, dealing somewhat of a blow to C.I.R.'s efforts (Gose & Schmidt, 2001). On the other side of the spectrum, in 2001, the University of Georgia's affirmative action program was found unconstitutional by the U.S. Court of Appeals for the 11th Circuit. The court ruled that Georgia's admissions policy was not narrowly tailored enough (Gose & Schmidt, 2001). This ruling applies not only to the state of Georgia, but to Alabama and Florida as well.

In both of the cases against the University of Michigan, the defense relies most heavily on the *Bakke* precedent of the argument from diversity to justify affirmative action in its undergraduate and law school admissions (Elgass, 2000). Like the lawyers for Bakke in 1978, the plaintiffs' C.I.R. lawyers maintain that Michigan's use of race as a factor in admissions violates the equal protection clause of the 14th Amendment and Title VI of the Civil Rights Act. *Gratz v. Bollinger*, in which two white students are challenging the undergraduate admissions policy, is the first case that is not centered on law or medical school admissions. The first court battle was won by the university. In December 2000, a U.S. District Court judge ruled against the students and C.I.R. This case, as well as *Grutter v. Bollinger*, centering on the law school, are also unique in that they name current and former presidents of the University of Michigan as personally liable. The results of the cases have been somewhat contradictory. As in the *Smith* case, the U.S. District Court adjudicating *Gratz* ruled in favor of the university (Schmidt, 2001). However, another U.S. District Court judge ruled against the University of Michigan Law School in *Grutter*, citing the admissions policy as unconstitutional (Selingo, 2001). Officials at the University of Michigan are strong in their stance that the university will not back down from its commitment to affirmative action.[13]

Institutions that are not facing court challenges to their affirmative action programs have begun to change their policies. For example, the prominent women's research center, the Mary Ingraham Bunting Institute at Radcliffe College has announced that it will accept male scholars as well. This action was likely spurred on by the fear of gender-bias lawsuits. The politics of intimidation are working, even against programs like the Bunting Institute, which serve to combat the professional isolation and stress that women may have as a minority on college and university faculties (Young, 1990a). Similarly, the University of Massachusetts at Amherst announced a preemptive strike on its affirmative action policy. Following the 1st Circuit's ruling against Boston Latin School's affirmative action program, the University of Massachusetts made race and ethnicity less significant qualifying factors for admissions (Healy, 1999b).

Court Challenges Beyond Higher Education

Challenges to affirmative action policies in admissions are no longer the sole purview of higher education. In 1998, the distinguished Boston Latin School's affirmative action policy was struck down by the U.S. Court of Appeals for the 1st Circuit in *Wessmann v. Gittens*. Judges for the federal appeals court ruled two to one in favor of Sarah Wessmann, a white student who sued the Boston School Committee after she was not admitted to Boston Latin, a very prestigious public exam school in Boston, Massachusetts. The judges stated that the Boston School Committee did not prove that their affirmative action program was constitutional according to the *Bakke* standards and that they should admit Wessmann (Gray, 2001). It is important to note that the judges ruled against Boston Latin because their affirmative action program included a specific numerical goal. Admissions officers had been working to ensure that Latino and African American students would make up around 35 percent of each first-year class. The judges deemed this practice a violation of the *Bakke* standards, and within the deciding opinion, they specifically upheld the *Bakke* ruling (Healy, 1998b). Therefore, the *Wessmann* ruling sends a clear message against numerical affirmative action goals. What is most important for higher education is that the ruling also strongly upholds the *Bakke* standards; race can be considered as a plus factor within admissions processes.

Another case with important implications is *Taxman v. Piscataway Township Board of Education*, a case centering on affirmative action in employment. In 1989, the school board of Piscataway Township, New Jersey, needed to let go of one teacher in a high school business department. In the interests of diversity, it decided to lay off Sharon Taxman, a white teacher, rather than Debra Williams, her African American colleague, even though the two women were judged to be equal in qualifications and seniority. Within their explanation of the decision, the board admitted that race was the final deciding factor (Pulley, 1997). In so doing, they faced accusations of blatant reverse discrimination leading to a white teacher losing and an African American teacher keeping a teaching job. This fueled white people's deepest fears about affirmative action by providing an example of a scarce resource seemingly allocated on the basis of race. The board's action and subsequent handling of it resulted in an uproar that led to Taxman's lawsuit. After losing the case, the school board appealed to the U.S. Court of Appeals for the 3rd Circuit, where in 1996 Taxman again won. The appeals court stated that diversity could not be cited as the reason employment decisions are made. Institutions within the 3rd Circuit states of New Jersey, Delaware, and Pennsylvania were left with the task of determining the ruling's implications for their affirmative action policies. As in the *Boston Latin* case, the Supreme Court did not get a chance to hear the case. Although the Piscataway school board did appeal to the Supreme Court, civil rights groups helped raise some $433,000 for an acceptable settlement so that the case would not be adjudicated by the Supreme Court.

The evasive tactics used by proponents of affirmative action in the *Wessmann* and *Taxman* cases may stave off a Supreme Court ruling on affirmative action, but probably not for long. The court cases demonstrate that the politics of intimidation threatens affirmative action policies, highlighting the need for even more compelling justifications for affirmative action such as the argument from self-determination.

CONCLUSION

Imagine, if you will, a world built over a long time by and for men, by and for whites. In that world there would be a thousand and one impediments to women and blacks working effectively and successfully. That world and its institutions would be suffused through and through with inhospitality to blacks and women. . . . That's the world we still live in, isn't it? (Fullinwider, 1991a, p. 13)

Indeed, that *is* the world we still live in. Affirmative action policies were implemented within higher education as part of an educational agenda for social justice that also includes bilingual education, multicultural curriculum, and remedial education policies.[14] In this chapter I have attempted to demonstrate that affirmative action is a crucial policy effort because it adds to students' meaningful self-determination by expanding their social contexts of choice. To a lesser extent, affirmative action fosters students' self-determination also by recognizing the worth of diverse cultures. A defense of affirmative action that rests on the ideal of self-determination goes beyond the established defenses of affirmative action because it has a good chance of widespread acceptance, and because it leads to social justice.

I did not argue that colleges and universities generally have affirmative action policies in place that are good and sound. As evidenced by the court victories against the University of Texas Law School and Boston Latin School, it is crucial for these policies to be well-drafted and in keeping with current law in order for them to withstand inevitable court challenges. Briefly, a sound admissions policy would include the following elements. First, it would consider students individually; race or ethnicity would be one qualifying factor, socioeconomic class or family wealth would be another. These would complement the traditional qualifications such as academic potential, leadership potential, talents, and activities and service. All factors would be relevant to the institution's role of educating leaders in the community and in their professions. Second, students' life circumstances should be taken into account. Are they first-generation college students? Did they have access to good neighborhood schools? Next, policies should rely less on standardized test scores as indicators of probable academic success. Lower test scores do not necessarily foreshadow academic failure. In fact, once admitted, students of color with lower scores do at least as well as their higher-scoring counterparts, especially at selective institutions (Bowen & Bok, 1998; K. Howe, 1997; Wightman, 1997). Admissions policies that put too much faith in test scores are vestiges of an old system for which today's colleges and universities have no use. In addition, an admissions policy cannot stand alone. College and university admissions must work in tandem with recruitment efforts, outreach programs, and programs aimed at retaining and graduating the students who decide to enroll. Finally, if a policy hopes to withstand a court challenge, it cannot include any numerical targets. As much as specific numerical targets help to speed the rate of change and to keep institutions accountable, they simply cannot today be part of a sound affirmative action program. Of course, even a good affirmative action policy cannot work magic for the project of justice in American education; the dominant institutional systems and structures that are oppressive to people of color and women must be challenged as well.

It is no accident that President Johnson is seen as having significantly advanced the civil rights agenda in the United States. During his tenure most liberal civil rights legislation was passed. It is essential to recognize the deeply symbolic nature of race-conscious civil rights policies such as affirmative action. Federal affirmative action policy is at a crossroads. The ongoing dissatisfaction with affirmative action programs shows that many Americans want a more palatable alternative. Supporters stress the importance of affirmative action to ensure that oppressive practices against people of color are abated. Otherwise, as history has shown, the United States would surely retreat to a more discriminatory and oppressive time (West, 1993). As early as 1972, scholars said that in order to have sound affirmative action programs, "universities will have to develop and continually monitor and revise their affirmative action programs" (Shulman, 1972, p. 37). To that end, affirmative action must be reconceptualized in the public consciousness as a policy that creates more favorable social contexts of choice and thus a greater sense of possibility for people of color and women. Sound affirmative action policies successfully combat oppression against people of color, with the aim of promoting students' self-determination and, ultimately, social justice.

NOTES

1. See President Clinton's July 19, 1995, speech on affirmative action. The text may be found at http://clinton6.nara.gov/1995/07/1995-07-19-president-remarks-on-affirmative-action.html.

2. In arguing for affirmative action I primarily have the interests of students of color and female students in mind, although there are important instances where white students and male students would also benefit from an expanded context of choice. I will address this issue in a later section.

3. For example, in President Clinton's July 19, 1995, speech on affirmative action, he began by saying that affirmative action policy had been in existence for 25 years, yet the correct number of years was 34.

4. This quote is from the Howard University speech titled "To Fulfill These Rights."

5. There are some exceptions to this, such as when being male may be seen as a qualification for posts as elementary school teachers, which I will discuss in the next section.

6. Related to this, the idea that standardized tests should be a major criterion of selection has been vigorously challenged. While I will not delve into this line of argument in detail here, see Sturm and Guinier (1996) for a well-considered critique of higher education selection practices.

7. This example owes to Edley (1996).

8. Graduation from a selective institution would expand his opportunities even further (Bowen & Bok, 1998; Velez, 1985).

9. I have been focusing on selective institutions of higher education for that reason. Selective institutions aim to educate future community leaders. In addition, because they admit almost all who apply, affirmative action is unnecessary in less selective or nonselective institutions.

10. These ideas owe substantially to the work of Ronald Dworkin (1978, 1998) as well, but herein I rely specifically on Gutmann's interpretations.

11. Note once again that the principle of nonoppression is conceptualized by K. Howe (1997) and is stronger than Gutmann's (1987) principle of nonrepression.

12. Yale Law School was ranked as the number one law school in the nation by *U.S. News and World Report* in April 2001.

13. See the website: www.umich.edu/~urel/admissions/index.html for further information from the University of Michigan.

14. Perhaps it should not go without saying that decent health care, public schools, and academic preparation are needed for all students.

6

Remedial Education

Shante Proctor attends a high-poverty school in New York City, where students routinely experience high teacher and administrator turnover, as well as high student turnover (Holloway, 2000). While Shante is a bright 11-year-old, she is already on a path away from real educational opportunity. If she beats the odds and aspires to a 4-year college, such an opportunity may be closed to her. She would likely need remedial education to raise her skill level in certain areas. If policymakers within higher education across the United States continue to sour to the idea of remedial education as a legitimate part of 4-year institutions, then, at best, Shante would be able to attend a community college. While community college is a step in the right direction, a bachelor's degree would afford Shante greater life opportunities (Dougherty, 1987; Karabel, 1972; Institute for Higher Education Policy, 1998; Lavin & Hyllegard, 1996).

In Shante's case, the absence of remedial programs would constrain her choices and thus her educational opportunities. In essence, the policymakers, educators, and politicians who are opposed to remedial education may end up punishing students like Shante for coming from poor schools in low-income and often predominantly African American and Latino neighborhoods. They say that they are simply trying to raise standards at 4-year institutions. However, another effect is the exclusion of students who have had the misfortune to attend bad public schools.

Ernest House (1999) points out that "Americans have defined their educational system in such a way as to ensure that African Americans (and often other minorities) are treated in an exclusionary way" (pp. 10–11). As a result of the civil rights movement, education policies such as remedial education[1] emerged in response to the exclusion House describes. As previous chapters on bilingual education, multicultural curricula, and affirmative action have shown, policies designed to benefit primarily students of color and low-income students have been facing increased attacks. Remedial education, though open to students of all

153

races and ethnicities can nonetheless be considered a race-conscious policy in that it disproportionately benefits students of color, and has become controversial for that reason among others (Guernsey, 1996). The purpose of this chapter is to provide a theoretically grounded examination of the current controversy over remedial education policy at the 4-year college level.[2]

Two perspectives dominate the current literature. On one side, scholars maintain that the students who need remedial courses should be attending community colleges instead, and that students are harmed when admitted to institutions at which they cannot compete (Manno, 1995; Steinberg, 1998). Part of the argument is that although remedial programs may be well intentioned, ultimately they are political programs, and not educational ones (Cronholm, 1999a, 1999b). On the other side, scholars argue that remedial education centers on creating opportunities, increased retention, and better graduation outcomes for students who may be underprepared for some college-level courses (Adelman, 1998; Ponitz, 1998; Roueche & Roueche, 1999). The backlash against these programs is cloaked in the rhetoric of standards and quality, but really stems from old notions of meritocracy. When one digs below the surface justifications for abolishing remedial education, race and class are exposed as key issues.

Researchers at the National Center for Education Statistics found that 78 percent of all colleges in the United States (including 2-year schools) offer remedial courses, and that 29 percent of first-time freshmen students take these courses (Lewis & Farris, 1996). The percentage is slightly lower for all 4-year institutions of higher education, at 72.5 percent. Often the students taking these remedial courses are students of color or poor students whose K–12 education was lacking and whose social context of choice was constrained as a result.

Prima facie, remedial programs hardly seem worth feuding over. Relatively few students are affected, and remedial programs cost less than 1 percent of public colleges' yearly budgets (Breneman, 1998; Woodhams, 1998). Nevertheless, the remediation controversy seems to fit into the larger discomfort with race-conscious education policies such as affirmative action and bilingual education. In entering the conversation about remedial education, I seek to answer the following questions: (1) How does remedial education fit into the aims of an education in a democratic society concerned with social justice for disadvantaged students? (2) What will the elimination of remedial education within 4-year colleges mean for the development of self-determination for students of color?

Like the three other policies I have examined thus far, I analyze remedial education within the philosophical framework that holds the contemporary liberal ideal of self-determination to be a primary aim of an education for social justice as outlined in Chapter 2. I explore whether or not remedial education fosters students' self-determination by playing a role in expanding their social contexts of choice, as students and afterwards (Kymlicka, 1991). When a student is able to gain admittance to a 4-year college and take needed remedial coursework, the context from which that student makes her or his choices in life may be greatly expanded. And when a more favorable context of choice is fostered by education policy, students are better able to become self-determining persons. I investigate whether a strong case can be made that remedial education policies are justifiable because they play a central role in the development of self-determination of students who otherwise are left with decreased educational opportunities and, consequently, with fewer life opportunities. In so doing, it is important to consider the context within which remedial education policies were formulated, as well as the most common points of argument surrounding remedial education.

There has been some contention about terms, about how to describe the courses that fall under the "remedial" or "developmental" label. Loosely, *remedial courses* are defined as courses dealing with precollege material, which are centered on addressing academic weaknesses (Boylan & White, 1987; Cross, 1976; Roueche & Roueche, 1999). Just what material counts as precollege versus college level varies greatly from institution to institution. *Developmental courses* are defined as college-level courses that focus on academic development in areas such as study skills and critical analysis, and thus on developing students' talents (Cross, 1976; Roueche & Roueche, 1999). It seems that educators who specialize in this type of education have increasingly preferred the term *developmental*, though *remedial* is widely used as well. Most public commentaries outside of academe refer to remedial education, especially when discussing the various criticisms and debates surrounding it. For that reason, remedial education will be referred to herein.

HISTORICAL CONTEXT

The history of remedial education highlights two prominent issues within the debate. The first issue is a conflicting idea about the mission of a 4-year institution of higher education. Should the main aim be individual student development and opportunity, or should it be high-level research and scholarship? If it should be both, which should take priority? For example, as early as 1851, the president of the University of

Michigan, Henry Tappan, suggested that all freshmen and sophomores be taught at the junior college level, thus relieving the university of the burden of general and vocational education and allowing it to focus energy on higher order scholarship (Cohen & Brawer, 1989). The idea never really took hold, despite support from other high-level administrators. However, Tappan's idea illustrates the historical roots of the tension surrounding the purpose of higher education's various institutions. At that time, however, the question was not about whether remedial education should be provided within higher education, but about where it should be provided.

The second main issue may be derived from the first. It appears that remedial education is least controversial or contested when all or most of the participating students are white. Harvard provided remedial tutoring to its upper-class, white male students already during the seventeenth century. In 1849, the University of Wisconsin offered remedial courses in reading, writing, and mathematics through their newly formed college preparatory department (Boylan & White, 1987; Schrag, 1999). Similarly, early remedial classes were offered at Wellesley College in the late 1800s (Cross, 1976). By 1889, at least 80 percent of U.S. colleges and universities provided at least some type of basic college preparatory programs (Boylan & White, 1987). There is no evidence of controversy surrounding these remedial education efforts. Later, the Veteran's Adjustment Act of 1944 gave federal support to World War II veterans who wanted to attend college. Colleges and universities were hesitant to deny the veterans admission even to selective institutions, and chose to accommodate them by providing basic skills and reading classes whenever needed (Boylan, 1988). Indeed, the bulk of the debate and controversy has occurred since the civil rights movement and anti-poverty activism of the 1960s. Race and class have surfaced as key factors in the acceptance of remedial education policy. Proponents of college access and equity for students of color highlight the social mission of public higher education in a democratic society.

The City University of New York (CUNY) system provides one example of the controversy over remedial education that covers both of the issues mentioned above. In the fall of 1970, the 15 colleges in the CUNY system changed their selective admissions policy to one where all high school graduates would be admitted; the era of open admissions at CUNY began (Rossmann, H. Astin, A. Astin, & El-Khawas, 1975). The overwhelming impetus for this change was the commitment of policymakers at one of the largest public urban (and no-tuition) university systems in the United States to making a direct connection between public higher education and the struggle against poverty and oppression. This change in admissions policy resulted in the establishment of a two-tier system of 2- and 4-year colleges. The 4-year colleges would admit all students with 80 percent high school averages or rankings in the top half of their graduating classes. The 2-year colleges would accept the rest of the high school graduates. Any graduate of a CUNY 2-year college could transfer to a 4-year college (Lavin, Alba, & Silberstein, 1981). The idea was to create an open door to college, not just a revolving door; a large remedial program and other student support services were thus established. These programs underscored an institutional concern for educational outcomes as well as access, which would prove quite controversial as debates about open admissions and remedial education policy inevitably moved to the fore. By 1994, 75 percent of City College's entering first-year students took at least one remedial course in reading, writing, or mathematics (Traub, 1994).[3]

Most remedial courses were eliminated at CUNY's eleven 4-year campuses by the fall of 2001 (Hebel, 2001). States such as Florida, Missouri, and South Carolina have also abolished remedial courses from their 4-year colleges and universities (Roueche & Roueche, 1999). California, Massachusetts, Georgia, Texas, and Virginia are moving in the direction of placing remedial programs solely at community colleges (Shaw, 1997). As Mayor of New York City, Rudolph Giuliani proposed that CUNY take another step away from remedial education by hiring a private firm to provide remedial services for 2002 (Hebel, 2001).

The reasons for the backlash against remedial education are varied and complex. At issue are the primary purposes of colleges and universities in the United States. Should status and standards be emphasized or should educational opportunity be emphasized? Is there a way to transcend this dichotomous view and attend to both concerns? If so, what is the place of remedial education?

THE DEBATE OVER REMEDIAL EDUCATION

The current debate about remedial courses has involved most prominently colleges in Massachusetts, New York, and California, and centers on the question of whether or not the students who may need such courses actually deserve to attend 4-year colleges (Hebel, 1999b, 2000; Lively, 1995). Consider the California State University system. It had proposed to eliminate most remedial education by 1995. As the deadline approached and administrators recognized the enormity of the disruption that this would cause, they softened the goal. California State University officials proposed instead to reduce the percentage of students taking remedial courses to 10 percent of all students by 2007 (Lively, 1995).

Opponents of remedial education maintain that these students do not deserve to be enrolled in 4-year institutions of higher education, and that neither students nor universities are well served by remedial education policy. As it stands, the discussion of remedial education policy has not taken into account the possibility that its elimination will have dire consequences for some students' contexts of choice and development of self-determination, both crucial pieces of a just education system. In order to explore that possibility, I undertake an analysis of the most commonly debated issues surrounding remedial education. These are as follows: (1) the impact of remedial courses on academic standards; (2) whether or not remedial education policy condones poor academic achievement by students and public schools; and (3) the cost of remedial programs.

ACADEMIC STANDARDS

Do remedial courses degrade academic standards? Those opposed to remedial education at 4-year colleges argue that remediation undercuts high academic standards and status (Cronholm, 1999a, 1999b; Manno, 1995; Steinberg, 1998). They say that they are concerned with raising standards at 4-year institutions that should not be reduced to providing remediation. Basic-skill-level courses do not belong at 4-year colleges, opponents maintain. Such courses are seen as negatively affecting the overall curriculum and forcing faculty to spend less time on higher level knowledge production (Cronholm, 1999b). In addition to the contention that basic skills courses ought to be offered only at community colleges, critics contend that remedial education demoralizes its intended beneficiaries as well as the faculty because of the negative stigma attached to basic-skill-level courses. Worries include curricular deflation and grade inflation (Cronholm, 1999a). Bruno Manno (1995), for one, maintains that in the name of high standards, colleges need to maintain a clear distinction between remedial-level and college-level work. If they do not, the inevitable lowering of standards would result in a degree with less value. Manno also observes that "sadly, with declining standards comes the decline of an institution's prestige" (p. 48). Institutional prestige, or the perception of prestige, seems to be a key issue for remedial education's foes, just as it is for those opposed to multicultural curricula. James Traub (1994), for example, pejoratively refers to the "remedial underworld" (p. 81) and the "nurturing and nondemanding environment of remediation" (p. 107). He critiques what he calls a remedial college model of higher education as one that supports and even promotes low academic standards for disadvantaged students in the name of opportunity. According to Traub, the model is the "inadvertent confirmation of the conservative argument that the intellectual values treasured in the academy cannot survive the onslaught of the new student" (p. 203). Somewhat hidden within the critiques is a preoccupation with smartness. Teaching underprepared, often low-income (Traub calls them new) students, is perceived as a low-status activity. As Alexander Astin (1998) points out, those worried about maintaining high academic standards "value *being* smart much more than . . . *developing* smartness" (p. 12). Again, the issue of institutional priorities comes to the surface.

What remedial education critics neglect to consider is that not all or even most students who need remedial coursework are necessarily academically less able than those who do not. Some are, to be sure, but there are a variety of other factors that cause students to lack academic preparation for college (Hardin, 1998). Some students may have followed the wrong track or curriculum in high school, that is, they may have made some unwise academic choices or received poor advice or counseling. This is related to having an adequate context of choice. Other students may be returning to school after time in the workforce, so that certain academic skills are not fresh in their minds. Still others may have a learning disability. In fact, few students who take remedial courses at 4-year colleges fall into the severely underprepared category (Hardin, 1998). On average, college students take approximately five remedial credits, which amounts to one or two courses, before moving on to nonremedial-level courses (Roueche & Roueche, 1999). This is not to say that there are not sometimes grave academic barriers, just that they are not necessarily insurmountable when they exist. Academic quality is seen as somehow contingent upon the exclusion of many from the university, rather than upon other, internal university factors such as faculty caliber, funding levels, curriculum, and so forth (Rossmann et al., 1975). The standards issue rests on perceptions of institutional reputation, instead of on more substantive factors.

Opponents also gloss over the possibility that the elimination of remedial courses may result not only in higher standards for admission, but in the exclusion of a diverse group of students who have had the misfortune to attend worse-than-average public schools as well. The catch is that the state of the public educational system in low-income areas is not these students' fault. Nevertheless, the abolishment of remedial programs serves to blame and punish some students for circumstances over which they have no control.

Still, those concerned with how remedial courses affect an institution's academic standards argue that attending community college is hardly a punishment. They argue that students with academic deficiencies are well served by the opportunity to catch up before going on to 4-year institutions. Indeed, community colleges provide educational opportunities to many students who might not otherwise pursue postsecondary education. An argument for remedial education at the 4-year-college level does not discount the importance of community colleges. However, the fact remains that where a student first goes to college has a serious impact on whether that student will obtain a baccalaureate degree (Velez, 1985). From their research on CUNY student data, David Lavin and David Hyllegard (1996) suggest that fears about lowered academic standards may be misguided. Twelve years after CUNY began open admissions, the researchers found that there remained great talent among the graduates, who were often accepted for and succeeded in graduate study at other institutions of higher education. In considering proposals to move all remedial education to community colleges, Mike Rose (1990) observes:

> what's troubling is that among the counterarguments—which are mostly political and economic—you rarely hear concerns about the astounding inbreeding and narrowness that would result: a faculty already conceptually isolated along disciplinary lines talking in more self-referenced ways to less and less diverse audiences. (p. 197)

Community colleges serve a vital purpose. The availability of remedial courses at the 4-year-college level also serves a vital purpose. One need not preclude the other in the name of academic standards.

STUDENTS' ACADEMIC PERFORMANCE

Opponents of remedial education worry that remedial education policy condones poor academic achievement by individual students and by public schools (Cronholm, 1999a, 1999b; Manno, 1995). Critics tend to blame individual students for not being able to score high enough on entrance and placement examinations. One main argument here is that these students are irresponsible and have chosen not to take the demanding high school courses that would have better prepared them for the levels of writing, reading, and mathematics expected of college students at 4-year institutions. Manno (1995) in particular calls remedial offerings a "disincentive to learn" in K–12 (p. 47). He says that students get the message that it is unimportant to work hard in K–12 because their efforts will not matter; public schools get the message that they need not bother with reform because their students are accepted by 4-year colleges anyway. A former president of Baruch College, Lois Cronholm (1999a) similarly claims that traditional-aged high school graduates who need remedial courses do not deserve another opportunity to master precollege material within a 4-year institution. In addition, by providing remedial opportunities for such students, colleges condone and accept the substandard academic preparation provided by public schools. Critics therefore believe that eliminating opportunities for remediation at 4-year institutions will force both students and public schools to change their ways.

For example, the trustees of CUNY, the institution most embattled over the remedial education issue, felt that abolishing remedial education would somehow shock such students into becoming more academically prepared in high school. This, in turn, they reasoned, would result in a much-decreased need for remedial courses, and therefore, their new policy would be a success (Cronholm, 1999b; Schmidt, 1998). Students who did still need remedial coursework would be forced to attend community college instead. The problem is that the action of CUNY's board may also have other significant consequences. Because on average students who enter 4-year colleges from the outset are more likely to obtain a bachelor's degree, they have greater options for choice than those who enter into community colleges (Alba & Lavin, 1981). Consequently, when a lack of remedial courses forces some students to go to community colleges or no college at all, the context within which they make their life choices becomes constrained, and their development of self-determination is negatively affected.

It would certainly be better, or more desirable, if there were no need for remediation at all, so perhaps the goal of abolishing remedial education is not fully negative. However, it is wrongheaded to try to use the threat of the elimination of remedial education in order to force public school improvement. It is true that many public schools need to improve, but it is unlikely that this type of threat, from CUNY or any other university system, will promote rapid change. Other comprehensive school reform efforts have had difficulty finding success, so why would these threats better spur public school improvements? It is more likely that the retrenchment of remedial programs will harm a substantial number of students. Even those with strong high school records may have been underprepared for high-level college work in some areas (Lavin et al., 1981). Consider that in 1994, approximately half of all freshmen in the California State University system were placed in remedial courses in English or math (Ignash, 1997). In puzzling over the simultaneous importance of remedial offerings and the stress they place on institutions of higher education, Traub (1994) notes:

> [City College] students know the ghetto life around them firsthand. They look on City College as their best chance at salvation from that life. That's a great deal to ask of a college, or of any institution; but those are the stakes. (p. 3)

Traub rightly points out that the stakes are high for many students who look to education as their main source of opportunity in life. Remedial programs serve an important need that is not being sufficiently filled through other avenues. Rather than condoning poor public school performance, remedial education policy places a high priority on the educational opportunities of disadvantaged students.

THE COST OF REMEDIAL EDUCATION

Remedial education's opponents raise another major question: Are remedial programs too expensive? Supporters such as John Roueche and Suanne Roueche (1999) and David Ponitz (1998) contend that remedial education is crucial for educational access and therefore worth the expense.

Critics of remedial education at the 4-year-college level contend that remedial programs end up costing taxpayers a large amount of money (Manno, 1995). Not only are taxpayers paying for students to learn this material in high school, but they must also pay for some students to be taught the same material in public colleges and universities as well. This results in a double cost. In addition, critics argue, it is very difficult to accurately estimate the full cost of remedial education programs due to the stigma associated with them and often fuzzy definitions of what constitutes a remedial program (Phipps, 1998).

Although it may be quite difficult to estimate the full cost of remedial programs, it is equally difficult to estimate the cost of their elimination. Lavin & Hyllegard (1996) found that open admissions, with its concomitant remedial courses, greatly increased opportunity for students of color. That is, of the students admitted at the senior-college level, the number of black students earning bachelor's degrees tripled and the number of Latino students increased by 1.7 times; the increases continued for postgraduate educational and employment activities as well. These figures show that remedial programs (and open admissions programs) likely lead to greater economic equality among ethnic groups. I should note that because Lavin & Hyllegard studied only open admissions students from CUNY, the students likely needed to take more remedial courses than students admitted to 4-year colleges through traditional admissions procedures. Lavin & Hyllegard go on to report that nonmaterial outcomes such as high levels of civic and cultural involvement, good self-esteem, good health, and feelings of control over one's life are positively affected as well. According to these factors, open admissions and remedial programs are worth the cost.

Remedial education generally costs slightly less than 1 percent of an institution's yearly budget (Breneman, 1998). In raw numbers, this means that remedial programs cost approximately $1 billion per year of an overall public higher education budget of $115 billion. The overall figure of less than 1 percent varies by state and by institution (Phipps, 1998). The courses, usually in math or language arts, often are taught by graduate students. As such, they may cost universities very little to administer and run. And the gains in terms of student diversity and opportunity are substantial. One of the reasons remedial education policy was established at so many institutions is that it seemed like a good investment, both socially and economically.

This line of reasoning calls to question the actual motives of those who would abolish remedial education courses. It would not be popular to say that poor students and students of color are causing a general decline in academic standards in (selective) 4-year institutions of higher education, so remedial education programs, along with affirmative action programs, are targeted instead.

REMEDIAL EDUCATION AS FOSTERING SELF-DETERMINATION

During a period of serious debate about remedial programs, it is worthwhile to take a step back and ask a further question: does remedial education contribute to the aims of education in a liberal democracy? Insofar as the development of self-determination by students is a legitimate and worthwhile aim of education, the answer is yes. I contend that remedial education, as a policy that significantly affects students of color and students from low-income communities, is defensible because it plays a critical role in the development of self-determination among needy students. Like affirmative action policy, remedial education policy does so primarily by increasing students' options for choice, that is, expanding choices that were previously limited by unjust social structures. Its link with helping students to have authenticity is more symbolic. The existence of remedial courses at 4-year institutions of higher education provides an acknowledgement that there are structural social and educational factors beyond individual students' control that may affect their preparedness for college. This acknowledgment, or recognition, of systemic inequalities allows students to understand that it is not personal or cultural factors such as race, ethnicity, or socioeconomic status that has limited their academic preparedness. They need not feel that they must eschew their cultural identity in order to succeed within selective higher education.

To review, my contention relies on liberal political theory, which has developed several strands of thought. One strand, which I call contemporary liberalism, acknowledges the continued importance of individual liberty, but moves beyond that focus to emphasize the social and cultural context of individuals' lives. Contemporary liberalism is thus distinguishable from the classical strands of liberalism that value individualism and neutrality to the exclusion of community context and cultural identity. Contemporary liberalism allows for transcendence of liberal neutrality about the good so that certain ideals may be held up as constituent of the good life. One such ideal is self-determination, the development of which is fostered by the availability of remedial education, or so I argue.

The ideal of self-determination is characterized by a capacity to make important life choices without being limited by social factors that are outside of one's control. Two conditions are associated with the development of self-determination. First, self-determining persons need to have a favorable social context within which to make those important life choices. It is the character of people's choices that matters, for even if a choice is not directly forced, it still cannot properly be considered a meaningful choice if it is made within a constrained context. Second, self-determining persons need to maintain or develop authentic cultural identities. In this case, to have an authentic identity means that the identity that persons embrace is one that they want to have, rather than merely one that they accept due to oppression or coercion. When the second condition is satisfied, persons do not have to sacrifice their authentic identities in order to achieve success.

REMEDIAL EDUCATION AND THE SOCIAL CONTEXT OF CHOICE

The previous three chapters have examined how certain race-conscious education policies foster more favorable contexts of choice for students of color, which in turn help to ensure students' self-determination. Remedial education policy serves a similar aim. I have been arguing that education policies ought to play a purposeful part in helping students to develop self-determination. Remedial education fosters the development of self-determination by students most directly by helping to meet the first condition described above. The availability of remedial education contributes to a more favorable context of choice for disadvantaged students.

Colleges generally place students in remedial courses based on their scores on the college's own placement exams, which usually are given after students have gained admission and have enrolled for the first term. This is not a trivial point. When policymakers and others call for the elimination of remedial courses at the 4-year-college level, they are in essence saying that certain admitted students should be excluded from participation at the 4-year institution to which they have been admitted and which they have chosen to attend. As mentioned earlier, a good number of the students in remedial courses come from disadvantaged educational backgrounds. Education in general, and real educational opportunities in particular constitute one important way for students to overcome structural societal inequalities and begin to enjoy a more expansive social context of choice. Elimination of remedial programs, on the other hand, would serve to impede opportunities and severely constrain the contexts within which students make their life choices.

The argument against remedial education within higher education seems to be an argument against individuals who are perceived as irresponsible or unintelligent. The below-the-surface sentiment is that students in remedial courses are each individually responsible for their underpreparedness; they squandered their K–12 educational opportunities and do not deserve so-called second chances at the postsecondary level. To be sure, some students have thrown away opportunities to become well prepared for college. Nonetheless, the sheer numbers of students taking remedial courses demonstrate a systemic rather than individual problem at the K–12 level (or for that matter, at the postsecondary level). Individual students who did not have the chance to receive adequate academic college preparation in high school do not deserve to be blamed and punished for that fact.

Consider the story of an African American student named Tammy, who Traub (1994) calls "a miraculous survivor," hinting at both her survival in life and in the academic world (p. 121). The youngest of ten, Tammy lived with her mother in housing projects in the South Bronx. One of her sisters was an alcoholic and one brother was homeless. She did not attend an exemplary New York City public school. Her grades in high school were low, but she was still admitted to City College through a special opportunity program. Tammy, then, represents the most severe case of a student needing remediation. Traub describes that

Tammy was ill prepared for college in a variety of ways, as she had never done homework or taken notes of her own initiative, never written any papers longer than five paragraphs, never even read an entire book. With much remediation and support, Tammy was able to persist at a senior college. She did not become a star student (her GPA was approximately a C+) but she had a firm commitment to graduate no matter how long it took. Traub, a presumable critic of remedial programs, concludes that her survival was due to "purely personal characteristics" (p. 127). Her personal characteristics must have been a big part of her survival against the odds, but why didn't Traub go a few steps further in his analysis? Her academic success was likely also a testimony to something else as well—the presence of real opportunity given by the special admissions program and by the availability of remedial courses and support programs. Just being admitted to a senior college boosted Tammy's context of choice and sense of self-determination. Traub points out that "virtually no one Tammy knew had ever received a degree from a 4-year college. 'I was so *proud* to get in here,' Tammy recalled" (p. 125). Remedial course offerings widened Tammy's options for choice.

Lavin et al. (1981) found that exposure to remedial courses made no significant negative or positive differences for students in terms of academic achievement, GPAs, retention, or graduation. They also found that success in remedial courses did make a difference for students who passed their remedial courses. Such students, like Tammy, were more likely to persist and graduate than comparable students who did not take remedial courses. However, when students failed their remedial courses, they were much more likely to drop out of college. Even with this negative finding, there is hopeful news as well. If success at remedial courses correlates with overall college success, and failure at remedial courses correlates with overall college failure, then we have one intriguing response to some of the basic criticisms of remedial education discussed earlier. Conservative critics may be satisfied because there is evidence that standards are not substantially lowered by remedial courses. Yet contemporary liberals may be satisfied because students' context of choice is expanded by the availability of remedial courses. Furthermore, these findings suggest that there could be a resolution for the conflicting goal priorities within institutions of higher education. Institutions can strive both to contribute to an expansive opportunity structure for all students, and to foster high-level academic research and scholarship. The pool of community leaders and office holders is expanded. The contexts within which students make choices for their education and beyond are more favorable. Both goals contribute to the social functions of an institution of higher education (Gutmann, 1987).

REMEDIAL EDUCATION'S LINK WITH AUTHENTICITY

As I argued previously, the second main condition associated with the development of self-determination among students of color is the development or maintenance of authenticity in identity. Whereas a policy like bilingual education is linked closely with students' cultural identities, remedial education is less directly linked with helping students to maintain or develop their identities. Nevertheless, the existence of remedial education courses symbolizes an institution's commitment to educational equality. By opening doors, remedial education policy supports students' sense of themselves and their communities. With remedial course availability, students do not feel limited either because of their circumstances of birth or because of the systemic factors that lessen their chances for equal educational opportunity.

From his role as a tutor for students in remedial classes at the University of California at Los Angeles (UCLA), Rose (1990) observed that most of the freshmen who needed remediation were leaders in their high schools—students who were class officers, honor roll members, in short, academic successes. If remedial courses were no longer offered at institutions like UCLA, these students would lose out. The problem with this is, as Rose puts it, "that they might not be able to separate out their particular problems with calculus or critical writing from their own image of themselves as thinkers, from their intellectual self-worth" (p. 173). These are students who did work hard in high school in order to gain entry to a selective university and the reasons they may need some remedial courses are varied as mentioned above. Remedial offerings help students to transcend the less favorable circumstances of their backgrounds, like a struggling public high school or poor advising. In addition, the opportunities extended by virtue of the remedial offerings underscore students' personal and cultural worth. Regardless of their arbitrary background characteristics, students receive the message that they deserve real opportunities. It is this way that remedial education contributes to students' sense of identity; they need not be ashamed of or try to change who they are. Consider once more the story of Angel, the Chicano student from the film *Stand and Deliver*. Angel's success in mathematics will likely propel him to enroll in a 4-year institution of higher education, but because his high school preparation was not as strong in language arts, he may need to take a remedial class. It seems ludicrous and unjust to deny Angel the best possibility of a bachelor's degree and future success by sending him first to a community college. Such action may damage his sense of self, as Rose (1990) fears, and steer him away from higher education altogether. The point here is that a

168

Embracing Race

lack of remedial education hinders meaningful equality of educational opportunity by reverting the education system back to one with no formal barriers, but many real obstacles for students with morally arbitrary educational circumstances (K. Howe, 1997).

Manno (1995) claims that remedial education undermines the "fundamental American belief" that persons move ahead in life due to their own abilities—their merit (p. 47). It is difficult to see how he can plausibly make this argument, especially when we consider a case like Angel's. Students' abilities gain them admission to universities; a remedial course offering is one way among many less controversial ways to provide students with the support necessary to help them succeed within higher education. Students of color like Angel deserve no less than, for instance, a student who needs counseling for an emotional issue. Yet no one suggests that students attend community college until they are emotionally ready for life at a 4-year institution.

Many years ago Jerome Karabel (1972) argued that community colleges function as a systematic way to divert poor students and students of color from 4-year institutions of higher education and therefore from limitless possibilities. He called the antiremedial position one of a set of "politically driven proposals which will particularly affect poor and minority students" (p. 5). Although the community college degree has more economic benefits than the high school degree only, income is most improved by a 4-year college degree. Students who enter community colleges with hopes of eventually earning a bachelor's degree have a severely decreased chance of doing so when compared with students who enter a 4-year institution at the start for their college careers (Alba & Lavin, 1981; Dougherty, 1987). Alba and Lavin go as far as to say that their study of the CUNY system shows that junior and community colleges function as a separate, lower academic track.

Simply put, without remedial education, there will be fewer good choices for less advantaged students. They will be forced to clear another hurdle (e.g., transferring from a community college to a 4-year institution) on the way to selective higher education, a bachelor's degree, and the attendant benefits. Students' social context of choice and their sense of identity may be compromised. The abolishment of remedial education thus diminishes students' self-determination.

CONCLUSION

Policies that have a positive impact on students of color and poor students are the most likely to get criticized and face attempts at abolishment, all without discussion of the deeper aims of education in U.S. society. The liberal system of education in the United States is burdened with a variety of different aims. One such aim is the development of self-determination among all students, so that they may make meaningful choices among different conceptions of the good and be able to participate effectively in a democratic system of government. Remedial education is one policy that helps disadvantaged students overcome structural inequalities so that they might pursue higher education at 4-year colleges. The best remedial programs are complemented by an array of important student services such as financial aid counseling, mentoring, and academic advising, all of which are crucial for most students (Roueche & Roueche, 1999).

The remedial education debate would be moot if in fact empirical research on community college attendance, graduation, and transfer to 4-year institutions were more hopeful. In actuality, when students attend community colleges rather than universities, they are less likely to go on to obtain a bachelor's degree (Dougherty, 1987; Velez, 1985). Students of color, when separated out, are even less likely.

The key to solving the remedial education controversy is to keep the interests of students as the top priority. Perhaps this chapter's defense of remedial education through its theoretically grounded account of the importance and worth of remedial programs at the 4-year-college level, will compel policymakers to ensure that students like Shante Proctor have a real opportunity to fulfill their dreams.

NOTES

1. Within the literature the type of program I am concerned with herein is alternately referred to as compensatory, remedial, or developmental. I will be using the term remedial, as it is the term most frequently cited in the current debate by both the media and education policy scholars. In addition, it evokes the issue of academic underpreparedness, which is central to my argument.

2. Most controversial and under attack across the nation are the remedial education policies at 4-year institutions of higher education, rather than such programs at 2-year or community colleges. As such, it is the programs at 4-year institutions with which I am concerned in this chapter. Unless otherwise noted, when I mention remedial education throughout this chapter, I am referring to the remedial education policies and programs at 4-year institutions of higher education.

3. Learners of English as a Second Language are not included in this group.

7

Conclusion

I refuse to believe that education must be painful and cruel....
Simply put, I am a rare bird trying to combine a traditional
Muscogee life with an Ivy League education. When I go to work
... I go to war. I seek to protect people and cultures that are
beautiful and unique and timeless. But mostly I seek to protect
children who should not have to kneel; children who might be
my grandmother, my son, my friend Val—or me.

—Bill Bray

Indeed, education should not cause pain and suffering among students. Instead, as I have argued in the previous pages, it ought to help students develop personal autonomy in such a way that they can conceptualize and pursue life's best possibilities. Unfortunately, as Native American educator Bill Bray (1997) suggests, the U.S. educational system is oppressive for far too many students of color. Through my arguments herein, I have endeavored to defend those education policies that strongly combat oppression. Education policies that are race-conscious, either explicitly or implicitly, have a tremendous impact on whether or not students of color receive an education that serves to enhance their possibilities in life. Thus, I have argued that race-conscious education policies, in general, and bilingual education, multicultural curricula, affirmative action, and remedial education policies, in particular, are crucial components of an educational system that is deeply concerned with and committed to social justice.

In making this argument, I conceptualized a contemporary liberal theoretical framework centered on the ideal of self-determination as a fundamental aim of a just education. I relied on contemporary liberal political theory, which supports a particular idea of the good. In Chapter 2, I defended a notion of the good life that entails that persons will be respected for who they authentically are within their own particular social and cultural context. This idea of the good life places the ideal of personal autonomy as self-determination at its center; an authentic cultural identity and a favorable social context of choice are the two factors required in order for persons to develop meaningful self-determination. The educational system often has a tremendous impact on students' ability to become self-determining.

With this framework in mind, I proceeded to craft a defense of race-conscious education policy. The argument went as follows: (1) Self-determination is a key aim of an education committed to social justice; (2) a favorable social context of choice and a sense of authenticity are required for the development of self-determination; (3) in varied ways, race-conscious education policy contributes greatly to students' favorable contexts of choice and feelings of authenticity; (4) therefore, race-conscious education policy is required in the name of justice because it significantly promotes students' development of self-determination.

In Chapters 3, 4, 5, and 6, I applied my framework to particular race-conscious policies: bilingual education, multicultural curricula, affirmative action in higher education admissions, and remedial education. Each in its own way helps to create more favorable social contexts of choice and feelings of authentic cultural identity for students of color. None of these policies is perfect, and considered separately, each is a weaker effort in the fight for equal educational opportunity for students of color. These policies are the best efforts thus far; they do not solve the underlying societal problems that have resulted in the need for them. Bilingual education cannot erase xenophobia and racism. Multicultural curricula cannot rid society of exclusion and distortion. Affirmative action cannot wipe out racism, oppression, and classism. And remedial education cannot erase years of inadequate public schooling. However, when they are taken together, these four policies make up a systematic agenda for social justice in education. The common and crucial thread is that they all contribute to an educational system that helps students of color to become self-determining.

Bilingual education policy does this in perhaps the strongest way. It fosters English language learners' self-determination by helping them affirm the worth of their native language and culture, and by helping expand the contexts within which students make important life choices. Without bilingual education, English language learners are likely to be harmed by academic failure or by the sacrifices they would be forced to make in order to succeed within mainstream education. Bilingual education, then, is one way that schools adjust to the needs of English language learners and contribute to social justice in the process.

Just as bilingual education policy helps to ensure a nonoppressive educational environment for K–12 English language learners, multicultural curriculum policy combats oppression for all students at the K–12 and college levels. Multicultural curricula enrich the quality of students' educational experiences and their sense of authentic cultural identity. Whether or not students receive a multicultural education has a profound impact on their development of self-determination. Multicultural education provides important public recognition of diverse racial and ethnic identities. With this type of cultural recognition, students of color gain an expanded range of options from which to choose in pursuing the good life. They would be much less likely to be faced only with the empty choice of total cultural assimilation in order to succeed academically and beyond.

While bilingual education and multicultural curriculum policies help students to become self-determining by strongly enhancing both their sense of authenticity and their social contexts of choice, affirmative action and remedial education policy foster self-determination primarily by expanding students' contexts of choice. They play lesser roles in supporting students' authentic identities. When students' race and ethnicity are used as factors in university admissions, their educational opportunities are widened, as are their possibilities for high-status positions in society. Both affirmative action and remedial education policy take into consideration systemic disparities in students' lives due to racism, classism, and other oppressive and exclusive societal structures that may contribute to impoverished social contexts of choice. In so doing, they expand the range of options from which students of color can make educational and career choices. As a result, the students who benefit from affirmative action gain access to selective higher education and a greater ability to meaningfully determine the way their lives ultimately will go. Students who are able to take remedial courses at the 4-year-college level benefit from the increased opportunities and goods available to those with a bachelor's degree. With the opportunities provided by higher education, they are much better able to conceive of possibilities for themselves and then act upon those possibilities to reach lofty goals.

Apart from the fact that these policies have in common the goal of helping students to develop self-determination, they are also connected because they are more effective when taken together, in combination. This is the main reason why I have examined the four policies herein. The weaknesses of one policy can be offset by the strengths of another. Consider the point I made about affirmative action and remedial education and the fact that they play lesser roles in fostering authenticity. When they are conjoined with a commitment to multicultural education, students' authentic identities are strongly supported by the curriculum. This way, affirmative action and remedial education can be defended for what they do best—expand students' social contexts of choice—and we know that we can rely on multicultural curricula to support students' authenticity. Bilingual education, multicultural curricula, affirmative action, and remedial education policies work in combination; they complement each other in striving for social justice. To take another example, a criticism of affirmative action is that it serves to benefit primarily middle-class students of color. Again, if we look at the educational system and education policies holistically, then we can tolerate what may be a weakness in one policy because other policies contribute to that holistic agenda for social justice. Bilingual education, multicultural curricula, and remedial education policies all provide substantial educational opportunities to poor and low-income students of color. In combination, the four policies examined in this book ensure that all students are reached.

So often, educators, scholars, and policymakers committed to social justice are left with the question of whether it is even realistic to believe that the educational system can do anything to counter the negative social factors that affect students' lives outside of school. Answers are difficult to come by, and negativity often prevails (Traub, 2000). The analysis of race-conscious education policy provided in this book shows that we can indeed do something—many things, in fact—within the policy arena to promote social justice through education. Not only can we, we must. Anyon (1997) insightfully reminds us that "to believe that fundamental social change is impossible is to be overly oppressed by the parameters of the present" (pp. 164–165). There are few social policies in the United States that explicitly counteract racial oppression. The ones in place ought to be utilized. Race-conscious policies such as bilingual education, multicultural curricula, affirmative action, and remedial education positively affect students' sense of self-determination and what is possible in life. Federal and local education policies contribute to social justice when they serve to protect students who would otherwise not benefit from the educational system. Educational institutions have an obligation to enact the agenda for social justice that I advocate herein. It will ensure that educators and educational institutions help all students feel worthy of equal respect, be capable of dreaming, and know that their dreams are possible.

CREATING A SENSE OF POSSIBILITY

In genetic, or biological, terms, race does not really exist (McDonald, 1998). It is a social construct rather than a biological determiner. But socially, culturally, and politically, it is indeed very real. It affects the way we see ourselves and others, the way we construct (or do not construct) our personal and cultural identities, the way we are treated within educational institutions and otherwise.

If they are truly concerned with creating a just educational system, educators and policymakers need to be conscious of race. The knowledge that race does not really exist fails to correct disparities in educational opportunity that are obviously related to racism and oppression. The dissolution of race-conscious education policies with no proper or meaningful alternatives leaves us in a kind of educational quicksand. The educational system continues to oppress students of color, who internalize the exclusive norms of the dominant culture. As they slip further into the quicksand, they come to believe that they are somehow inferior, to doubt that they are capable of success, and then cease trying to dream of a greater world. It is as if through education, they are swallowed up, sunk. Good race-conscious education policies, on the other hand, prompt educators to regain their faith in all students' possibilities, and help students of color rise above the muck.

I hope that out of the debates and political campaigns against bilingual education, multicultural curricula, affirmative action, and remedial education can come a sharp period of renewal—that the outrage at the inequality resulting from the abolishment of these policies will ignite deeper passions to protect the ideals they uphold. For race-conscious education policies were born out of the effort for civil rights in the United States, as a long-awaited response by the establishment to the demands and desires of oppressed peoples. It was the stories and struggles of individual persons of color that helped mainstream educators and policymakers first realize the need for race-conscious policy. Yet, their staunchest opponents fail to remember that real persons are intimately harmed by the elimination of race-conscious policies—persons who for a short while in U.S. history have been able to have hope that their education would no longer serve to truncate their sense of themselves or their dreams of the good life. With race-conscious education policies strongly in place, the U.S. educational system fulfills its democratic promise by helping students create a meaningful sense of possibility for their lives.

References

Ackerman, B. A. (1980). *Social justice in the liberal state*. New Haven, CT: Yale University Press.

Adelman, C. (1998). The kiss of death? An alternative view of college remediation. *Cross Talk, 6*(3), 11.

Alba, R. D., & Lavin, D. E. (1981, October). Community colleges and tracking in higher education. *Sociology of Education, 54*, 223-237.

Altbach, P. G., & Lomotey, K. (Eds.). (1991). *The racial crisis in American higher education*. Albany, NY: State University of New York Press.

Amaker, N. C. (1988). *Civil rights and the Reagan administration*. Washington, DC: The Urban Institute Press.

American Council on Education. (1996). *Making the case for affirmative action in higher education*. Washington, DC: American Council on Education.

Anderson, G. (1989). Critical ethnography in education: Origins, current status, and new directions. *Review of Educational Research, 59*(3), 249-270.

Anderson, J. D. (1988). *The education of blacks in the South*. Chapel Hill: University of North Carolina Press.

Andersson, T., & Boyer, M. (1976). *Bilingual schooling in the United States: History, rationale, implications, and planning*. Austin, Texas: Southwest Educational Development Laboratory

Anyon, J. (1997). *Ghetto schooling: A political economy of urban educational reform*. New York: Teachers College Press.

Appiah, K. A. (1994). Identity, authenticity, survival: multicultural societies and social reproduction. In A. Gutmann (Ed.), *Multiculturalism: Examining the politics of recognition* (pp. 149-163). Princeton, NJ: Princeton University Press.

Appiah, K. A. (1996). Culture, subculture, multiculturalism: Educational options. In R. K. Fullinwider (Ed.), *Public education in a multicultural society* (pp. 65-89). Cambridge, England: Cambridge University Press.

Appiah, K. A., & Gutmann, A. (1996). *Color conscious: The political morality of race*. Princeton, NJ: Princeton University Press.

Applewhite, S. R. (1979). The legal dialect of bilingual education. In R. V. Padilla (Ed.), *Bilingual education and public policy in the United States* (Vol. 1, pp. 3-17). Ypsilanti, Michigan: Eastern Michigan University Press.

175

Arthur, J., & Shaw, W. H. (Eds.). (1991). *Justice and economic distribution* (2d ed.). Englewood Cliffs, NJ: Prentice-Hall.

Aspira of New York, Inc. v. Board of Education of the City of New York, 423F Supp. 647 (S.D.N.Y. 1976).

Astin, A. (1993, March/April). Diversity and multiculturalism on campus: How are students affected? *Change, 25,* 44–49.

Astin, A. (1998). Remedial education and civic responsibility. *Crosstalk, 6*(3), 12–13.

Banks, J. A. (1994). *Multiethnic education: Theory and practice* (3rd ed.). Boston: Allyn and Bacon.

Baron, D. (1990). *The English-only question: An official language for Americans?* New Haven, CT: Yale University Press.

Basinger, J. (1998, May 29). Eighty-eight students arrested in protest at UCLA. *The Chronicle of Higher Education*, p. A32.

Bell, D. (1992). *Faces at the bottom of the well*. New York: Basic Books.

Bell, D. (1993). *Communitarianism and its critics*. Oxford: Clarendon Press.

Belz, H. (1991). *Equality transformed: A quarter-century of affirmative action*. New Brunswick, NJ: Transaction.

Bennett, W., & Eastland, T. (1979). *Counting by race: Equality from the founding fathers to Bakke and Weber*. New York: Basic Books.

Berliner, D. C., & Biddle, B. J. (1995). *The manufactured crisis: Myths, fraud, and the attack on America's public schools*. White Plains, NY: Longman.

Berman, M. (1970). *The politics of authenticity: Radical individualism and the emergence of modern society*. New York: Atheneum.

Bernal, E. M., Cabrera, A. F., & Terenzini, P. T. (1999, November). Class-based affirmative action admissions policies: A viable alternative to race-based programs? Paper presented at the annual meeting of the Association for the Study of Higher Education, San Antonio, TX.

Bernstein, R. (1994). *Dictatorship of virtue: Multiculturalism and the battle for America's future*. New York: Knopf.

Berry, M. F. (1983). Civil rights enforcement in higher education. *Integrated Education*, 2.

Beykont, Z. F. (2000). Introduction. In Z. F. Beykont (Ed.), *Lifting every voice: Pedagogy and politics of bilingualism* (pp. vii–xix). Cambridge, MA: Harvard Educational Publishing Group.

Bloom, A. (1987). *The closing of the American mind*. New York: Simon and Schuster.

Bork, R. H. (1996). *Slouching towards Gomorrah: Modern liberalism and American decline*. New York: HarperCollins.

Botstein, L. (1991). The undergraduate curriculum and the issue of race: Opportunities and obligations. In P. G. Altbach & K. Lomotey (Eds.), *The racial crisis in American higher education* (pp. 89–105). Albany, NY: State University of New York Press.

Bowen, W. G., & Bok, D. (1998). *The shape of the river: Long-term consequences of considering race in college and university admissions*. Princeton, NJ: Princeton University Press.

Boylan, H. R. (1988). The historical roots of developmental education, part III. *Review of Research on Developmental Education, 5*(3), 1-3.

Boylan, H. R., & White, W. G. (1987). Educating the nation's people: The historical roots of developmental education, part I. *Review of Research on Developmental Education, 4*(4), 1-4.

Bray, B. (1997). Refuse to kneel. In A. Garrod & C. Larimore (Eds.), *First persons, first peoples: Native American graduates tell their life stories* (pp. 23-42). Ithaca, NY: Cornell University Press.

Breneman, D. W. (1998). The extent and cost of remediation in higher education. In D. Ravitch (Ed.), *Brookings papers on education policy: 1998* (pp. 359-383). Washington, DC: Brookings Institution Press.

Brock, C., & Tulasiewicz, W. (Eds.). (1985). *Cultural identity and educational policy.* New York: St. Martin's Press.

Bronner, E. (1999, January 26). Conservatives open drive against affirmative action. *New York Times*, p. A10.

Brown v. Board of Education of the City of Topeka, 347 U.S. 483 (1954).

Cage, M. C. (1996, May 24). Faculty at University of Washington opposes proposed diversity rule. *The Chronicle of Higher Education*, p. A17.

Callan, E. (1988). *Autonomy and schooling.* Montreal: McGill-Queen's University Press.

Carmines, E. G., & Stimson, J. A. (1989). *Issue evolution: Race and the transformation of American politics.* Princeton, NJ: Princeton University Press.

Castaneda v. Pickard, 648 F. 2d 989 (5th Cir. 1981).

Castellanos, D. (1985). *The best of two worlds: Bilingual-bicultural education in the U.S.* Trenton: New Jersey State Department of Education.

Chang, M., Witt, D., Jones, J., & Hakuta, K. (Eds.). (1999). *Compelling interest: Examining the evidence on racial dynamics in higher education.* Washington, DC: American Educational Research Association.

Chavez, L. (1991). *Out of the barrio: Toward a new politics of Hispanic assimilation.* New York: Basic Books.

Chavez, L. (2000, March 22). Nation's new dual-immersion plan revives languishing bilingual ed. *Tucson Citizen*

Chávez, L. (1998). *The color bind: California's battle to end affirmative action.* Berkeley: University of California press.

Chenoweth, K. (1997, October 30). Not guilty! *Black Issues in Higher Education, 14*, 10-13.

Chockley, A. L. (1997). *Self-authored life stories: A narrative conception of personal autonomy.* Unpublished master's thesis, University of Colorado-Boulder, Boulder, CO.

Christman, J. (Ed.). (1989). *The inner citadel: Essays on individual autonomy.* New York: Oxford University Press.

The Chronicle of Higher Education. (1997a, May 30). At Stanford University, it's finally all quiet on the Western-canon front, p. A20.

The Chronicle of Higher Education. (1997b, June 6). It can no longer give special consideration to black applicants, but the admissions office at the University of California at Berkeley is still swayed by the sight of green, p. A26.

The Chronicle of Higher Education. (1998a, July 17). Which students talk the most in law school? White men, p. A53.

The Chronicle of Higher Education. (1998b, November 20). Racial issues prompt protests on 4 campuses, p. A8.

The Chronicle of Higher Education. (1998c, November 27). Cornell students protest report, p. A8.

The Chronicle of Higher Education. (1999, March 5). Hispanic students at Michigan State hold books hostage in protest, p. A10.

Cohen, A. M., & Brawer, F. B. (1989). *The American community college* (2d ed.). San Francisco: Jossey-Bass.

Cohen, J. (1993). Constructing race at an urban high school: In their minds, their mouths, their hearts. In L. Weis & M. Fine (Eds.), *Beyond silenced voices: Class, race, and gender in United States schools* (pp. 289–308). Albany, NY: State University of New York Press.

Connerly, W. (2000). *Creating equal: My fight against race preferences.* San Francisco: Encounter Books.

Connolly, W. E. (1991). *Identity/difference: Democratic negotiations of political paradox.* Ithaca, NY: Cornell University Press.

Cortés, C. (Ed.). (1986). *Beyond language: Social and cultural factors in schooling language minority students.* Los Angeles: Evaluation, Dissemination and Assessment Center, California State University.

Cose, E. (1993). *The rage of a privileged class.* New York: HarperCollins.

Crawford, J. (1991). *Bilingual education: History, politics, theory, and practice* (2d ed.). Los Angeles: Bilingual Educational Services.

Crawford, J. (1998). *Anatomy of the English-only movement: Social and ideological sources of language restrictionism in the United States* [on-line]. Available: http://www.ourworld.compuserve.com/homepages/jwcrawford.

Crawford, J. (1999). What now for bilingual education? *Rethinking Schools, 13*(2), 1–5.

Crawford, J. (2000). Bilingual education: Strike two. *Rethinking Schools, 15*(2), 3, 8.

Cronholm, L. (1999a). *The assault on remediation: The triumph of logic over emotion* [on-line]. Baruch College. Available: http://www.baruch.cuny.-edu/president/remediation.html.

Cronholm, L. (1999b, September 24). Why one college jettisoned all its remedial courses. *The Chronicle of Higher Education,* pp. B6–B7.

Cross, P. (1976). *Accent on learning.* San Francisco: Jossey-Bass.

Cummins, J. (1981). The role of primary language development in promoting educational success for language minority students. In *Schooling and language minority students: A theoretical framework* (pp. 3–49). Los Angeles: Evaluation, Dissemination and Assessment Center, California State University.

Darling-Hammond, L. (1998). Unequal opportunity: Race and education. *The Brookings Review, 16*(2), 28–32.

Davidson, R. C., & Lewis, E. L. (1997). Affirmative action and other special consideration admissions at the University of California, Davis School of

Medicine. *Journal of the American Medical Association, 278*(14), 1153–1158.

de Beauvoir, S. (1952). *The second sex* (H. M. Parshley, Trans.). New York: Knopf.

DeFunis v. Odegaard, 94 S. Ct. 1704 (1974).

Della Piana, L. (1999, Spring). Reading, writing, race and resegregation. *Colorlines, 2*, 9–14.

Delpit, L. (1993). The silenced dialogue: Power and pedagogy in educating other people's children. In L. Weis & M. Fine (Eds.), *Beyond silenced voices: Class, race, and gender in United States schools* (pp. 119–139). Albany: State University of New York Press.

Dennett, D. (1984). *Elbow room: The varieties of free will worth wanting.* Cambridge, MA: MIT Press.

Dettmar, K. J. H. (1998, September 11). What's so great about great books? *The Chronicle of Higher Education*, pp. B6–B7.

Dewey, J. (1927). *The public and its problems.* New York: Capricorn.

Dewey, J. (1930). *Individualism old and new.* New York: Capricorn.

Dewey, J. (1938). *Experience and education.* New York: Collier.

Donato, R. (1997). *The other struggle for equal schools: Mexican Americans during the civil rights era.* Albany, NY: State University of New York Press.

Dougherty, K. (1987). The effects of community colleges: Aid or hindrance to socioeconomic attainment? *Sociology of Education, 60*(April), 86–103.

D'Souza, D. (1991). *Illiberal education: The politics of race and sex on campus.* New York: Free Press.

Duarte, E. M. (1998). Expanding the borders of liberal democracy: Multicultural education and the struggle for cultural identity. *Educational Foundations, 12*(2), 5–30.

Dworkin, G. (1989). The concept of autonomy. In J. Christman (Ed.), *The inner citadel: Essays on individual autonomy* (pp. 54–62). New York: Oxford University Press.

Dworkin, R. (1978). *Taking rights seriously.* Cambridge, MA: Harvard University Press.

Dworkin, R. (1998, October 22). Affirming affirmative action. *New York Review of Books, XLV,* 91–102.

Edley, C. J. (1996). *Not all black and white: Affirmative action, race, and American values.* New York: Hill and Wang.

Elgass, J. R. (2000). University lawsuit gets court hearing. *The University Record.* Ann Arbor: University of Michigan.

English language education for children in public schools. (1998, February 1). *NABE [National Association for Bilingual Education] News,* 12–14.

Ethridge, R. W. (1997). There is much more to do. In M. García (Ed.), *Affirmative action's testament of hope: Strategies for a new era in higher education* (pp. 47–74). Albany, NY: State University of New York Press.

Farley, C. J. (1997, November 24). Kids and race. *Time,* 88–91.

Feinberg, J. (1989). Autonomy. In J. Christman (Ed.), *The inner citadel: Essays on individual autonomy* (pp. 27–53). New York: Oxford University Press.

Feinberg, W. (1998). *On higher ground: Education and the case for affirmative action*. New York: Teachers College Press.

Ferrara, A. (1994). Authenticity and the project of modernity. *European Journal of Philosophy, 2*(3), 241-273.

Fletcher, S. (2000). *Education and emancipation: Theory and practice in a new constellation*. New York: Teachers College Press.

Ford Foundation. (1997). *Campus diversity initiative*. Seattle: Author.

Fránquiz, M., & Reyes, M. (1998). Creating inclusive learning communities through English language arts: From "chanclas" to "canicas." *Language Arts, 75*(3), 211-220.

Freire, P. (1970). *The pedagogy of the oppressed*. New York: Continuum.

Friedman, M. (1991). Feminism and modern friendship: Dislocating the community. In J. Arthur & W. H. Shaw (Eds.), *Justice and economic distribution* (2d ed., pp. 304-319). Englewood Cliffs, NJ: Prentice-Hall.

Fullinwider, R. K. (1991a). Affirmative action and fairness. *Report from the Institute for Philosophy and Public Policy, 11*(1), 10-13.

Fullinwider, R. K. (1991b). Multicultural education. *Report from the Institute for Philosophy and Public Policy, 11*(3), 12-14.

Fullinwider, R. K. (1994). Ethnocentrism and education in judgment. *Report from the Institute for Philosophy and Public Policy, 14*(1 & 2).

Fullinwider, R. K. (Ed.). (1996). *Public education in a multicultural society*. New York: Cambridge University Press.

Fullinwider, R. K. (1999). Open admissions and remedial education at CUNY. *Report from the Institute for Philosophy and Public Policy, 19*(1), 7-13.

Gándara, P. (1995). *Over the ivy walls: The educational mobility of low-income Chicanos*. Albany, NY: State University of New York Press.

Garvin, G. (1998). Loco, completamente loco. *Reason, 29*(8), 18-29.

Gates, H. L. (1990). The master's pieces: On canon formation and the African-American tradition. *The South-Atlantic Quarterly, 89*(1), 89-111.

Gay, G. (1983, April). Multiethnic education: Historical developments and future prospects. *Phi Delta Kappan, 64,* 560-563.

Geraghty, M. (1997, January 17). Finances are becoming more crucial in students' college choice, survey finds. *The Chronicle of Higher Education*, pp. A41-A43.

Gill, G. R. (1980). *Meanness mania: The changed mood*. Washington, DC: Howard University Press.

Ginsberg, E. K. (Ed.). (1996). *Passing and the fictions of identity*. Durham, NC: Duke University Press.

Glazer, N. (1997). *We are all multiculturalists now*. Cambridge, MA: Harvard University Press.

Gonzalez, G. G. (1990). *Chicano education in the era of segregation*. Philadelphia: Balch Institute Press.

Gose, B. (1997, September 19). Tutoring companies take over remedial teaching at some colleges. *The Chronicle of Higher Education*, pp. A44-A45.

Gose, B., & Schmidt, P. (2001, September 7). Ruling against affirmative action could alter legal debate and admissions practices. *The Chronicle of Higher Education*, pp. A36–A37.

Graham, H. D. (1990). *The civil rights era: Origins and development of national policy 1960–1972*. New York: Oxford University Press.

Gratz v. Bollinger. 122 F. Supp.2d 811, 819–21 (ED Mich. 2000).

Gray, M. J., Rolph, E., & Melamid, E. (1996). *Immigration and higher education: Institutional responses to changing demographics*. Santa Monica, CA: Rand.

Gray, W. R. (2001). *The four faces of affirmative action: Fundamental answers and actions*. Westport, CT: Greenwood Press.

Greve, M. S. (1999, March 19). The demise of race-based admissions policies. *The Chronicle of Higher Education*, pp. B6–B7.

Grutter v. Bollinger, No. 97-75928, 2001 WL 293196 (ED Mich. 2001).

Guernsey, L. (1996, November 1). Study finds that 29 percent of freshmen take remedial instruction. *The Chronicle of Higher Education*, p. A23.

Gurin, P. (1999). Selections from the compelling need for diversity in higher education: Expert report of Patricia Gurin. *Equity and Excellence in Education, 32*(2), 36–62.

Gutmann, A. (1987). *Democratic education*. Princeton, NJ: Princeton University Press.

Gutmann, A. (1994). Introduction. In A. Gutmann (Ed.), *Multiculturalism: Examining the Politics of Recognition* (pp. 3–24). Princeton, NJ: Princeton University Press.

Gutmann, A., & Thompson, D. (1996). *Democracy and disagreement: Why moral conflict cannot be avoided in politics, and what should be done about it*. Cambridge, MA: Belknap Press.

Hakuta, K. (1986). *Mirror of language: The debate on bilingualism*. New York: Basic Books.

Halcón, J. J., & Reyes, M. (1991). Bilingual education, public policy, and the trickle-down reform agenda. In R. Padilla & A. Benavidez (Eds.), *Critical perspectives on bilingual research* (pp. 303–323). Phoenix, AZ: Bilingual Review Press.

Hardin, C. J. (1998). Who belongs in college: A second look. In J. L. Higbee & P. L. Dwinell (Eds.), *Developmental education: Preparing successful college students* (pp. 15–24). Columbia, SC: University of South Carolina.

Harris, D. K. (1998). Exploding the Western canon: San Francisco adopts diversity requirement. *Rethinking Schools, 12*(4), 12–13.

Hawkesworth, M. E. (1990). *Beyond oppression: Feminist theory and political strategy*. New York: Continuum.

Healy, P. (1998a, May 29). Berkeley struggles to stay diverse in post-affirmative action era. *The Chronicle of Higher Education*, pp. A31–A33.

Healy, P. (1998b, December 4). U.S. appeals court ruling may imperil university defenses for affirmative action. *The Chronicle of Higher Education*, pp. A29–A30.

Healy, P. (1999a, February 5). A group attacking affirmative action seeks help from trustees and students. *The Chronicle of Higher Education*, pp. A36–A37.

Healy, P. (1999b, March 5). U. of Mass. limits racial preferences, despite vow to increase minority enrollment. *The Chronicle of Higher Education*, pp. A30–A31.

Heath, S. B. (1986). Sociocultural contexts of language development. In C. Cortés (Ed.), *Beyond language: Social and cultural factors in schooling language minority students* (pp. 143–186). Los Angeles: Evaluation, Dissemination and Assessment Center, California State University.

Hebel, S. (1999a, February 19). How liable are trustees in affirmative-action suits? *The Chronicle of Higher Education*, pp. A35–A36.

Hebel, S. (1999b, December 10). In CUNY remediation debate, the numbers—and the strategy—are in dispute. *The Chronicle of Higher Education*, pp. A36–A37.

Hebel, S. (2000, February 18). U. Va. sees drop in black applicants. *The Chronicle of Higher Education*, p. A44.

Hebel, S. (2001, May 11). Mayor asks that CUNY outsource remediation. *The Chronicle of Higher Education*, p. A31.

Heidegger, M. (1927). *Being and time*. London: SCM Press.

Hirsch, E. D. (1987). *Cultural literacy*. New York: Vintage Books.

Hirsch, E. D. (1996). *The schools we need and why we don't have them*. New York: Doubleday.

Holloway, L. (2000, May 25). As poverty shifts students, getting lessons to stick proves a tough task. *New York Times*, p. A29.

hooks, b. (1994). *Teaching to transgress: Education as the practice of freedom*. London: Routledge.

Hopwood v. Texas, 78 F, 3d 932 (5th Cir. 1996), certiorari denied, 116 S. Ct. 2582 (1996).

House, E. R. (1999). Race and policy. *Education Policy Analysis Archives*, 7(16), 1–13.

Howe, I. (1991). The value of the canon. *Liberal Education, 77*(3), 8–9.

Howe, K. R. (1992). Liberal democracy, equal educational opportunity, and the challenge of multiculturalism. *American Educational Research Journal, 29*(3), 455–470.

Howe, K. R. (1997). *Understanding equal educational opportunity: Social justice, democracy, and schooling*. New York: Teachers College Press.

Huddy, L., & Sears, D. O. (1990). Qualified public support for bilingual education: Some policy implications. *Annals of the American Academy of Psychology and Social Science, 508*, 119–134.

Hurtado, S., & Navia, C. (1997). Reconciling college access and the affirmative action debate. In M. García (Ed.), *Affirmative action's testament of hope: Strategies for a new era in higher education* (pp. 105–130). Albany, NY: State University of New York Press.

Ignash, J. M. (1997). Who should provide postsecondary remedial/developmental education? In J. M. Ignash (Ed.), *Implementing effective policies for remedial and developmental education* (pp. 5-20). San Francisco: Jossey-Bass.

Institute for Higher Education Policy. (1998). *Reaping the benefits: Defining the public and private value of going to college.* Washington, DC: New Millennium Project on Higher Education Costs, Pricing, and Productivity.

Kallen, H. (1924). *Culture and democracy in the United States.* New York: Boni and Liveright.

Kane, T. J. (1998). Misconceptions in the debate over affirmative action in college admissions. In G. Orfield & E. Miller (Eds.), *Chilling admissions: The affirmative action crisis and the search for alternatives* (pp. 17-31). Cambridge, MA: Harvard Education Publishing Group.

Karabel, J. (1972). Community colleges and social stratification. *Harvard Educational Review, 42*(4), 521-562.

Karen, D. (1998, November 16). Go to the head of the class. *The Nation, 46-50.*

Katzenbach, N., & Marshall, B. (1998, February 22). Not color blind: Just blind. *New York Times Magazine, 42-45.*

Kauffman, A. H., & Gonzalez, R. (1997). The Hopwood case: What it says and what it doesn't. In M. García (Ed.), *Affirmative action's testament of hope: Strategies for a new era in higher education* (pp. 227-248). Albany, NY: State University of New York Press.

Kimball, R. (1990). *Tenured radicals: How politics has corrupted higher education.* New York: Harper and Row.

King, R. D. (1997, April). Should English be the law? *The Atlantic Monthly,* 55-64.

Knowledge of English and Spanish helps Latino children succeed in school. (1998, May/June). *LMRI [Linguistic Minority Research Institute] News, 1.*

Kozol, J. (1991). *Savage inequalities: Children in America's schools.* New York: Harper.

Krashen, S. D. (1996). *Under attack: The case against bilingual education.* Culver City, CA: Language Education Associates.

Krashen, S., Park, G., & Seldin, D. (2000, September/October). Bilingual education in Arizona. *NABE [National Association for Bilingual Education] News,* 12-14.

Kull, A. (1992). *The color-blind constitution.* Cambridge, MA: Harvard University Press.

Kymlicka, W. (1991). *Liberalism, community, and culture.* Oxford: Clarendon Press.

Kymlicka, W. (1992). *Contemporary political philosophy.* Oxford: Clarendon Press.

Kymlicka, W. (1995). *Multicultural citizenship.* Oxford: Clarendon Press.

Ladson-Billings, G. (1998). Toward a theory of culturally relevant pedagogy. In L. E. Beyer & M. W. Apple (Eds.), *The curriculum: Problems, politics, and possibilities* (pp. 201-229). Albany, NY: State University of New York Press.

Lau v. Nichols, 414 U.S. 563 (1974).

Lavin, D. E., Alba, R. D., & Silberstein, R. A. (1981). *Right versus privilege: The open-admissions experiment at the City University of New York.* New York: Free Press.

Lavin, D. E., & Hyllegard, D. (1996). *Changing the odds: Open admission and the life chances of the disadvantaged.* New Haven, CT: Yale University Press.

Lawrence, C. R., & Matsuda, M. J. (1996). *We won't go back: Making the case for affirmative action.* New York: Houghton Mifflin.

Leahy, R. (1994). Authenticity: From philosophic concept to literary character. *Educational Theory, 44*(4), 447–461.

Leatherman, C. (2000, September 18). College drops rule calling for multicultural component in all new courses. *The Chronicle of Higher Education* [on-line]. Available: http://chronicle.com.

Lederman, D. (1997, November 14). Supreme Court refuses appeal on California measure barring affirmative action. *The Chronicle of Higher Education,* pp. A27-A28.

Leistyna, P. (1999). *Presence of mind: Education and the politics of deception.* Boulder, CO: Westview Press.

Lewis, L., & Farris, E. (1996). *Remedial Education at Higher Education Institutions in Fall 1995.* Washington, DC: U.S. Department of Education.

Lindenberger, H. (1989, Fall). The western culture debate at Stanford University. *Comparative Criticism, 11,* 225–234.

Liu, E. (1998). *The accidental Asian: Notes of a native speaker.* New York: Random House.

Liu, G. (1998). Affirmative action in higher education: The diversity rationale and the compelling interest test. *Harvard Civil Rights–Civil Liberties Law Review, 33,* 381–442.

Lively, K. (1995, December 15). Cal. State U. revises plan for ending remedial education. *The Chronicle of Higher Education,* p. A27.

Lyons, J. J. (1998, February 1). Untruthfulness of the California "English for the children" campaign. *NABE [National Association for Bilingual Education] News, 21,* 1, 6.

Ma, K. (1999, May 28). U. of Wash. expects fewer black freshmen. *The Chronicle of Higher Education,* pp. A33.

MacIntyre, A. (1981). *After virtue: A study in moral theory.* South Bend, IN: University of Notre Dame Press.

MacKinnon, C. A. (1989). *Toward a feminist theory of the state.* Cambridge, MA: Harvard University Press.

MacLean, D., & Mills, C. (Eds.). (1983). *Liberalism reconsidered.* Totowa, NJ: Rowman and Allanheld.

Maddux, D. (1997). The miseducation of African Americans in public high schools. In K. Lomotey (Ed.), *Sailing against the wind: African Americans and women in U.S. education* (pp. 63–69). Albany, NY: State University Press of New York.

Magner, D. K. (1996, November 15). Wellesley experiments with a new approach to its multicultural requirement. *The Chronicle of Higher Education*, p. A14.

Mangan, K. S. (1997, September 15). Lawmakers call on U. of Texas professor to quit over remarks on race and success. *The Chronicle of Higher Education* [on-line]. Available: http://chronicle.com.

Manno, B. V. (1995, May/June). Remedial education: Replacing the double standard with real standards. *Change, 27*, 47–49.

Marable, M. (1995). *Beyond black and white: Transforming African-American politics*. London: Verso.

Marin, P. (2000). The educational possibility of multi-racial/multi-ethnic college classrooms. In American Council on Education (Ed.), *Does diversity make a difference: Three research studies on diversity in college classrooms* (pp. 61–83). Washington, DC: American Council on Education and American Association of University Professors.

McCarthy, C. (1994). Multicultural discourses and curriculum reform: A critical perspective. *Educational Theory, 44*(1), 81–98.

McCloy, M. (1999, January 7). Showdown over language. *The Arizona Republic* [on-line]. Available: http://ourworld.compuserve.com/homepages/JWCRAWFORDAR4.html

McDonald, K. A. (1998, October 30). Genetically speaking, race doesn't exist. *The Chronicle of Higher Education*, p. A19.

McIntosh, P. (1989, July/August). White privilege: Unpacking the invisible knapsack. *Peace and Freedom*, 10–12.

McKenna, T., & Ortiz, F. I. (Eds.). (1988). *The broken web: The educational experience of Hispanic American women*. Claremont, CA: The Tomás Rivera Center and Floricanto Press.

McLaren, P., & Muñoz, J. S. (2000). Contesting whiteness: Critical perspectives on the struggle for social justice. In C. J. Ovando & P. McLaren (Eds.), *The politics of multiculturalism and bilingual education: Students and teachers caught in the cross fire* (pp. 22–49). New York: McGraw-Hill.

McWhorter, J. H. (2000). *Losing the race: Self-sabotage in black America*. New York: Free Press.

Meyer v. Nebraska, 262 U.S. 390 (1923).

Meyers, D. T. (1989). *Self, society, and personal choice*. New York: Columbia University Press.

Milem, J. F. (1999). The educational benefits of diversity: Evidence from multiple sectors. In M. Chang, D. Witt, J. Jones, & K. Hakuta (Eds.), *Compelling interest: Examining the evidence on racial dynamics in higher education* (pp. 1–41). Washington, DC: American Educational Research Association.

Milem, J. F., & Hakuta, K. (2000). *The Benefits of Racial and Ethnic Diversity in Higher Education*. Washington, DC: American Council on Education.

Mill, J. S. (1974). *On liberty*. London: Penguin Books. (Originally published 1859).

Mills, C. (1995). Politics and manipulation. *Social Theory and Practice, 21*(1), 97–112.

Miner, B. (1999). Bilingual education: New visions for a new era. *Rethinking Schools, 13*(4), 1, 18–20.

Miramontes, O. B., Nadeau, A., & Commins, N. L. (1997). *Restructuring schools for linguistic diversity: Linking decision making to effective programs.* New York: Teachers College Press.

Mogdil, S., Verma, G., Mallick, K., & Mogdil, C. (Eds.). (1986). *Multicultural education: The interminable debate.* London: Falmer Press.

Moses, M. S. (1997). Multicultural education as fostering individual autonomy. *Studies in Philosophy and Education, 16*(4), 373–388.

Moses, M. S. (2000, Fall). Why bilingual education policy is needed: A philosophical response to the critics. *Bilingual Research Journal, 24*(4), 333–354.

Moses, M. S. (2001a). The relationship between self-determination, the social context of choice, and authenticity. In L. Stone (Ed.), *Philosophy of Education 2000* (pp. 294–302). Urbana, IL: Philosophy of Education Society.

Moses, M. S. (2001b). Affirmative action and the creation of more favorable contexts of choice. *American Educational Research Journal, 38*(1), 3–36.

Mowatt, R. V. (1992). What revolution at Stanford? In P. Aufderheide (Ed.), *Beyond PC: Toward a politics of understanding* (pp. 129–132). St. Paul, MN: Graywolf Press.

Moya, P. M. L. (2002). *Learning from experience: Minority identities, multicultural struggles.* Berkeley: University of California Press.

National Labor Relations Act of 1935, 74 P.L. 198, 74 Cong. Ch. 372; 49 Stat. 449.

Nieto, S. (1992). *Affirming diversity: The sociopolitical context of multicultural education.* New York: Longman.

Noddings, N. (1992). *The challenge to care in schools: An alternative approach to education.* New York: Teachers College Press.

Noffke, S. E. (1998). Multicultural curricula: "Whose knowledge?" and beyond. In L. E. Beyer & M. W. Apple (Eds.), *The curriculum: Problems, politics, and possibilities* (pp. 101–116). Albany, NY: State University of New York Press.

Nussbaum, M. C. (1991, Autumn). The literary imagination in public life. *New Literary History, 22,* 877–910.

Nussbaum, M. C. (1997). *Cultivating humanity: A classical defense of reform in liberal education.* Cambridge, MA: Harvard University Press.

Oboler, S. (1995). *Ethnic labels, Latino lives: Identity and the politics of (re) presentation in the United States.* Minneapolis: University of Minnesota Press.

Ogbu, J. U. (1992). Understanding cultural diversity and learning. *Educational Researcher, 21*(8), 5–14, 24.

Ogbu, J. U., & Gibson, M. A. (Eds.). (1991). *Minority status and schooling : A comparative study of immigrant and involuntary minorities.* New York: Garland.

Omi, M., & Winant, H. (1994). *Racial formation in the United States: From the 1960s to the 1990s* (2d ed.). New York: Routledge.

O'Neill, T. J. (1985). *Bakke and the politics of equality: Friends and foes in the classroom of litigation.* Middletown, CT: Wesleyan University Press.

Ovando, C. J., & McLaren, P. (2000). Cultural recognition and civil discourse in a democracy. In C. J. Ovando & P. McLaren (Eds.), *The politics of multiculturalism and bilingual education: Students and teachers caught in the cross fire* (pp. xvii–xxiv). New York: McGraw-Hill.

Parekh, B. (1986). The concept of multicultural education. In S. Mogdil, G. Verma, K. Mallick, & C. Mogdil (Eds.), *Multicultural education: The interminable debate* (pp. 19–31). London: Falmer Press.

Peters, R. S. (1967). *Ethics and education.* Atlanta: Scott, Foresman.

Philips, B. (1987, July 17). Official English drive misunderstood. *Rocky Mountain News.*

Phipps, R. (1998). *College remediation: What it is, what it costs, what's at stake.* Washington, DC: The Institute for Higher Education Policy.

Piper, A. (1996). Passing for white, passing for black, *Passing and the fictions of identity.* Durham, NC: Duke University Press.

Ponitz, D. H. (1998). Commentary. In C. E. Finn (Ed.), *Remediation in higher education: A symposium* (pp. 35–37). Dayton, OH: Fordham Foundation.

Pottinger, J. S. (1972). Equality for Spanish-surnamed students. *Integrated Education, 10*(6), 48–53.

Pratt, M. L. (1992). Humanities for the future: Reflections on the western culture debate at Stanford. In D. J. Gless & B. H. Smith (Eds.), *The politics of liberal education* (pp. 13–31). Durham, NC: Duke University Press.

Pulley, B. (1997, August 3). A reverse discrimination suit shatters two teachers' lives. *New York Times,* pp. 1, 18.

Purdum, T. S. (1995, July 20). President shows fervent support for goals of affirmative action. *New York Times,* p. A1.

Ramírez, J. D. (1992). Executive summary. *Bilingual Research Journal, 16*(1 & 2), 1–62.

Ravitch, D. (1983). *The troubled crusade: American education 1945–1980.* New York: Basic Books.

Ravitch, D. (1995). Multiculturalism· E pluribus plures. In K. Ryan & J. M. Cooper (Eds.), *Kaleidoscope: Readings in education* (7th ed., pp. 458–464). Boston: Houghton Mifflin.

Rawls, J. (1971). *A theory of justice.* Cambridge, MA: Harvard University Press.

Raz, J. (1986). *The morality of freedom.* Oxford: Clarendon Press.

Regents of the University of California v. Bakke, 98 S. Ct. 2733 (1978).

Reich, R. (2002). *Bridging liberalism and multiculturalism in American education.* Chicago: University of Chicago Press.

Reisberg, L. (1999, January 29). Survey of freshmen finds a decline in support for abortion and casual sex. *The Chronicle of Higher Education,* pp. A47–A50.

Reyes, M. (1992). Challenging venerable assumptions: Literacy instruction for linguistically different students. *Harvard Educational Review, 62*(4), 427–446.

Rhoads, R. A. (1995). Critical multiculturalism, border knowledge, and the canon: Implications for general education. *Journal of General Education, 44*(4), 256–273.

Richards, D. A. J. (1989). Rights and autonomy. In J. Christman (Ed.), *The inner citadel: Essays on individual autonomy* (pp. 203–220). New York: Oxford University Press.

Rios v. Read, 73 F.R.D. 589 (1977).

Rodriguez, R. (1982). *Hunger of memory: The education of Richard Rodriguez*. New York: Bantam.

Rodriguez, R. (1996). The dirty little secret of college admissions. *Black Issues in Higher Education, 12*(13), 12–14.

Rodriguez, R. (1998). California has another proposition: This one would prohibit bilingual education. *Black Issues in Higher Education, 14*(23), 11.

Rose, M. (1990). *Lives on the boundary: A moving account of the struggles and achievements of America's educational underclass*. New York: Penguin Books.

Rossmann, J. E., Astin, H. S., Astin, A. W., & El-Khawas, E. H. (1975). *Open admissions at City University of New York: An analysis of the first year*. Englewood Cliffs, NJ: Prentice-Hall.

Roueche, J. E., & Roueche, S. D. (1999). *High stakes, high performance: Making remedial education work*. Washington, DC: Community College Press.

Salins, P. D. (1997). *Assimilating, American-style*. New York: Basic Books.

Salomone, R. (1986). *Equal education under law*. New York: St. Martin's Press.

Sandel, M. J. (1982). *Liberalism and the limits of justice*. Cambridge, England: Cambridge University Press.

Sandel, M. J. (1991). Morality and the liberal ideal. In J. Arthur & W. H. Shaw (Eds.), *Justice and economic distribution* (2d ed., pp. 244–249). Englewood Cliffs, NJ: Prentice-Hall.

Sandel, M. J. (1997, December 1). Picking winners. *The New Republic*, pp. 13–16.

Scanlon, T. M. (1979). Freedom of expression and categories of expression. *University of Pittsburgh Law Review, 40*(4), 519–550.

Schevitz, T. (2001, May 16). Critics say plan fails to counter image of bias. *San Francisco Chronicle*, p. A4.

Schlesinger, A. (1992). *The disuniting of America: Reflections on a multicultural society*. New York: Norton.

Schmidt, P. (1997, October 31). U.S. to let people choose multiple races on forms; big changes expected in data. *The Chronicle of Higher Education* [on-line]. Available: http://chronicle. com.

Schmidt, P. (1998, March 20). A clash of values at CUNY over remedial education. *The Chronicle of Higher Education*, pp. A33–A34.

Schmidt, P. (2001, January 5). Federal judge upholds use of race in admissions. *The Chronicle of Higher Education*, p. A32.

Schneider, A. (1997, May 9). Stanford revisits the course that set off the culture wars. *The Chronicle of Higher Education*, pp. A10–A12.

Schrag, P. (1999, May/June). End of the second chance? *The American Prospect, 44.*

Schroeder, S. A. (1996, November 1). Doctors and diversity: Improving the health of poor and minority people. *The Chronicle of Higher Education,* p. B5.

Selingo, J. (1997, August 8). No blacks are admitted by Cal. medical school. *The Chronicle of Higher Education,* p. A32.

Selingo, J. (1999, March 26). Washington law school loses black applicants. *The Chronicle of Higher Education,* p. A45.

Selingo, J. (2000, January 20). Sit-in forces delay in vote on Florida plan to end use of race in admissions. *The Chronicle of Higher Education* [on-line]. Available: http://chronicle.com.

Selingo, J. (2001, April 6). Michigan law school's admissions policies found to be unconstitutional. *The Chronicle of Higher Education,* p. A29.

Serna v. Portales Municipal Schools, 351 F. Supp. 1279 (1972).

Shaw, K. M. (1997). Remedial education as ideological battleground: Emerging remedial education policies in the community college. *Educational Evaluation and Policy Analysis, 19*(3), 284-296.

Shulman, C. H. (1972). *Affirmative action: Women's rights on campus.* Washington, DC: American Association for Higher Education.

Sindler, A. P. (1978). *Bakke, DeFunis, and minority admissions: The quest for equal opportunity.* New York: Longman.

Sleeter, C. E., & Grant, C. (1987). An analysis of multicultural education. *Harvard Educational Review, 57*(4), 421-442.

Sleeter, C. E., & McLaren, P. L. (Eds.). (1995). *Multicultural education, critical pedagogy, and the politics of difference.* Albany, NY: State University of New York Press.

Smith, B. H. (1990). Cultural literacy: Hirsch, literacy, and the "national culture." *The South-Atlantic Quarterly, 89*(1), 69-88.

Smith, R. R. (1978). Bakke's case vs. the case for affirmative action. *New York University Education Quarterly, 9*(2), 2-8.

Smith v. University of Washington Law School. 233 F.3d 1188 (4th Cir. 2000).

Sobel, L. (Ed.). (1980). *Quotas and affirmative action.* New York: Facts on File.

Solomon, R. C. (Ed.). (1974). *Existentialism.* New York: McGraw-Hill.

Sovern, M. I. (1966). *Legal restraints on racial discrimination in employment.* New York: Twentieth Century Fund.

Sowell, T. (1981). *Ethnic America.* New York: Free Press.

Sowell, T. (1993). *Inside American education: The decline, the deception, the dogmas.* New York: Free Press.

Spring, J. (1997). *Deculturalization and the struggle for equality: A brief history of dominated cultures in the United States* (2d ed.). New York: McGraw-Hill.

Springer, L., Palmer, B., Terenzini, P., Pascarella, E. T., & Nora, A. (1997, April). The impact of ethnic and women's studies courses on students' attitudes toward diversity on campus. Paper presented at the meeting of the American Educational Research Association, Chicago.

Srinivasan, K. (1997, November 2). Medical school minorities decline. *Denver Post,* p. 18A.

Steele, C. M. (1999, August). Thin ice: "Stereotype threat" and black college students. *The Atlantic Monthly, 284,* 44-54.

Steele, S. (1990). *The content of our character: A new vision of race in America.* New York: St. Martin's Press.

Steinberg, L. (1998). Commentary. In C. E. Finn (Ed.), *Remediation in higher education: A symposium* (pp. 37-41). Dayton, OH: Fordham Foundation.

Stewart, J. (1998, March 13). Employment in colleges and universities. *The Chronicle of Higher Education,* p. A15.

Sturm, S., & Guinier, L. (1996). The future of affirmative action: Reclaiming the innovative ideal. *California Law Review, 84*(4), 953-1036.

Sue, S., & Padilla, A. (1986). Ethnic minority issues in the United States: Challenges for the educational system. In C. Cortés (Ed.), *Beyond language: Social and cultural factors in schooling language minority students* (pp. 35-72). Los Angeles: Evaluation, Dissemination and Assessment Center, California State University.

Takaki, R. (1993). *A different mirror: A history of multicultural America.* Boston: Little, Brown.

Takaki, R. (1998, October 5). California's big squeeze. *The Nation,* 21-23.

Taxman v. Board of Education of the Township of Piscataway, NJ, 91 F.3d 1547 (3rd Cir. 1996).

Taylor, C. (1989). *Sources of the self: The making of the modern identity.* Cambridge, MA: Harvard University Press.

Taylor, C. (1991). *The ethics of authenticity.* Cambridge, MA: Harvard University Press.

Taylor, C. (1994). The politics of recognition. In A. Gutmann (Ed.), *Multiculturalism: Examining the politics of recognition.* Princeton, NJ: Princeton University Press.

Taylor, C. (1995). *Philosophical arguments.* Cambridge, MA: Harvard University Press.

Tennant, E. A. (1992, August). The "eye of awareness": Probing the hidden dimension of bilingual education. Paper presented at the Third National Research Symposium on Limited English Proficient Student Issues, Washington, DC.

Thernstrom, S., & Thernstrom, A. (1997). *America in black and white.* New York: Simon and Schuster.

Tierney, W. G. (1993). The college experience of Native Americans: A critical analysis. In L. Weis & M. Fine (Eds.), *Beyond silenced voices: Class, race, and gender in United States schools* (pp. 309-324). Albany, NY: State University of New York Press.

Tierney, W. G. (1997). The parameters of affirmative action: Equity and excellence in the academy. *Review of Educational Research, 67*(2), 165-196.

Torres, A. (1986). English-only movement fosters divisiveness. *Interracial Books for Children Bulletin, 17*(3/4), 18-19.

Traub, J. (1994). *City on a hill.* Reading, MA: Addison-Wesley.

Traub, J. (2000, January 16). Schools are not the answer. *New York Times Magazine,* 52-57, 68, 81, 90-91.

Trueba, H., Jacobs, L., & Kirton, E. (1990). *Cultural conflict and adaptation: The case of Hmong children in American society.* New York: Falmer Press.

Turner, M. E., & Pratkanis, A. R. (1994). Affirmative action: Insights from social psychological and organizational research. *Basic and Applied Social Psychology, 15*(1/2), 43–69.

Tyack, D. (1967). *Turning points in American educational history.* Waltham, MA: Blaisdell.

U.S. Department of Education. (2001, January 29). *No child left behind: Reauthorization of the Elementary and Secondary Education Act* [on-line]. U.S. Department of Education. Available: http://www.ed.gov.

United States v. Fordice, 505 U.S. 717 (1992).

Unz, R. K. (2001, March 2). Bilingual education lives on. *New York Times.*

Valdés, G. (1997). Dual-language immersion programs: A cautionary note concerning the education of language-minority students. *Harvard Educational Review, 67*(3), 391–429.

Velez, W. (1985, July). Finishing college: The effects of college type. *Sociology of Education, 58,* 191–200.

Watkins, W. H. (1994). Multicultural education: Toward a history and political inquiry. *Educational Theory, 44*(1), 99–117.

Weber, B. (2000, July 11). Bilingual issue misleading to parents, state high court says. *Rocky Mountain News.*

Weis, L., & Fine, M. (Eds.). (1993). *Beyond silenced voices: Class, race, and gender in United States schools.* Albany, NY: State University of New York Press.

Wessman v. Gittens, 160 F.3d 790 (1st Cir. 1998).

West, C. (1993). *Race matters.* Boston: Beacon Press.

Wheeler, S. (1997, August 29). Program seeks to put more minorities on college track. *Denver Post.*

White, J. (1991). *Education and the good life: Autonomy, altruism, and the national curriculum.* New York: Teachers College Press.

Wightman, L. F. (1997). The threat to diversity in legal education: An empirical analysis of the consequences of abandoning race as a factor in law school admission decisions. *New York University Law Review, 72*(1), 1–53.

Wilkins, D. B. (1996). Introduction. The context of race. In K. A. Appiah & A. Gutmann (Eds.), *Color conscious: The political morality of race* (pp. 3–29). Cambridge, MA: Belknap Press.

Williams, P. J. (1991). *The alchemy of race and rights.* Cambridge, MA: Harvard University Press.

Wilson, R. (1998, May 15). A single commencement expands the pool of new black Ph.D.'s in engineering. *The Chronicle of Higher Education,* pp. A14–A16.

Winkler, K. J. (1995, November 17). A sociologist's research finds little evidence of white backlash. *The Chronicle of Higher Education,* p. A15.

Wolf, S. (1994). Comment. In A. Gutmann (Ed.), *Multiculturalism: Examining the politics of recognition.* Princeton, NJ: Princeton University Press.

Wolfe, C., & Hittinger, J. (Eds.). (1994). *Liberalism at the crossroads.* Lanham, MD: Rowman and Littlefield.

Wong Fillmore, L. (1991). When learning a second language means losing the first. *Early Childhood Research Quarterly, 6,* 324–346.

Woodhams, F. (1998, December 11). Report finds remedial classes cost-effective. *The Chronicle of Higher Education,* pp. A54.

Young, I. M. (1990a). *Justice and the politics of difference.* Princeton, NJ: Princeton University Press.

Young, I. M. (1990b). Polity and group difference: A critique of the ideal of universal citizenship. In C. R. Sunstein (Ed.), *Feminism and political theory* (pp. 117–141). Chicago: University of Chicago Press.

Zangwill, I. (1908). *The melting-pot.* New York: Ayer.

Index

193

About the Author

Michele S. Moses is Assistant Professor in the Division of Educational Leadership and Policy Studies, College of Education, at the Arizona State University.